GETTING TO KNOW
THE MAN
—IN THE—
MIRROR

An Interactive Guide for Men

GETTING TO KNOW THE MAN —IN THE— MIRROR

An Interactive Guide for Men

Patrick M. Morley

Thomas Nelson Publishers

NASHVILLE • ATLANTA • LONDON • VANCOUVER

Published in Nashville, Tennessee, by Thomas Nelson, Inc., Publishers, and distributed in Canada by Word Communications, Ltd., Richmond, British Columbia, and in the United Kingdom by Word (UK), Ltd., Milton Keynes, England.

ISBN 0-7852-8061-8
Printed in the United States of America

1 2 3 4 5 6 7 — 00 99 98 97 96 95 94

To my brothers, Pete and Bill.
I pray that you will experience the full
measure of God's Grace.

Contents

PART FIVE: SOLVING OUR TEMPERAMENT PROBLEMS

PART SIX: SOLVING OUR INTEGRITY PROBLEMS

PART SEVEN: CONCLUSION

Acknowledgments

I would like to express my deepest appreciation to someone who really breathed life into this workbook. The efforts of Ruth Ford have been nothing short of mind boggling. She got her head into this project and wrote questions and made changes to the original *The Man in the Mirror* that, frankly, I could not improve upon. Thank you, Ruth.

Sincere thanks also go to Mike Hyatt and Robert Wolgemuth for the way they have looked after me. Special thanks to Betty Feiler and B. J. Belton at my office, whose remarkable administrative skills made it possible for me to devote large blocks of time to this ministry of Christian literature.

Introduction

I struck up a new business relationship with a man that required me to call him at approximate six-month intervals to put the deal together.

The first time I called him I said, "Hi, Tom, how are you doing?"

"Perfect, just perfect!" came his response.

Okay, sure, I thought to myself. *Whatever you say,* and we went ahead and talked business.

Six months later I called again, asking, "Hi, Tom, how are you doing?"

"Perfect! Pat, I'm just perfect."

Yeah, right. Sure you are, I thought, and I finished up the second leg of our transaction. But I started thinking about his canned responses.

After another six months I rang him up to do the final leg of our business deal. "Hi, Tom, this is Pat. How are you doing?"

"Perfect. I'm just perfect."

Because I had been thinking about our previous exchanges of shallow greetings I said, "Tom, I don't think you understand the question I'm asking you. I'm not just asking, 'How are you doing?' but I'm interested in how you are *really* doing."

He said, "Oh," which was followed by a long, pregnant five-second pause. "Well, okay then," he said, and then Tom launched into a thirty minute long monologue—he didn't come up for air one time, not once—in which he described one of the most agonizing, tortured kinds of business problems that any man could ever be expected to endure. What's most interesting about this is that he had been going through this jawbreaking problem all the months we had been speaking on the phone: "Perfect, just perfect."

Something akin to this scene repeats itself every day in the lives of most men. We don't tell people how we are really doing because we don't think they really want the answer. In truth, most people don't. Why is that? Why do we not seem to care about how people are *really* doing?

We Americans are so busy, so overcommitted, so up to our ears in duties and debts—we just don't want to know. We have so many problems of our own, there is no time left for anyone else—we just don't have the time to "want an answer."

More than a few men are swamped—they are in over their heads. After taking care of their own problems they have no capacity left over to help anyone else. Most men don't understand why they are so caught up in the rat race, and their lives are frequently spinning out of control.

Other men sense that something isn't quite right about their lives, but they can't quite put their finger on the answer. An eerie feeling lingers that they may be running in the wrong race. They see that they are more *financially* successful than their parents, but they suspect that they may not be better off.

It was in 1939 when Christopher Morley penned these words in his novel *Kitty Foyle,* "Their own private life gets to be like a rat race." In the decades since, the term *rat race* has evolved to describe the hopeless pursuit of a good life always just out of reach—a treadmill upon which we can't stop walking or we will fall off. Many of us today are trying to win the wrong race.

We could view Tom's shallow talk above as an indictment, but instead, let's use it as a springboard to look into the problems, issues, and temptations that face the man in the mirror every day and see what practical solutions we can discover for winning the *right* race.

My sincere goal with this workbook is to walk and talk you through *The Man in the Mirror* and help you "digest" the twenty-four chapters. Actually, I want to *dialogue* with you. I want us to do this book together, if you will.

It's certainly true for me that I learn—and *remember*—more if I'm forced to think and write and participate in something (even challenging some of it) than if I simply read, perhaps never getting below the surface.

Therefore, this workbook should be good for those who haven't read the original book, as well as for those who have read it. The approaches are different, although the material is basically the same.

If my purpose for this workbook is to be accomplished, it will be important for you to answer the questions and to write out the materials requested. If you *do* answer the questions to the best of your ability and read all the material, you will have gotten deep into the issues, and you will find yourself coming to grips with that man in the mirror.

You will also note that I ask you to write out a lot of scripture. It will be time consuming, but it is extraordinarily important. The Scriptures will sink into your being, and you will find them written on your mind for the Holy Spirit to use as He wishes. Remember, rat race or not there is no big rush; we're dealing with eternity. Take the time to do the work.

Finally, this workbook can be done by one person at a time or by several, provided they have copies to go around. In a group setting, such as Bible studies and Sunday school, you will want to develop trust in one another. The material probes hard, and candid answers are required. You should talk about this in advance. But don't be afraid.

I am confident that you—alone or in a group—will be a happier, more focused man when you finish.

A Word from the Publisher

The foreword from the original *The Man in the Mirror* came from R.C. Sproul. Let us start you on the *right* race with his insightful words about Pat's book.

> The goal of knowledge is wisdom. The goal of wisdom is to lead a life that is pleasing to God. This book is a book that contains uncommon wisdom. It is stirring, disturbing, and abundantly encouraging all at the same time.
>
> *The Man in the Mirror* is a book written by a man's man. It is a book written by a man, for men. While I was reading this book, the thought kept occurring to me, "I can't wait for my wife, Vesta, to read this book." Vesta is a voracious reader. She reads more than I do. I get my best tips on what to read next from her (even with books of theology).
>
> I want my wife to read this book, not because I think she needs to read this book. I'm the one who needed to read it. I want my wife to read this book because I know my wife will be thrilled to read it. One last tip for you. If someone gives you this book or if you buy it yourself, be sure to read it. If you don't read it, by all means destroy it before your wife gets hold of it. If the unthinkable happens, if you don't read it, and your wife does, then my dear brother, you are in deep weeds.

PART ONE

Solving

Our

Identity

Problems

The Rat Race

Like a rat in a maze, the path before me lies. . . .

SIMON AND GARFUNKEL

You were running a good race. Who cut in on you and kept you from obeying the truth?

GALATIANS 5:7

T he timer clicked, the TV screen fluttered, and the speaker blared the morning news.

"Morning already?" groaned Larry, rolling over and squeezing the pillow tightly over his ears. Then the aroma of coffee from the timer-operated percolator lured him toward the kitchen.

Six hours of sleep may not have been the rule growing up, but success at the end of the twentieth century demanded a premium. A rising star like Larry couldn't squander time sleeping.

Steam curled from the bowl of instant oatmeal. The microwave had produced predictably perfect results in perfect cadence with his thirty-five-minute wake-up schedule.

Slouched in his chair, propped against his elbow, Larry noticed the computer screen blinking at him. Last night he balanced his checkbook after the eleven o'clock news, and, weary from the long day, he must have neglected to switch it off.

His wife, Carol, had a welcomed day off, so while she slept in, Larry rushed to get the kids off to school. After he dropped the two younger children off at day-care, he was alone in the car with Julie. She seemed troubled lately, as if there was a lot going on in her twelve-year-old head. As the car hit the speed limit again, Julie asked, "Daddy, do you love Mom anymore?"

The question seemed to come out of the blue. Larry didn't know Julie had been building the courage to ask it for several months. Their family life was changing, and Julie seemed to be the only one diagnosing the changes. Larry reassured her that he loved Mom very much.

Carol hadn't planned to go back to work when she started her MBA degree. Bored with her traditional, nonworking-housewife role, she just wanted more personal fulfillment. Other neighborhood women seemed to lead glamorous lives in the business world. And her magazines conferred no dignity on the role of mother and homemaker. She couldn't help questioning her traditional values. So, two nights each week for three and a half years she journeyed off to the local university.

Larry, a tenacious, carefree sales representative, advanced quickly in his

> **❝Today men are consumed by desires to buy things they don't need, with money they don't have, to impress people they don't like.❞**

company. Fifteen years of dream chasing rewarded him with a vice-president's title. The pay covered the essentials, but they both wanted more of the "good life."

"I've been thinking about going back to work," Carol told him. Larry didn't protest. Carol had earned extra money as a bank teller at the beginning of their marriage, and it helped furnish their honeymoon apartment. By mutual agreement, Carol had stopped working when Julie was born, and ever since they had been hard-pressed to make ends meet.

Although his own mother didn't work, Larry knew things were different now for women. He had mixed emotions about sending their two small children to day-care. But since money was always a problem, he just shrugged and kept silent when Carol announced she had started interviewing for a job.

Larry clearly understood the trade-off. More money, less family. More family, less money. Yet they really wanted the "good life."

Their neighbors bought a twenty-four-foot cabin cruiser. Larry was surprised to learn they could own one, too, for only $328 per month. By scrimping for five months they pulled together $1,000 which, when added to their savings, gave them enough for the $2,500 down payment.

Larry loved cars. His gentle dad had always loved cars—Chevys—but Larry's tastes had evolved with the times. If a shiny two-door pulled up next to him at a traffic light, Larry's heart always beat faster. He could just picture himself shifting through the gears of a fancy European import. By accident he discovered that for only $423 a month he could lease the car of his fantasies. Leasing never occurred to him before.

Carol desperately wanted to vacation in Hawaii that year; her Tuesday tennis partner went last spring. But they couldn't do both. "If you go along with me on this car, I'll make it up to you, Carol. I promise!" Larry told her, his infectious grin spreading across his face. She reminisced how that impish, little-boy smile had first attracted her to him. He had been good to her, she thought. "Okay, go ahead," she told him.

Carol dreamed of living in a two-story home with a swimming pool, but with car and boat payments so high, it remained a dream for years. Larry slaved twelve- and fourteen-hour days—always thinking of how to earn more money for Carol's dream house. When Carol went to work, they totaled the numbers and were elated to see they could finally move.

But the strain of keeping their household afloat discouraged them. There were bills to pay, kids to pick up from day-care, deadlines to meet, quotas to beat, but not much time to enjoy the possessions they had accumulated. Larry could not remember when they had last gone for a weekend outing on the boat.

Words from a Simon and Garfunkel song haunted Larry's thoughts: "Like a rat in a maze, the path before me lies. And the pattern never alters, until the rat dies." He was trapped.

Carol pressured out—she just couldn't take it anymore. She believed Larry had let her down. He was supposed to be strong. He was supposed to

We all want to improve our standard of living—that's normal. But the world where we live has implemented its own ideas about how to accomplish the good life.

Many men—Christian men included—have been lulled into mental and spiritual complacency.

know how to keep everything going. But Larry was just as confused about their situation as she was.

As the U-haul pulled away from the house, Larry couldn't quite believe she was actually doing it—Carol was moving out. She said she just needed some time and space to sort things out. The question Julie had asked a few months earlier burned in his mind, "Daddy, do you love Mom anymore?" Yes . . . yes, he loved her, but was it too late? How did things get so out of hand?

The Problem

I believe most men are caught up in "the rat race." Do you agree or disagree, and why? What symptoms do you see to support your position?

_____

_____

Do you know anyone who has ever actually won the rat race? Most of us have to answer no. If that's true, why do you think so many men run in it? What are they trying to accomplish?

_____

_____

_____

The proverbial questions of the rat race—*What's it all about?* and *Is this all there is?*—have tortured us all at one time or another. No matter how successful we become, these questions always lurk in the shadows, waiting to pounce when life's inevitable problems overtake us.

- Why do I exist? How do I find meaning?
- Why are my relationships in shambles?
- How did I get so far in debt?
- How did I get caught in the rat race in the first place?

We all want to improve our standard of living—that's normal. But the world where we live has implemented its own ideas about how to accomplish the good life. And those ideas are far different from God's order.

The dichotomy between God's order and the order of this world produces a strain on the Christian man trying to sort out his thinking. *Are there absolutes? Do biblical principles really apply to the twentieth century?*

The Standard of Living Fallacy

Any good business plan starts with a description of the current environment. So, let's begin our look at the problems of men by first getting a handle on the environment in which we live and work. The first question we need to delve into is "How do we measure our standard of living?"

It doesn't take much in-depth analysis to discover that our measurement and definition of the "good life" has changed over the past forty years. *Try to imagine how your father and grandfather might have described the "good life." What do you suppose they would envision?*

_____

_____

_____

_____

How is that different from the way our contemporary society, shown by Larry and Carol, measures and defines "the good life"?

_____

_____

_____

Figure 1.1 shows two components of our standard of living. They are on sharply different vectors. While our material standard of living has soared over the past forty years, our moral/spiritual/relational standard of living has plummeted. They have, more or less, traded places.

Remember "Leave It to Beaver," "Father Knows Best," traditional families, prayer in schools, happy pregnancies? Yes, there were problems. But they were Chevrolet problems for Chevrolet families who lived in Chevrolet neighborhoods and had Chevrolet paychecks. Life was gradual and linear: Chevy, Buick, Oldsmobile, Cadillac, gold watch, funeral.

The desire for instant gratification, however, has taken the place of deferring to a time when we can pay cash. Today men are consumed by desires to buy things they don't need, with money they don't have, to impress people they don't like.

Now look at Figure 1.1 again. In what ways has your material standard of living gone up since you were a child? In what ways do you think your moral/spiritual/relational standard of living has been affected?

_____

_____

_____

Figure 1.1

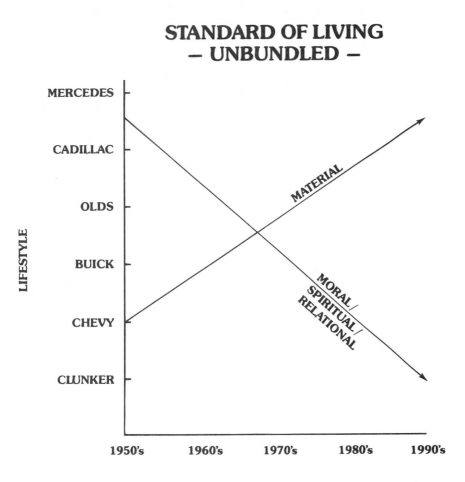

A Technological Explosion

The technological explosion of the last eighty years marks this century as the apex of human potential and achievement in all of history. We are blessed with enhancements in creature comforts, travel, communications, and jobs.

Do you remember how tedious it was putting together financial projections before personal computers? Can you recall what it was like to redo a marketing proposal before we had access to spreadsheets and word processors?

Truly, we have accumulated a winning score, but most of us are exhausted. And unfortunately, tired players are more easily injured. As individuals are injured, the whole team begins to lose its rhythm, courage, and will.

Men today are worn out. Do you feel worn out? Why?

_____

_____

_____

_____

Although our progress as a nation continues to grow, the souls of men continue to shrink. We can buy more and more things, but we are less satisfied with them. As I explained via the graph in Figure 1.1, our standard of living must be measured in more than one dimension.

The Dominant Economic Theory in America

We have exchanged our traditional values for a murky sort of prosperity.

The dominant economic theory in the United States for the past forty years or so has been *consumerism. Webster's* dictionary defines *consumerism* as "the economic theory that a progressively greater consumption of goods is beneficial." Judging by newspaper and TV ads, this certainly appears to be the philosophy of most businessmen.

In 1957 Vance Packard wrote a book, *The Hidden Persuaders,* which shocked and alarmed the nation. He discovered a large-scale effort to channel our unconscious habits and manipulate our purchasing behavior. The Madison Avenue pin-stripers formed an unholy alliance with the practitioners of psychology to manipulate the American consumer.

Have you ever wondered why, after only two or three years, you begin to itch for a shiny new car? The reason is *psychological obsolescence.* Madison Avenue figured out how to make us feel ashamed to own a slightly used car when the manufacturer could provide a new, more aerodynamically shaped and powerful one.

The Influence of the Media

Madison Avenue wouldn't have such strong influence if it weren't for the media. No single factor impacts our thinking more, but unfortunately, the media is controlled by secular humanists. The slant of most print copy, programming, advertising, and news portrays a secular life view.

We'll explore the secular humanist life view in greater detail in the next chapter, but let's use this working definition for now:

Secular humanism is the view that man establishes his own moral values apart from the influence of anyone (including God), and he self-determines his destiny—he is the "master of his own fate."

The problem with such a life view is that it has no absolutes—no eternal reference points. We can make up our own rules as we go. But how do we know if sexual promiscuity is immoral or not? Why shouldn't we cheat in business? Why should family life be valued higher than career?

How has this life view affected our society?

_____

_____

_____

Could this be happening in areas of your life? What indications do you see that this humanism is taking over in your personal experience?

_____

_____

_____

Through media and advertising, which rely heavily on subliminal suggestions, we are consciously and unconsciously lured to go for the *Madison Avenue lifestyle.* You see, we can at least somewhat defend ourselves at the conscious level, but most of consumerism's appeals are directed to our unconscious mind.

The media has been so effective in promoting this life view through sitcoms, movies, and talk shows, that even Christians are unconsciously buying into it. *Many men—Christian men included—have been lulled into mental and spiritual complacency. How has consumerism and the media impacted your own values and the way you spend your time and money?*

_____

_____

_____

Today's media-driven, humanistic society naturally devalues the Bible. How should we value what the Bible teaches us, according to 2 Timothy 3:16–17?

_____

_____

_____

Look up Philippians 4:8. According to that verse, what should be our guideline for evaluating what we view on television or read in books and newspapers?

_____

_____

_____

Perhaps the only way to overcome this dilemma is to reevaluate our sources of entertainment and information. Personally, I have virtually stopped watching television, and I am trying to read more books. *I have adopted the credo offered in 1 Corinthians 6:12. Write that verse here:*

_____

_____

_____

What does that imply for your television-watching or reading habits?

_____

_____

My own concern is that my unconscious mind will be mastered in an area where I have no ability to resist. Our unconscious mind has no walls around it and no sentinel at the gate.

Just watch TV commercials one evening and ask yourself, "If these commercials are true, then who am I, and what am I?" The life portrayed on the tube loves pleasure and sensuality. It doesn't deny itself anything, and it has a right to whatever goal it sets. If you do that, I believe you will come to the same conclusion I did.

The Beautiful, Wrinkle-Free Life

Unfortunately, in today's consumer-driven economy, more of us are trying to achieve the Madison Avenue lifestyle (we'll call it the beautiful, wrinkle-free life) than the economy will support. The lifestyle and image we strive for is a media-generated, artificial standard of living. The media creates the lifestyle image that the producers of goods and services want to sell, but only a few achieve it.

Solomon issued a warning in Ecclesiastes 5:10. Look it up and paraphrase it, showing how it applies to those who pursue the Madison Avenue lifestyle.

_____

_____

Figure 1.2

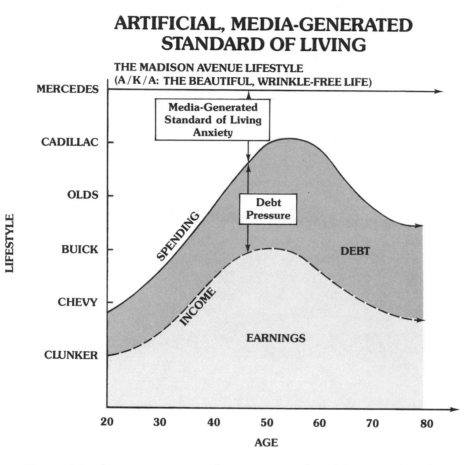

ARTIFICIAL, MEDIA-GENERATED STANDARD OF LIVING

Figure 1.2 shows two types of pressure produced by pursuing the beautiful, wrinkle-free life. First is *media-generated standard of living anxiety.* This is the extent to which our total spending still doesn't achieve the lifestyle level we set as our goal.

The result of trying to achieve the beautiful, wrinkle-free life, and failing, is an excruciating anxiety level not just among men, but also among their wives and children. When expectations do not match results, as in Larry and Carol's case, wives may take drastic action.

What expectations, both personal and on the part of your wife or children, have you been unable to meet?

_____

_____

_____

_____

The second category is *debt pressure*. Notice the difference between our spending and our income. To the extent that spending exceeds income, we accumulate debt.

Unfortunately, borrowing has become a national pastime. Easy credit seems like a good idea. Mixing easy credit and consumerism, however, is a highly volatile compound, producing a highly combustible formula. Essentially, we have exchanged our traditional values for a murky sort of prosperity financed by a remarkable increase in productivity and by a suffocating load of personal, corporate, and public debt.

The Rat Race Defined

We can define the rat race, then, as the pursuit of this beautiful, wrinkle-free life. Since there are no winners, the aftermath of running the race and losing takes a heavy toll.

The double whammy of media-generated standard of living anxiety and debt pressure is enormously depressing. We have the tension of not reaching the lifestyle we set as our goal, and we also have the pressure of the debt we accumulated trying to get there. Beyond that, our relationships have been fractured in the process. Could we define the rat race any more succinctly?

The way we measure our standard of living indicates the race we have decided to run. Look up Hebrews 12:1 and record it in the space provided.

_____

_____

_____

The number one reason men fail when they are promoted is that they keep doing the old job.

In keeping with that verse, the American Christian faces a true dilemma. We each make our own choice, but the pressure to make the wrong choice should not be underestimated. And, as my first Bible study leader used to say, "You can choose your way, but you can't choose the results."

Doing the New Job

The number one reason why men fail when they are promoted is that they keep doing the old job. In other words, since what they have done in the past is comfortable, they simply continue the old job description instead of taking on new challenges.

The same is true in the spiritual realm. Instead of letting biblical values penetrate the issues of their lives, and responding biblically, they continue to live an impotent life as if nothing had happened. Maybe the language is cleaned up a little, but essentially there is no change.

The apostle Paul describes what ought to happen in 2 Corinthians

5:17: "Therefore, if anyone is in Christ, he is a new creation; the old has gone, the new has come." We are promised a new spiritual nature, but we must be faithful—we must do our part.

What are some ways in which you have been faithful?

_____

_____

_____

What are some things you regret?

_____

_____

_____

ooking Closer in the Mirror:

Think back to Larry's story. In your mind, outline his morning routine. Now take a moment to describe your morning routine.

_____

_____

_____

_____

_____

Do you like the way your mornings flow? If not, what specific steps can you think of that might improve it?

_____

_____

_____

_____

If you go by how Larry spent his money, what were his priorities?

_____

_____

■ *THINK ABOUT YOUR WIFE*

Do you have a solid enough friendship with your wife, whether she is a stay-at-home mother or a working mother, to ask about how fulfilled she feels? If so, record her answer.

_____

_____

_____

Discuss some specific adjustments in your schedule or activities that could show your wife that you do love and cherish her. Record what you agree upon, preferably in order of priority.

_____

_____

_____

(You'll want to come back to this after you have worked your way through this book and see whether there is any change in her feelings.)

What might a marriage retreat like a Family Life weekend or a Marriage Encounter weekend have done for Larry and Carol's relationship?

_____

_____

_____

If you are married, is it time for you to consider such an intensive focus on your relationship? Are you satisfied with your marriage?

■ *THINK ABOUT YOUR CHILDREN*

Do you have the courage to ask your children whether they sense that there is something wrong relationally in your home? Now might be the time to take one or two of the children in elementary, junior high, or high school for a drive or to one of their favorite eating places. Casually ask them if they sense anything going wrong between them and you, or between Mom and Dad. Record the key responses:

_____

_____

_____

_____

_____

MIRROR WORK

*L*ord Jesus, give me insight into how I have been influenced by the society in which I live. Help me to see what is not of You and give me courage to change it. And help me to live each moment with You as my Standard for living. Amen.

In the next chapter . . .

With this consideration of the environment in which we live, let's now turn to the specific problems men face, see what solutions might be available, and see if we can discover a new track upon which we can run in the race that really counts.

2 Leading an Unexamined Life

The life which is unexamined is not worth living.

PLATO

Let us examine our ways and test them, and let us return to the LORD.

LAMENTATIONS 3:40

"To see ourselves as we really are, we must acknowledge our inability to do so without God's help."

He is Dempsey—a tough New York cop. After a reliable police informer reports that the mob has placed a contract on his life, his boss sends Dempsey—a gruff, head-busting maverick—to London for safekeeping.

She is Makepeace—a very feminine, very proper, very British policewoman. They become partners in the English cops-and-robbers television series "Dempsey and Makepeace."

On each week's lead-in, they run from burning cars. They dive to the pavement to avoid machine-gun fire. They roll across the ground and return gunfire at the bad guys.

Then the screen suddenly quiets. The camera zooms in on Dempsey's face. He glares into the lens for what seems like a long time. Then, matter-of-factly, he summarizes his view of the world: "Life is hard, and then you die."

You don't get the impression that Dempsey represents the profound, intellectual sort, but his statement has a certain ring of truth. Dempsey takes life one episode at a time, never considering tomorrow.

Do you share Dempsey's view of life? Does his statement reflect your approach to each day? Explain your answer.

If you answered yes, you certainly are not alone. A lot of us are like Dempsey. There comes a day, however, when you want *real* answers to *real* questions: "Why is life so hard?" and "What happens when I die?"

Do you have real answers for that type of gut-level inquiry? If you don't, do you know where to find them?

_____

_____

The Problem

When we progress along the trajectory we set for ourselves, we don't give much thought to the *why* questions of life. But when we hit the target and still aren't satisfied, the questions start to come.

- "Who am I?"
- "Why do I exist?"
- "Is this all there is?"
- "If I'm so successful, why do I feel so empty?"

And if we don't hit our target, the list grows even longer. "Why me, God? If You love me, where are You when I need You?" Our hurt feelings erode to anger and bitterness, or fear and guilt, or some of each.
Recall the last two times you felt any of these negative emotions.

(1) _____

(2) _____

Those caught in the rat race have a very basic problem. They haven't paid attention to the questions that really matter. *Most men lead unexamined lives. We have not carefully chiseled our life views by a personal search for truth and by obedience to God.*

Instead, we rush from task to task without calling time-outs to reflect on life's larger meaning and purpose. We live myopically under the tyranny of today. Our lives, like Dempsey's, are consumed in action and reaction to a seemingly endless menu of options vying for attention, time, and money.

As Gandhi said, "There is more to life than increasing its speed." Be honest with yourself. Are you taking time to reflect on the basic questions of life? Or have you been increasing life's speed? Explain how you arrived at your conclusion regarding these questions.

_____

_____

_____

_____

Most men lead unexamined lives. We have not carefully chiseled our life views by a personal search for truth and by obedience to God.

For many, even Sunday doesn't make a real difference. We show up at church, but the service doesn't do for us what it does for others. We don't know exactly why, but before we spend much time thinking about it, our minds wander to the office problems chewing at our guts. We speed off to the next task, and by Monday afternoon, Sunday is as distant as last year's vacation.

How unfortunate. We admit that a lawyer or accountant is no better than the effort he puts into keeping up with his profession. Why can't we see that the Christian is no better than the effort he puts into self-examination of life's big questions?

Two Life Views

In the previous chapter we introduced the life view of the secular humanist, who holds that man is the central figure who shapes events. In contrast, the biblical life view sees God as sovereign and active in everyday life.

With that in mind, check which of the following you agree with:

_____ *Man is intrinsically good.*
_____ *Man can master his own fate.*
_____ *Man can determine the boundaries of his achievements.*
_____ *Man can establish the limits of his own knowledge.*
_____ *Man sets his own moral standards.*

If you checked any of these, you are holding at least one position of the secular life view.

Now check which of the following is your personal position:

_____ *An all-powerful God created the universe.*
_____ *This living God possesses all knowledge.*
_____ *God established moral standards by which He expects man to live.*
_____ *God is holy, loving, and personal.*

The items you checked in that list put you in harmony with the Christian life view.

It is simple to see the differences in these two views when they are spelled out in this kind of format. It isn't always easy, though, in real life. And so Christian men often apply the wrong set of principles to their problems.

Unfortunately, this is intensified by our fragmented understanding of how God intends for us to live. Christians often see things in bits and pieces instead of totals. We have sounded alarms over permissiveness, pornography, prayer in public schools, the family, and abortion. But, as the late Dr.

Francis Schaeffer pointed out, we "have not seen this as a totality—each thing being a part, a symptom, of a much larger problem."[1]

This larger problem is the basic shift in values mentioned in Chapter 1. It's a fundamental change in how we view life and the world. We have moved away from traditional Judeo-Christian values toward a life view that lets us self-select values based on whether they serve our self-interests.

Without careful examination, we tend to see the Christian and secular views as being close to one another, like two horses ridden at the same time by a circus performer. But when the horses move apart, the performer must pick one or the other. So it is with life views. Careful examination reveals unmistakable contrasts, and we must pick one or the other.

Describe two times where you found the secular and Christian life views diverging so greatly, you had to make a choice.

(1) _____

(2) _____

The Results of Leading an Unexamined Life

The choice between Christian and secular life views is a choice between God's race and the rat race.

*C*onsider John and Betty, for instance. For seven years I watched them struggle with lifestyle and life view issues. They sincerely sought peace and contentment, yet they endured constant tension because of their material appetites. Betty, in particular, always wanted more.

They lived in a comfortable home, but like so many, they clutched the hope of buying their dream house. John knew the payments weren't manageable, but Betty seemed so anxious. Eventually they plunged in and bought a real showplace.

Still, John just couldn't seem to satisfy Betty's desire for possessions. He worked hard enough, but Betty honestly believed he was unambitious. When he worked on Christian tasks, Betty felt he was copping out on his responsibility to work and save for the family they talked of starting.

Then Betty went home to visit her parents for a few weeks. One day she phoned home. "I've taken a job," she said simply.

"What does that mean?" John, though gasping for breath, was able to ask.

She didn't respond in terms of their relationship, but spoke only of her ambition to earn more money. The upshot was a divorce and the loss of their dream house.

How can a Christian couple go so far astray? Simply put, the secular life view competes directly with the Christian life view, and the disciples of secularism work just as hard as Christians do to make converts!

Christians in Captivity

Scripture issues a stern warning to Christians who are drawn to the secular worldview. Look up Colossians 2:8 and write it in the space provided. Then I encourage you to memorize it.

_____

_____

_____

_____

Unfortunately, many American Christians have not yet found the freedom of that verse. In the meantime, secular humanists have been doing a much better job of influencing our culture than we Christians have. School prayer was banned in 1961, and abortion was legalized in 1973. Since those two watershed decisions, virtually every other valued institution has endured significant erosion. *Today, Christians are a minority in America. We are as much of a minority, and our values and views as impotent, as any minority group at any time in modern history.*

In what ways do you recognize that, as a Christian, you are in the minority in the area where you live?

_____

_____

What about the place where you work?

_____

_____

How has this become a general characterization for American society? It has happened because we Christians lead unexamined lives. Many good men—Christian men—have been taken "captive through hollow and deceptive philosophy, which depends on human tradition and the basic principles of this world" (Colossians 2:8).

As I noted, we often see societal issues in fragments. This applies to our personal lives as well. We see things in bits and pieces instead of totals. Archaeologists search the ruins of long-forgotten civilizations looking for, among other things, shards. A shard is a piece of broken pottery which the archaeologist studies. Then he visualizes what the object must have looked like by projecting from the broken pieces.

This is how we should examine our lives. We should look at every shard—every idea flowing through our minds—and see which life view it represents. Too often we see events and circumstances as unrelated and isolated when, instead, we should visualize how they fit into the big picture of our lives.

If John and Betty had done that—if they had examined the shard of their materialism to determine its origin and effect—how could that have improved their relationship and perhaps saved their marriage?

The first step to knowing God's plan for our lives is to commit to see ourselves as we really are and to stop living an unexamined life. *Will you make that commitment? Write it in your own words. Then date it and sign it for future reference.*

The Two You's

You may find it harder than you think to live out that commitment. You see, there is more than one you to examine. There is at least one visible you, and there is the real you.

The visible you is the you known by others. We learn instinctively from our experiences how to act and speak to fit in with our peer groups. We often act differently from one peer group to the next.

In high school I was in three different peer groups. One was the jock crowd. When I worked out with the athletes I talked tough and wouldn't smoke or drink.

Another peer group was the academics. I was an honor student and liked these high-brows. We would discuss Darwinian theory and talk about the importance of science to the future of mankind.

The third group was the hell-raisers. All weekend I would smoke, drink beer, cruise the drive-in restaurants, and look for girls. Frankly, I was a nervous wreck around campus. When I walked the halls with one peer group, my eyes constantly darted around. I feared seeing a friend from a different peer group—then I would be exposed as an impostor!

And even beyond all that, a fourth Pat Morley showed up at home every day after school.

> *Christians are a minority in America. We are as much of a minority, and our values and views as impotent, as any minority group at any time in modern history.*

I was a walking identity crisis. I was trying to balance four "visible me's." How many visible you's do you see in your experience? What are they like?

_____

_____

_____

If you are like me, none of those visible you's is the real you. *The real you is the you known by God. You may not even know the real you. How can I say that? Find Jeremiah 17:9 and record it in the space provided.*

_____

_____

To protect our self-images, we kid, trick, and fool ourselves into believing the *visible* you is somehow *real*. To see ourselves as we really are, we must acknowledge our inability to do so without God's help.

The Battle Rages

Our speech and actions flow from our thinking, thus battle for the real you occurs in the mind. It's the battle between the majority secular life view and the minority Christian life view.

Ephesians 6:12 describes this battle. Write this verse and memorize it:

_____

_____

_____

_____

Because we don't take this invisible war seriously, many of us are losing the battle for our minds. But we can win them back by committing ourselves to self-examination through studying the Scriptures. You *can* know the real you, the you who is known by God. And you can affect that real you for the better.

Now let's take a look at a tool to help you in the quest to understand yourself.

"Look at the Fish"

At a young age Louis Agassiz gained an international reputation as a natural scientist. He also had a magic touch with people. Swiss-born, he arrived in Boston in 1846 with boundless imagination and enthusiasm. He accepted a teaching post at Harvard, where he conducted seemingly infinite investigations of fish and fossils.

As great as was the genius of Agassiz in the study of fossils and fishes, his genius as a teacher was of far greater significance. The lesson he left for the man who wants to examine his life is considerable, as noted in this account by one of his students, Mr. Scudder, who later became a professor of near equal popularity.

He asked me a few questions about my object in coming. . . . "When do you wish to begin?" he asked.

"Now," I replied.

This seemed to please him, and with an energetic "very well!" he reached from a shelf a huge jar of specimen in yellow alcohol.

"Take this fish," said he, "and look at it. . . . By and by I will ask what you have seen." In ten minutes I had seen all that could be seen in that fish, and started in search of the Professor—who had, however, left the Museum. . . . Half an hour passed—an hour—another hour; the fish began to look loathsome. I turned it over and around; looked it in the face—ghastly; from behind, beneath, above, sideways, at a three-quarter's view—just as ghastly. I was in despair; at an early hour I concluded that lunch was necessary; so, with infinite relief, the fish was carefully replaced in the jar, and for an hour I was free.

On my return, I learned that Professor Agassiz had been at the Museum, but had gone and would not return for several hours. . . . Slowly I drew forth that hideous fish, and with a feeling of desperation again looked at it. . . . I pushed my finger down its throat to feel how sharp the teeth were. I began to count the scales in the different rows, until I was convinced that that was nonsense. At last a happy thought struck me—I would draw the fish; and now with surprise I began to discover new features in the creature. Just then the Professor returned.

"That is right," said he: "A pencil is one of the best of eyes. Well, what is it like?"

He listened attentively to my brief rehearsal. . . .

When I had finished, he waited as if expecting more, and then, with an air of disappointment:

"You have not looked very carefully . . . look again, look again!" And he left me to my misery. . . .

I ventured to ask what I should do next.

"Oh, look at your fish!" he said. . . . And so for three long days he

By the end of this workbook, you will be able to find God's principles for every aspect of your life. You will be able to bring bits and pieces of your life into connection with the general laws of God.

placed that fish before my eyes, forbidding me to look at anything else, or to use any artificial aid. "Look, look, look," was his repeated injunction.

This was the best entomological lesson I ever had—a lesson whose influence has extended to the details of every subsequent study; a legacy the Professor has left to me, as he has left it to many others, of inestimable value, which we could not buy, with which we cannot part. . . .

Agassiz's training in the method of observing facts and their orderly arrangement was ever accompanied by the urgent exhortation not to be content with them.

"Facts are stupid things," he would say, "until brought into connection with some general law."

At the end of eight months, it was almost with reluctance that I left these friends and turned to insects; but what I had gained by this outside experience has been of greater value than years of later investigation in my favorite groups.[2]

Learning to Look

The main reason we lead unexamined lives is that we do not take time to "look at the fish"—ourselves—carefully looking for more and more.

Have you ever looked at yourself with this intensity and integrity? List any barriers you sense in yourself that could prevent a thorough examination.

_____

_____

_____

Even if you believe you have examined yourself very carefully, let me assure you that we can always see more. Soon we discover the professor's criticism is just—we have not examined our lives carefully. With any good fortune we will soon be able to say, "No, I am certain I don't see it yet, but I see how little I saw before."

By the end of this workbook, I hope it will be with Mr. Scudder's reluctance that you leave this study and turn to some new area of self-examination. With the Bible as your resource book, you will be able to find God's principles for every aspect of your life. You will be able to bring the bits and pieces of your life into connection with the general laws of God.

Looking Closer in the Mirror:

When you die, what do you want your tombstone to say?

_____

_____

If you were to die today, could someone honestly request that statement for your tombstone? _____ *Yes* _____ *No*

If not, what changes do you need to make for that statement to be a reality in your life?

_____

_____

_____

List the people who have had the greatest influence on how you think, speak, and act.

_____

_____

_____

List the experiences that have had the greatest influence on how you think, speak, and act.

_____

_____

_____

Has their influence been good or bad? Explain your answer.

_____

_____

_____

Regarding the Christian life view and the secular life view, what percentage of each makes up your thinking? For instance, you may find that 60 percent of your life view is actually Christian and the other 40 percent is secular. Explain how you came to that conclusion.

_____

_____

_____

Are you content or discontent with your life as it is? How does that affect your desire to examine your life?

_____

_____

Read Psalm 139:1–4. According to those verses, how well does God know the real you?

_____

_____

Read Psalm 139:23–24. Are you prepared to make that your prayer?
_____ Yes   _____ No

If you ask God to show you yourself as you really are, what are some of the things you might find out about yourself? How do they make you feel?

_____

_____

MIRROR WORK

*L*ord Jesus, help me not to lose sight of You in this process of examining myself. Keep me from fear of what I will find, so I will not stop looking, and help me to change whatever I find that displeases You. Amen.

In the next chapter . . .

Our material standard of living is up. Many men see that financially we are better off than our parents. But are we really better off in the ways that matter? Consumerism and media influence have caused a basic shift in values. How is it affecting our lives?

Biblical Christian or Cultural Christian?

A whole new generation of Christians has come up believing that it is possible to "accept" Christ without forsaking the world.

A. W. TOZER

Anyone who listens to the word but does not do what it says is like a man who looks at his face in a mirror and, after looking at himself, goes away and immediately forgets what he looks like.

JAMES 1:23–24

L et's begin this discussion by recalling two couples mentioned earlier —Larry and Carol in the first chapter and John and Betty in the second. They were all Christians.

I believe the forces at work in Larry and Carol's lives and in John and Betty's lives are the rule rather than the exception among Christian households. Going a step further, I would also tell you that after counseling hundreds of men, I can't name ten whose marriages are working the way they should.

Have you known Christians who were similarly caught in the assault on the family? Recall the family values that were hit the hardest.

> **Many of us are busy 'doing' God's things but not keeping our personal relationships with God in tune.**

In situations like the one you just recounted, you may ask, "How could that happen to a Christian couple?" It's easier than you might think.

The Problem

As we have already seen, our material standard of living is up. Many men see they are more financially successful than their parents, but they suspect they may not be better off. What is really going on?

As we noted in the first chapter, forty years of consumerism and media influence have caused a basic shift in values. Overall, we live in a culture dominated by the secular life view. It's not just happening to Larry and Carol, or to John and Betty. *It's happening to us too.*

Two Impoverished Values

In the previous chapter we examined some differences between the secular and Christian life views. In a nutshell, one is man-based, the other God-based. A 1976 book by the late Dr. Francis Schaeffer, *How Should We Then Live?*, noted how changes in art, music, drama, theology, and the mass media have negatively affected our values. Dr. Schaeffer underscored that the majority of people have adopted two impoverished values: *personal peace* and *affluence.* Here are his definitions for those two values:

> Personal peace means just to be let alone, not to be troubled by the troubles of other people, whether across the world or across the city—to live one's life with minimal possibilities of being personally disturbed. Personal peace means wanting to have my personal life pattern undisturbed in my lifetime, regardless of what the result will be in the lifetimes of my children and grandchildren.[1]

The Christian life view, according to 2 Corinthians 1:3–4, opposes that value. Record that passage in the space provided.

_____

_____

_____

_____

_____

> Affluence means an overwhelming and ever-increasing prosperity—a life made up of things, things, and more things—a success judged by an ever-higher level of material abundance.[2]

Again, the Christian life view opposes that definition. In the space provided, record Matthew 6:19–21 and memorize verse 21.

_____

_____

_____

_____

_____

A Third Impoverished Value

The year 1976 was a watershed year. In addition to Schaeffer's writings, Chuck Colson's _Born Again,_ the personal story of his encounter with God and his Watergate experiences, was published. Many believe his book had a dynamic and powerful influence in building contemporary interest in Christianity.

America also elected a _born-again_ president that year. Not since the Great Depression had a country so needed a catharsis—a healing of our Watergate and Vietnam wounds. Jimmy Carter offered integrity, all in the form of a committed Christian who used the moniker "born again."

So it became socially acceptable to be a Christian. A Gallup Poll in 1986 revealed that an incredible 32 percent of Americans classified themselves as "born again" or evangelical Christians. Another 1986 Gallup Poll showed 57 percent of Americans believing religion could answer all or most of today's problems. Gallup surveys also found that 71 percent reported church membership, while 42 percent said they attended church in a typical week.

Here is the question, then: If religion is such a big part of our lives, why hasn't it made more of an impact on our society? Explain your answer.

> _If religion is such a big part of our lives, why hasn't it made more of an impact on our society?_

_____

_____

I believe that, as it became okay—even popular—to be "born again," the price of identifying oneself as a Christian dropped. Cheap Christianity. More and more people bought in because the personal cost was lower. The unfortunate result of this religious popularity is that since the mid-seventies a third impoverished value has evolved: _cultural Christianity._

Cultural Christianity means pursuing the God we want instead of the God who is. It is the tendency to be shallow in our understanding of God, wanting Him to be a gentle grandfather type who spoils us and lets us have our own way. It is wanting the God we have underlined in our Bibles without wanting the rest of Him too. It is God relative instead of God absolute.

Cultural Christianity is Christianity made impotent. It is Christianity with little or no impact on the values or beliefs of our society. When the secular life view is merged into the Christian life view, neither survives. Cultural Christianity is God love, but not God holy.

Given that explanation, where would you place you and your family on a scale of one to ten, with 1 being cultural Christianity and 10 being biblical Christianity? _____

What are your reasons for giving that rating?

_____

_____

_____

Now rate your church on the same scale. _____
Give your reasons.

_____

_____

_____

Actually, God loves us so much that He will cleanse the cultural Christianity from our lives, as the silversmith purifies silver by burning off the dross, if we will call on Him. *Assuming you did not rate yourself perfectly, do you intend to call upon and cooperate with Him?*

Four Groups of Hearers

Categorizing people according to their life view certainly is not a new concept. Jesus, in fact, was the first to clarify the different types of people who would or would not associate with Him. His parable of the sower, recorded in Luke 8, reveals four groups of hearers of the Word of God.

Group 1—The Non-Christian

Write Luke 8:12 and read it through twice.

_____

_____

_____

_____

Jesus clearly points out that not everyone who hears about salvation will believe.

Group 2—The Cultural Christian Type "C"

Record Luke 8:13 and read it through twice.

_____

_____

_____

_____

Modern thinking correctly believes that once a man is saved he is always saved. Christ affirms this by saying, "My sheep listen to my voice; I know them, and they follow me. I give them eternal life, and they shall never perish; no one can snatch them out of my hand" (John 10:27–28).

Modern thinking breaks down, though, by advertising that all people need to do is "pray a prayer" and they will be saved—born again. Everyone, it seems, has "prayed a prayer"! Prayers don't save; faith saves. We'll cover that in more detail in the next chapter.

Type "C" stands for "counterfeit" faith. Some among us profess to be Christians, but in reality they are not Christians at all. They are cultural Christians—*type "C."* Jesus said, "Not everyone who says to me, 'Lord, Lord,' will enter the kingdom of heaven, but only he who does the will of my Father who is in heaven" (Matthew 7:21).

> **Prayers don't save; faith saves.**

The apostle Paul urges, "Examine yourselves to see whether you are in the faith; test yourselves. Do you not realize that Christ Jesus is in you— unless, of course, you fail the test?" (2 Corinthians 13:5). *Close your eyes and test yourself right now. What do you find?*

_____

_____

In love, I encourage every man who finds himself to be a cultural Christian not to be discouraged. God loves you with an everlasting love and wants to reconcile with you. In the next chapter, I will show you how to get on the right track.

Group 3—The Cultural Christian Type "D"

Write Luke 8:14 and read it through twice.

_____

_____

_____

I have observed and evaluated the differences in purchasing patterns between born-again Christians and the secular society at large. The results are startling: Most of the time there is no difference. Why is this significant? The typical U.S. family spends 23 percent of its after-tax income to repay debts. When Christians are bogged down with debts and run the race to acquire material possessions, worries choke the Word and make it unfruitful.

How does your debt load compare to the typical U.S. family described above?

_____

If we are to be salt and light in this confused world, how should our spending patterns differ from those of the secular family?

_____

_____

_____

Type "D" in this category stands for "defeated" faith. The cultural Christian of type "D" lives in defeat, with only marginal differences between his lifestyle and that of a person who makes no claim to be a Christian.

Test yourself again. Do you see any symptoms of defeated faith? Name them, as painful as it might be.

_____

_____

_____

Once again, be hopeful. This book will be especially helpful for the man with the "defeated" faith. This is the category I flirted with before God brought me to my senses.

Group 4—The Biblical Christian

Write Luke 8:15 and this time MEMORIZE it.

_____

_____

_____

Biblical Christians don't live by their own ideas, but by penetrating, understanding, and applying the Word of God. By the Spirit, they discover the success and peace to which we each aspire.

A biblical Christian has done more than trust Christ, and Christ alone, for his salvation. He has moved on from saving faith to "obedient" faith (Romans 1:5). He has made Christ the Lord of his life and allowed the Holy Spirit to empower him.

Remember, among cultural Christians are those who have a "counterfeit" faith and those who have a "defeated" faith. Now in your own words, reviewing what we have discussed so far, define the following terms:

—*Biblical Christian* _____

—*Cultural Christian*

    Type "C" _____

    Type "D" _____

> *When Christians are bogged down with debts and run the race to acquire material possessions, worries choke the Word and make it unfruitful.*

An Ambiguity of Terms

Today calling yourself a Christian is similar to calling yourself a Republican or a Democrat. The label reveals far less about your thoughts and beliefs than it did fifty years ago.

Perhaps you remember your elementary teacher demonstrating the principle of diffusion. Probably she started with a clear glass of water. With an eyedropper she squeezed one drop of red food dye into the glass. Within moments the water was tainted with a pinkish hue as the dye permeated it.

To be a cultural Christian today is like having the whole bottle of red dye poured in the glass. Secular culture is so polluted that to be a cultural Christian means your life view and lifestyle are not tainted a pinkish hue but completely contaminated to a bright red.

Cooking a Frog

Malcolm Muggeridge once explained how to cook a frog. If you toss a frog in a pot of boiling water, it will immediately feel the heat and leap out.

But if you put the frog in a pot of cold water and slowly turn up the heat, the frog won't notice the change in temperature. Eventually it'll be cooked.

Like an unsuspecting frog in a cold pot, our values have been slowly "cooked" over the last few decades. We took a long time to realize everything had changed, and we felt helpless once we *did* realize. If someone had been cryonically frozen forty years ago and brought back to life today, that person would jump right out of this boiling pot!

In your case, how have you responded to these bits of value "cooking"?

Choice of television viewing: _____

Choice of reading material: _____

Choice of music you listen to: _____

Meeting the neighbors: _____

Be honest. Is there any marginal difference between the way you deal with the world's problems and the way the non-Christian does? Does your life offer hope?

Jesus had a word for cultural Christians whose attitudes and actions reflect the bankrupt values of a shallow, hurting society. That word to a specific church is found in Revelation 3:15–17. Write those verses and memorize them.

_____

_____

_____

_____

Does that message describe you? Yes _____ *No* _____ *If the answer is yes, you have been living the life of a cultural Christian.*

Too Busy

Many of us are busy "doing" God's things but not keeping our personal relationships with God in tune. We can become so busy for Christ that we live in defeat in important areas of our personal lives, similar to another group addressed by Jesus in Revelation 2:2–4. *Write those verses in the space provided.*

_____

_____

_____

_____

_____

Relativism Versus Truth

One of the clearest descriptions of the "cooking" of American values is found in the words of a Chief Justice of the Supreme Court, Frederick Moore Vinson: "Nothing is more certain in modern society than the principle that there are no absolutes."

Cultural Christians often think truth, even biblical truth, changes with circumstances. Biblical Christians, on the other hand, say there are truths—absolutes—that never change, even when times change.

Relativism is really a dead end, a cul-de-sac. Each person simply ends up fighting for his or her own opinion. _Are you a cultural Christian in your decision making? How can relativistic thinking influence your life?_

_____

_____

The biblical Christian finds no fault in making modern application of the Bible's teachings. The lack of a high-tech appearance to the Scriptures is a source of strength and encouragement, not embarrassment. He is persuaded that the Bible, though often filled with mystery, reveals a personal God with unchanging, absolute principles and precepts.

What is your personal view of the Bible?

_____

_____

Is the biblical Christian ever permitted to question Scripture? Yes, of course. But there is a difference between wrestling with a verse to understand its truth and wrestling with it to decide whether you think it's true.

Looking Out for Number One

So, how do you really know if you are a cultural or a biblical Christian? Perhaps the easiest way is to ask yourself a simple question. _Who is number one in your life?_

Like an unsuspecting frog in a cold pot, our values have been slowly "cooked" over the last few decades.

Steve found his answer when he faced a difficult situation. He and his wife sold their business. He enrolled in graduate school out of state, and they purchased a home near the university. When they went to close the mortgage on the new house, the mortgage company wanted him to falsify some financial information.

"I can't do that," he told them.

"It's no big deal; everybody does it," was the reply.

"I don't think you understand. I can't do that."

"It just goes in the file; nobody will ever even look at it. Besides, if you don't, we can't give you the loan."

Steve really believed God had led them to the decision to return to school. *What would Steve gain by obliging the mortgage company?*

_____

_____

What would he lose by obliging the mortgage company?

_____

_____

What, honestly, would you do, and why?

_____

_____

Many Christian men have adopted the three impoverished values of our time: personal peace, affluence, and cultural Christianity. They become number one in their own lives. For the biblical Christian, Jesus heads the list. Obedience is the trademark of a biblical Christian. It demonstrates his love to God and God's truth to a weary culture.

Self-examination

The man who has been living as a cultural Christian can change by checking the *influences* on his life and the *values* he has adopted. He should begin with self-examination.

What about you? Examine the influences in your life:

Is your church biblical? _____

What life view do your friends represent? _____

What forms of entertainment do you expose yourself to? _____

In the space provided, note the positive and negative ways you have been influenced by:

Television: _____

Radio: _____

Music: _____

Art: _____

Literature: _____

Are some bad habits at work in you? List them:

_____

_____

Do you want to change? _____

Patient for Change

When I became a Christian, I asked God for help on two serious, practical problems. The first was cursing. Almost instantly, the cursing ceased.

I was flabbergasted. I had made no conscious effort to stop, nor was I aware a change had occurred. That's the silent, almost imperceptible work of the Holy Spirit.

My other serious struggle was with temper. Despite the speed of the Lord's work with cursing, my temper problem lingered for five tearful years. Virtually every day I would ask for forgiveness. There were many tears and long prayers, but five years passed before my anger became a normal person's anger.

The point is that we didn't get to be the men we are overnight, and we may need to allow some time, perhaps a long time, before we see our lives the way we want them to be.

ooking Closer in the Mirror:

> *The man in the mirror will never change until he is willing to see himself as he really is and to commit to know God as He really is.*

The man in the mirror will never change until he is willing to see himself as he really is and to commit to know God as He really is. This objectivity anchors a man. It gives him the clarity he needs to be a biblical Christian.

So what about you? Are you ready for some objectivity? Look up the Scrip-

tures listed below. For each passage, determine whether your life demonstrates the Christian values described, or whether it demonstrates secular values instead:

Integrity (Matthew 5:33–37) _____

_____

_____

Faithfulness (Galatians 5:22) _____

_____

_____

Considering others more important than yourself (Philippians 2:3) _____

_____

_____

Opinions toward ethnic minorities (Galatians 3:26–28) _____

_____

_____

Striving for unity (Ephesians 4:1–3) _____

_____

_____

Sharing your faith (2 Corinthians 5:17–20) _____

_____

_____

Go back and review the section in this chapter titled "An Ambiguity of Terms." Then consider what is the red dye in your life. What do you need to do to get it out?

_____

_____

MIRROR WORK

Lord Jesus, as I examine my life view, help me to discern the things that have come from secular culture rather than from You. Help me to establish my life view so that, as daily details are filtered through it, my actions and reactions will be in keeping with Your desires. Amen.

In the next chapter . . .

It's time to advance to the next step in objectivity. I think we can agree that, at the bottom line of life, a man's greatest need is to be significant. Together, we will focus our attention on finding meaning and purpose for life.

4 Significance: The Search for Meaning and Purpose

The mass of men live lives of quiet desperation.

HENRY DAVID THOREAU

I have come that they may have life, and have it to the full.

JESUS, JOHN 10:10B

> **Men cannot find significance in any lasting way apart from Christ. If a man is in Christ and is submitted to God's plan and purpose, he can satisfy his greatest need in the only way that endures.**

Freeport, the Bahamas. Howard Hughes, the richest man in the world. The Xanadu, a ten-story condominium on the ocean. Howard Hughes, shunning public contact, fled to this veritable fortress in self-exile.

Two years after his death, I walked up to the imposing front door of his penthouse compound. After considerable persuasion, a maid let me in. I don't know what I expected, but what I saw was a shock! I imagined the richest man in the world would import opulent chandeliers and expensive rare art. I visualized the influence of some famous European designer in the decor.

But the sparse, austere furnishings made it look more like a rustic mountain cabin. Worn, threadbare, olive-green plaid cushions rested in cut-rate priced wooden couch frames. The bathroom fixtures looked like a cheap motel.

Hughes's wealth, power, and fame had been unmatched by any man of his time. Yet his final hideaway, where he sequestered himself from reality, was a stark reminder that money is a mortal god. He died a prisoner in his own citadel of power, betrayed by his fame. His impact began to fade into the dusty pages of history the instant his flesh turned cold.

The Problem

Whether we speak of achieving our full potential, or merely surviving to the next paycheck, men invariably talk about their need to be significant.

A man's most innate need is to find his purpose and meaning. He expresses that need in various ways.

- "I want to make a difference."
- "I want to have an impact."
- "I want to make a contribution."
- "I want to be somebody."

The difference in men is in how we go about satisfying our need to be significant. List some ways men try to achieve significance:

With money _____

_____

With power _____

_____

With prestige _____

_____

With possessions _____

_____

With influence _____

_____

How we each answer the questions *"Who am I?"* and *"Why do I exist?"* determines how we pursue our significance. Our answers divide us succinctly into two groups: those who pursue significance in appropriate ways, and those who pursue significance in inappropriate ways. Our desire to satisfy this need can take us close to or far away from the things of God.

In John 15:5, Jesus indicates where true significance lies. Copy the verse here and think through Jesus' answer.

_____

_____

_____

Look at the last part of that verse. It clearly indicates that men cannot find significance in any lasting way apart from Christ. If a man is in Christ and is submitted to God's plan and purpose, he can satisfy his greatest need in the only way that endures. Otherwise his efforts, like those of Howard Hughes, will be inappropriate, and in the end, they won't satisfy.

Who or what have you been relying on to provide your sense of personal significance?

_____

_____

Has that proven to be an appropriate or inappropriate way to accomplish that goal? Explain your answer.

_____

_____

_____

A Man's Highest Hope

A man's most innate need is to find his purpose and meaning.

What is the highest hope of a man who does not have Christ? Most men will never see their names in the newspaper. If you were a really great man—someone of national reputation—what would be the best you might expect from history? You might expect a couple of paragraphs in the *World Book Encyclopedia*. Just look up Howard Hughes.

A man's ultimate desire is immortality. We read about it in Ecclesiastes 3:11. Write that verse in the space provided.

_____

That's part of what we mean when we say we want to be significant. We want something to survive us. And in the long run, how we answer the two earlier questions—*"Who am I?"* and *"Why do I exist?"*—is a choice between two time lines: one that's eighty years long and one that lasts forever.

If we don't ultimately find our significance in Christ, we won't survive the threshold between this world and the next. Our highest hopes will come to a screeching halt. It would be better if we had never been born.

Inappropriate Ways to Find Significance

No one can question that many people satisfy their need to be significant without Christ. *Name three people you think have satisfied their need to be significant, presumably without Christ:*

(1) _____

(2) _____

(3) _____

The difference in the *quality* and *durability* of significance outside of Christ, however, is monumental. Why settle for the crumbs beneath the table when you can join in the feast? Yet many of us pursue significance in inappropriate ways. Let's look at some common ways in which the world defines significance.

Fame: Short Memories

A few years ago my daughter and I went to the U.S. Open Tennis Tournament. Moments before the Ladies Championship final match began, they introduced the great women champions of yesteryear, from the oldest to the youngest.

As the first elderly lady was escorted to center court, a handful of fans offered a few polite claps. As the announcer introduced the next one, the applause picked up a little. This continued, with each succeeding star gaining a little more applause.

By the time they called Billie Jean King's name, the applause turned from polite to robust. And when they called out Chris Evert, the great lady of tennis, the stands went wild. I wondered how long it would be before Chris Evert was virtually forgotten, worthy of only a few polite claps from a handful of courteous fans.

Fame has wings and flies away at its own will. Have you ever experienced this? Describe the impact it had on your feeling of significance.

_____

_____

_____

> **If we don't ultimately find our significance in Christ, we won't survive the threshold between this world and the next.**

Memories are short. When we try to answer the question in terms of fame and worldly accomplishment, we select an identity that will fade like sun-bleached furniture.

Possessions: Unsatisfied Eyes

The most fleeting significance comes from things. Once I bought a new luxury car. I will always remember how the metallic-blue paint glistened in the sun. The aroma from the white leather seats was like sweet perfume to a young materialist.

But about three weeks later, the novelty wore off. I noticed the same car in a different color and wished I had bought that color instead!

Describe a time that you did something similar.

_____

_____

_____

What happens to our identity when we tie it to things?

_____

_____

> **Men who achieve significant positions of responsibility and authority run one of life's greatest risks. You may begin to identify who you are with the position you hold.**

Power: What's His Name Again?

Secretary of the Interior Donald Hodell remarked about the obscurity of former Cabinet members. As a member of President Reagan's Cabinet, he reminded his department heads not to be too enamored of their titles. After all, no one remembers former secretaries, much less department heads.

Men who achieve significant positions of responsibility and authority run one of life's greatest risks. *You may begin to identify who you are with the position you hold.* The heartache comes when you no longer have the position, and you realize people were not interested in you because of who you were, but because of the position you held. They believed you could benefit them in some way.

A recently retired man said, "We come into this world as babies, and that's the way we go out. I used to be able to pick up the phone and talk to anybody I wanted to. Enjoy your power while you can, because once you retire, they don't return your phone calls anymore."

Of all the positions you have held, which proved to be the most satisfying in terms of achieving personal significance? Why is that true?

_____

_____

How have you responded to the temptation to find your significance in position?

_____

_____

The Game of Tens

If you still think a man can find lasting significance through the pursuit of fame, possessions, or power, then try this quiz to check your "significance I.Q.":

1. Name the ten wealthiest men in the world.

_____

_____

2. How about ten of the most admired men in the world?

_____

_____

3. Try for ten of the ten top corporate executives in the country.

_____

_____

4. Now list the last ten presidents of the United States.

_____

_____

5. Name any ten winners of the Nobel Peace Prize.

_____

_____

6. How about ten members of the current President of the United States' Cabinet?

_____

_____

The Game of Tens is ruthless—a heartless, dispassionate, but objective illustrator of the folly of pursuing significance apart from Jesus Christ. Even the highest achievers of our society are, as James wrote, mists that appear for a little while and then vanish (James 4:14).

To go a step further in self-examination, play the Game of Tens this way:
1. Name your ten best friends.

_____

_____

2. Name ten family members who love you.

_____

_____

3. List the ten most memorable experiences of your life.

_____

_____

_____

_____

_____

4. Name ten people you think will attend your funeral.

_____

_____

5. List ten questions you want to ask God.

(1) _____

(2) _____

(3) _____

(4) _____

(5) _____

(6) _____

(7) _____

(8) _____

(9) _____

(10) _____

The Self-gratification/Significance Distinction

As the scales have tipped toward individual rights and away from Judeo-Christian values, our society has immersed itself in self-gratifying activity. *List some ways society has dropped Judeo-Christian values in favor of individual rights (for example: abortion-on-demand, rising divorce rates, father-less children).*

_____

_____

_____

Focus on personal peace and affluence has largely replaced self-sacrificing convictions (and the resulting community building causes) that benefit the human condition. We are encouraged to spend our energies to satisfy ourselves rather than to serve others. But *significance is not possible unless what we do contributes to the welfare of others.*

If what I do is only for self-gratification, I will never derive a lasting sense of purpose and meaning from it. But when I embark on a task that will survive the test of benefiting others, I know I am doing something important. And, if I make helping others my practice, a state of significance results.

Christ spelled this out in Matthew 16:24–26. Record that passage here.

_____

_____

_____

_____

_____

The difference between self-gratification and significance is in the motive and attitude rather than the task. Two men working side by side can fulfill the same job description, yet have entirely different impacts. One runs on the fast track, clawing his way to the top. The other finds his greatest reward in helping others in a Christ-like manner.

Here's a Significance Test to help you sort through your activities: *"Does what I am about to do contribute to the welfare of others in a demonstration of faith, love, obedience, and service to Christ?"* That amounts to putting wheels on denying self, taking up our cross, and following Jesus. Accumulating wealth, power, influence, and prestige is self-gratifying, but will not satisfy your need to be significant in a lasting way.

What are you now involved in that benefits others? List examples from work, church, or elsewhere in which you are:

Mentoring others _____

_____

> **We are encouraged to spend our energies to satisfy ourselves rather than to serve others.**

Encouraging sound risk-takers _____

_____

Counseling the discouraged _____

_____

Helping those who are failing _____

_____

What opportunities have you turned down that you ought to reconsider in terms of the eternal significance they offer?

_____

_____

_____

Being a Doer

Write out the words of James 1:22–24:

_____

_____

_____

_____

_____

Because one man, Martin Luther, examined Scripture and became a doer of what he read there, half of Europe's churches became Protestant over the next forty years, initiating the Protestant Reformation. The Roman Catholic Church itself made changes. Social, political, and economic structures were reformed.

In your search for significance, have you sought your life's purpose by studying the Scriptures, as Luther did? Certainly he had no idea of the impact— the significance—his life would have. But because he believed God, he found significance, and God gave him a purpose.

Looking Closer in the Mirror:

Are you a talker or a doer? Explain your answer.

_____

_____

Do you regularly study God's Word, so He can show you the purpose for your life? _____ *Yes* _____ *No*
What has He been telling you?

_____

_____

How are you going to act upon it and be a doer?

_____

_____

■ *FAITHFULNESS*

At lunch one day a deeply committed man related his discouragement with his profession, saying he thought God might have a full-time ministry for him. He led a Bible study discipling six men, but to his surprise, our discussion revealed he was not completely faithful to his responsibilities to care for these men.

He came to this conclusion: "Why should God give me a greater job when I am not yet a faithful doer of the job He has already given me?" Now he is achieving significance without a career change. What made the difference? Faithfulness to the task God had already given him.

What God-given assignment have you been struggling with?

_____

_____

What do you sense is the root problem?

_____

_____

■ *QUESTIONS WORTH ASKING*

As you struggle candidly with this chapter, does your life feel impotent? Are you achieving your full significance? I urge you to press on with the following questions:

Are you trying to win the rat race? _____ Yes   _____ No

How do you keep score? At the end of the day, how do you measure whether or not you have been successful?

_____

_____

How does your method compare to the way God keeps score?

_____

_____

Are you disillusioned with materialism? _____ Yes   _____ No

Are you pursuing significance or self-gratification? How do you know?

_____

_____

_____

Have you been looking for significance in inappropriate ways? _____ Yes _____ No

Are you contributing to God's agenda? _____ Yes   _____ No

Do you even know what God's agenda is? _____ Yes   _____ No

Has your passive indifference contributed to the decaying state of the nation? Give an example to support your answer.

_____

_____

Are you willing to pay the price if the cost of being a Christian goes up? _____ Yes _____ No

Are you leading a life of faith, love, obedience, and service? Explain how you came to that conclusion.

_____

_____

What is your highest hope?

_____

_____

Are you a cultural or a biblical Christian? _____

If you are *dissatisfied with your answers,* pause for a moment. Acknowledge to God that you have sinned, ask Him to forgive you, and thank Him for doing so.

If you have been a *cultural Christian* with a "defeated" faith, ask Christ to take control of your life. Rededicate yourself to Him.

If you have been *playing games with God,* confess that to Him. If you have been *guilty of the sin of partial surrender*—trying to have your cake and eat it too—totally surrender yourself to Him. Ask Him to lead and guide you by His Spirit to a purpose for your life that will give you lasting significance. And then ask Him to give you the power to be faithful. Take a moment and do this now.

If you have *never placed your faith in Jesus Christ,* or if you have been *a cultural Christian with a "counterfeit" faith,* there will never be a better time to receive Christ. He offers an identity that never fades, rusts, or rots away.

If you sincerely desire to become a Christian, invite Him into your heart and life. We receive Christ by faith and repentance. Prayer is an excellent way to express faith.

The difference between self-gratification and significance is in the motive and attitude rather than the task.

MIRROR WORK

Lord Jesus, I acknowledge that I have been attempting to find significance in inappropriate ways. I have sinned against You. Thank You for dying on the cross for me and for forgiving my sins. As an act of faith, I invite You to take control of my life, and make me the kind of person You want me to be. Amen.

If you sincerely prayed this prayer, I would like to say, "Congratulations!" You have just become a Christian. I encourage you to share your decision with someone close to you. It will help you to conceptualize your commitment better, and be an encouragement to the one you tell. Find a good Bible study group, read your Bible, pray, join a Bible-believing church.

In the next chapter . . .

There are two halves to finding significance. We have just looked at the first one—finding our identity and significance in Christ. But beyond that, we must also find the purpose for which God created us. Keep reading to discover how you can tap into the mission for which God created you.

Purpose: Why Do I Exist?

5

Man's chief end is to glorify God, and to enjoy Him forever.

WESTMINSTER CONFESSION OF FAITH

The LORD foils the plans of the nations; he thwarts the purposes of the peoples. / But the plans of the LORD stand firm forever, the purposes of his heart through all generations.

PSALM 33:10–11

The most surprising thing about Tom's call wasn't that he was crying; it wasn't even that he was fifty-eight years old and crying. It was his candor that got my attention.

Tom was one of Florida's most prominent attorneys. His list of credits revealed a Who's Who in the legal field. I would have imagined him to be satisfied, were it not for the stream of tears that diluted the value of those achievements.

"My life has no meaning—no purpose," he began. "It's as though I've been chasing the wind all these years."

Tom had reached the pinnacle of professional success, yet he still ached for a sense of purpose. He attained the rung on the ladder that every young lawyer aspires to, but found the ladder reached into the clouds of disillusionment. Success created more questions than it answered.

Tom spent a lifetime pursing the god he wanted. Then one day he woke up and realized he didn't have the slightest idea who God really is. Aware of just how unfulfilled he was, and not knowing why, he accepted an invitation from a friend to a prayer breakfast. "Maybe God will have some answers," he thought.

What interested Tom most was the peace he saw in some of the men involved with the breakfast. Over the next six months, he was surprised to learn these men attributed their sense of peace and purpose to a "personal" relationship with God through Jesus Christ.

Tom found the message of Jesus intriguing and called to say he was interested in the whole story. We made an appointment to talk about it.

> **❝Purpose is not about what I do today, but it's about 'Why do I exist?'❞**

The Lure of Churchmanship

Tom wasn't sure he needed this relationship the other men enjoyed. "I've always attended church," he insisted.

"We're not talking about attending church, although that's important," I replied. "We're talking about a relationship with the living, personal God. We aren't talking about working your way in. The only way into God's favor is to receive the free gift of eternal life that comes by trusting Christ with your life."

"Well, I've been a faithful churchman for over thirty years. Are you trying to tell me I've wasted all those years? I just can't believe you would even suggest such a thing!"

"Tom, if church has been such an important part of your life, why are we together today talking about your feelings of emptiness and lack of purpose?"

Tom is not alone. He lived the first fifty-eight years of his life without giving much attention to why he thought, said, and did things. He attended church because it was the expected thing to do, not because of a deeply held conviction. He was literally just "going through the motions."

Why do so many men resist the idea of going beyond churchmanship to enter into a personal relationship with God?

_____

_____

Describe a time when you responded to the lure of churchmanship rather than to the call of a personal relationship with God.

_____

_____

_____

_____

The Problem

In your opinion, what is the best part of achieving goals?

_____

_____

Sometimes, though, we all experience some frustration along with our achievement. Why do you think that is so?

We also experience frustration when we are unable to achieve our goals, and let's face it—no one is successful in meeting every goal he sets for himself. Describe one major unmet goal in your life.

Does failure to meet your goals make you angry at God? Why do you think God has not enabled you to meet all your goals?

I don't mean to imply that setting and achieving goals is bad. For me, achieving goals is intoxicating. A number of years ago I set a goal of achieving a certain income level. I felt a deep sense of personal satisfaction when I finally reached it, but after a few weeks, the novelty wore off, and I wanted more.

Why is it that achieving a goal doesn't necessarily bring lasting satisfaction? Why are we driven to set new goals rather than really enjoying our success?

Perhaps, for you, achievement has yielded an unrelated string of hollow victories. As the satisfaction of each success fades, you find you must set new goals to enjoy a new sense of accomplishment. The fleeting satisfaction begs the question, _"Is there something bigger for my life than the routine of setting and meeting goals?"_

To be truly satisfying, our goals must reflect our examination of life's larger meaning. Most men don't know their purpose in life, or their purpose is too small.

Identity Versus Purpose

In the previous chapter we came to terms with the fundamental question _"Who am I?"_ We know that we derive our identity and meaning from understanding _who we are_ in Christ. It's a _position_ we occupy, a _relationship_ with God.

What tries to crowd into your life to keep you from finding your identity in your relationship with God?

_____

_____

Perhaps you answered "money" and "possessions." Or perhaps it was "personal power." Or perhaps it was any number of things unique to you. Yet we know these *things* don't give meaning and identity. They also don't lead us to our purpose.

That is a crucial point, for beyond knowing who we are, we need to know *why we are alive.* We need to seek basic answers to anchor our process of setting and achieving goals. In the process, we will find lasting satisfaction.

These answers lie in our responses to two simple questions:

- Why do I exist?
- What is the purpose of my life?

God has a purpose for our lives—a mission, a destiny—which is why we exist. It is the direction God wants us to move. It is the other half of our search for significance.

But in continuing our search for true significance, it is important to note that only one kind of purpose will endure. In whatever version of the Bible you use most regularly, look up Proverbs 19:21 and write it here:

_____

_____

_____

_____

Compare it with Proverbs 16:9 and 21:30, as well as Psalm 33:10–11, which is quoted at the beginning of this chapter. According to those verses, what kinds of purposes will survive?

_____

_____

_____

Goals Versus Purpose

Once we understand the direction God wants us to take—the purpose for which He created us—we can begin to set goals to move us in that direction.

Define the word goal.

_____

By comparison, define the word purpose.

_____

To me, a *goal* is a specific objective to accomplish in the near term. We will know when we have achieved it. Some insist that goals are "hard," that they must be measurable and require a specific completion date. I suggest that goals can be "soft"—qualitative, not just quantitative. For example, becoming a more loving person, developing a more loving, empathetic spirit, is not a "hard" measurable goal, but it *is* a worthwhile goal.

A *purpose,* on the other hand, reflects life's larger questions. *Purpose is not about what I do today, but it's about "Why do I exist?"* A man's purpose is what God wants him to do long term.

Purposes are *threads of continuity* we weave into the long-term view of our lives. Goals come and go, but purposes survive. They pertain to the *why we exist* part of our lives.

Examine your own situation. What do you believe God wants you to do with your life? Describe your long-term purpose.

_____

_____

_____

How will this affect your process for setting goals?

_____

_____

> **We know that we derive our identity and meaning from understanding who we are *in Christ*. It's a position we occupy, a relationship with God.**

The What/Why Distinction

Goals are *what* we do. Purposes are *why* we do what we do. It is important to ask ourselves, "Why am I pursuing this goal?" The answer to this question reveals our purpose.
Write down a specific goal for yourself.

_____

_____

Now ask yourself why you are pursuing this goal.

_____

_____

How does the "why" question help you understand the purpose behind that goal?

_____

Eternal Purpose Versus Earthly Purpose

Perhaps you are familiar with the first statement quoted at the beginning of this chapter. This particular assertion came from an unusual seventeenth-century assembly called to clarify the doctrines of Christianity by carefully examining Holy Scripture. The Westminster Shorter Catechism, an important product of the Assembly, asks and answers one hundred four essential questions that form the basic tenets of the Christian faith.

Profoundly, the first question is "What is the chief end of man?" We might rephrase it, "What is man's purpose?" or "Why does man exist?" The answer is that classic statement, "Man's chief end is to glorify God and to enjoy him forever."

Based on that statement, we can draw a distinction between God's eternal purpose for us and His earthly purpose. This is in keeping with Scripture. Record Matthew 6:31–33 in the space provided.

_____

_____

_____

_____

_____

This passage outlines two purposes—earthly and eternal. *Describe the earthly purpose in this statement.*

_____

_____

Describe the eternal purpose.

_____

_____

The *kingdom* of God is the *unseen realm,* while the *righteousness* of God is the *seen.* We are instructed to seek both the seen and the unseen. God has an eternal purpose for us, which is part of His unseen kingdom. He also has an earthly purpose for us as we live in the tangible, here-and-now world.

In the Catechism's answer, we find the eternal purpose for which God created us all—to seek His kingdom by enjoying Him forever—and the earthly purpose for which He created us all—to seek His righteousness by glorifying Him. As the chief end of man, this means we are to give priority above all else to knowing and doing God's eternal and earthly purpose for us.

We find the eternal purpose for which God created us all—to seek His kingdom by enjoying Him forever—and the earthly purpose for which He created us all—to seek His righteousness by glorifying Him.

Eternal Purpose

When Jesus tells us to seek His kingdom, He is telling us to seek eternal life. The unseen kingdom is a volunteer kingdom. He does not force Himself upon us, but rather, through Jesus, we are offered a new birth. This new birth takes us into a realm that lasts forever.

This is the most important part of our relationship with God. If God did not have as His purpose to give us eternal life (so we can enjoy Him forever), our faith would be futile. It wouldn't get us beyond the threshold of death.

Earthly Purpose

God's earthly purpose for us is why we, the "eternal" man, continue to exist here. This is a subject about which Christian men are really hungry. They ask, "What does God want me to do with my life?"

The reason we exist is to emulate the perfect example of Christ's life—in the words of the Catechism, to glorify God. How do we pull this off? By searching, striving, aspiring, and yearning to understand His purpose for our lives. *And we must apply that at several levels.*

Level One—Universal Purpose

There is a sense in which all men are alike, and God gives all men the same universal earthly purpose. We can break this down into two areas:

1. What God wants us to be.
2. What God wants us to do.

You could say that our universal earthly purpose is wrapped up in character and conduct. We read in 2 Timothy 1:9 that God *"has saved us and called us to a holy life—not because of anything we have done but because of his own purpose and grace."*

That verse sums up our universal purpose. Paraphrase it in your own, everyday terms:

_____

_____

_____

Level Two—Personal Purpose

While all of us are called to adhere to a universal purpose, there also is a sense in which each of us is unique. Therefore, God also gives each of us a specific call. In other words, God has a personal, unique, and specific purpose for your life, and it's just waiting to be discovered. Could anything be more exciting?

But how can we discover that specific purpose? I believe every man should prepare a *Written Life Purpose Statement,* encompassing what he discovers as God's personal earthly purpose for his life. This statement is intensely personal. It doesn't matter whether it makes sense to others. Your Written Life Purpose Statement is like a mission statement for your business, only the business is your own life.

God's Word reveals His known will. If possible, your purpose should spring from Scripture so you can have confidence that it conforms to God's will.

Later on, I will help you through the process of writing your own Life Purpose Statement. In the meantime, let me tell you how I arrived at mine.

My first Written Life Purpose Statement was from Philippians 3:10: "I want to know Christ and the power of his resurrection and the fellowship of sharing in his sufferings."

I desperately wanted to know Christ intimately—not just know about Him, but really know Him. I wanted to penetrate His power—to truly understand the significance of His resurrection. And I wanted to know the fellowship of sharing in

Our universal earthly purpose is wrapped up in character and conduct.

His sufferings—not just read about them, but share in sweet fellowship with the living God, because I was willing to suffer for His sake.

Later I adopted a new purpose statement. All my adult life I've been tormented by migraine headaches. Several years ago, after trying every conceivable modern and medieval remedy, I discovered that I have severe food allergies—so much so that I have never been tested for anything to which I am not allergic.

Over several years I eliminated certain foods from my diet and measured the intake of others, and, on a trial-and-error basis, have been able to reduce these daily migraines to four or five manageable headaches per week. The verses that helped me survive those years of agonizing pain are 1 Peter 4:1–2:

> Therefore, since Christ suffered in his body, arm yourselves also with the same attitude, because he who has suffered in his body is done with sin. As a result, he does not live the rest of his earthly life for evil human desires, but rather for the will of God.

The idea that through my suffering I might overcome sin and spend the rest of my earthly life for the will of God ministered to me deep inside the speechless chambers of my tortured soul.

When I began to get well after fifteen years of sometimes hopeless despair, I sensed a new purpose. At first it was without form. Words wouldn't describe it, but as time passed, as I meditated on Scripture and asked God to reshape my life's purpose, I was drawn repeatedly back to 1 Peter 4:1–2.

Finally, on February 1, 1986, years of deep unutterable groanings flowed spontaneously from my heart through my pen onto the title page of my Bible: "I want to spend the rest of my earthly life for the will of God." And that became my Written Life Purpose Statement.

Now, I invite you to examine your own life. What experiences have you endured that may shape your Life Purpose Statement?

God has a personal, unique, and specific purpose for your life, and it's just waiting to be discovered.

_____

_____

_____

Arriving at your purpose statement may involve a difficult journey. Because of this, later in this chapter I will help you through the process of defining your own Written Life Purpose Statement.

Level Three—Other Life Purposes

In addition to your Written Life Purpose Statement, you can drop down a level and develop written purpose statements for specific areas of your life.

Think through the reasons why you exist. As you uncover nuggets of wisdom about different areas, jot them down and keep track of what God is saying to you about the why part of your life. *Here are some specific areas to consider. You will want to come back and upgrade them as you continue working through this book.*

Relationship with God: _____

_____

Relationship with family (wife, children, parents): _____

_____

Relationships on the job: _____

_____

Use of your gifts: _____

_____

Service for the Lord: _____

_____

Goals and Activities

Goals and activities put specific actions to our purposes. They are the natural result of a carefully examined life. For one of the categories listed above, work through the following exercise:

Purpose: _____

Goal: _____

Activities: _____

For example, one of mine, relating to relationships on the job, looks like this:

> *Purpose:* To be an encourager.
> *Goal:* Take one man to lunch each week.
> *Activities:* Write notes, call hurting men.

The Apostle Paul: A Life with Purpose

The apostle Paul remains one of the most exciting personalities in all of history. His fortitude boggles the mind. *Read 2 Corinthians 11:24–27 and record the hardships he endured.*

_____

_____

_____

_____

_____

_____

_____

What kind of life purpose statement would you expect from this kind of person? You'll find what I believe to be Paul's Written Life Purpose Statement in Colossians 1:28–29. In whatever version of the Bible you prefer, look up that passage and record it here.

_____

_____

_____

_____

_____

In your opinion, how did this purpose statement help the apostle Paul endure his "job-related stress" of opposition, persecution, and pain?

_____

Do you think you can have that same sense of mission, purpose, and destiny in your own life? Why or why not?

_____

ooking Closer in the Mirror:

Now it's your turn. I can almost guarantee that, if you put it off, you will not come back to develop your own Written Life Purpose Statement. So set aside some time to get started and tackle it now. It could be a truly life-transforming experience.

■ DEVELOPING A WRITTEN LIFE PURPOSE STATEMENT

Use this worksheet to help you discover God's purpose for your life. Your reward will be a sense of personal destiny and mission. Follow these practical steps:

(1) *Ask God to reveal your personal earthly purpose to you. Then find Psalm 32:8 and record it here:*

_____

_____

_____

Decide to buy something great with the rest of the days you have to spend.

Now claim that verse as a promise that He will answer.

(2) *Search the Bible for verses that capture your sense of God's purpose for your earthly life. Record verses that give a special sense of meaning and purpose.*

Here are some you can begin to explore: Joshua 24:15; Proverbs 3:5–6; Matthew 6:33; 22:37–40; 28:19–20; John 4:34; 15:1–9, 15; 17:4; Acts 20:24; 1 Corinthians 10:31; Ephesians 2:10; Philippians 3:10; Proverbs 30:7–9; Micah 6:8; Acts 1:8; Ecclesiastes 12:13. Write down any other verses you think are big enough to last a lifetime.

_____

_____

(3) *Be patient and wait for God to reveal Himself. It may take some time—perhaps days, weeks, or months.*

(4) *Once you find a verse you believe expresses God's earthly purpose for you, paraphrase it in your own words.*

_____

_____

Now use that verse to write a "draft" of your Written Life Purpose Statement.

_____

_____

Once you are satisfied that you have perfected it, write it in the front of your Bible and date it.

(5) *Do all of the above asking God to give you a passion for life so you will not be numbered among those timid souls who never know what it is like to taste His full measure. Decide to buy something great with the rest of the days you have to spend.*

And keep in mind that, as you encounter new experiences, God may change your purpose statement, just as He did mine. You will want to review this process occasionally.

MIRROR WORK

Lord God, I acknowledge that You are sovereign. I praise You because You have ordered eternal and earthly purposes for me. I confess that I have not sought Your purposes, or I have forgotten the sense of destiny and purpose I once knew. Forgive me for pursuing my goals without seeking Your purpose for my life, through the study of Scripture and prayer, to which I now pledge myself to do daily. Amen.

In the next chapter . . .

If significance and purpose come from our relationship with God through Christ, then other than financial gain, what can we really expect to gain from our employment? Together, we will discover how we can gain the proper sense of contentment that God intends for us to find in the workplace.

6 The Secret of Job Contentment

The most outstanding characteristic of Eastern civilization is to know contentment, whereas that of Western civilization is not to know contentment.

HU SHIH[1]

I have learned the secret of being content in any and every situation.

PAUL, PHILIPPIANS 4:12

"Work is how God intended us to occupy our time in the perfection of His plan for Creation."

The above quotations show a strange dichotomy between what is and what should be in our "Christianized" Western culture. *Why do we in Western civilization reveal such tension between the contentment we ought to experience and the discontent that so obviously characterizes us?*

The Answer in a Movie?

A good answer can be found in the Oscar-winning movie *Chariots of Fire*. This fact-based film depicts the quests of Harold Abrahams and Eric Liddell to win gold medals in the 1924 Olympics. Their similarities lay in their accomplishments. Their differences lay in their motivations. Abrahams did everything for himself. Liddell did everything for God.

"I Feel His Pleasure"

Eric Liddell's sister Jennie mistook her brother's love of running for rebellion against God. She pressed him to return to the mission field in China, where they had been born and where their parents lived. One day she became upset because he had missed a mission meeting, so Eric decided to talk with her.

Clutching her arms, trying to explain his calling to run, he said, "Jen-

nie, Jennie. You've got to understand. I believe God made me for a purpose
—China. But He also made me fast!—and when I run, I feel His pleasure!"

This beautiful statement reveals Eric's contentment in doing what he
knew God created him to do.

*Do a quick mental tour of the men you see regularly at church and at the
office. Who is doing things for God? Who is doing things for himself?*

---

*Now consider your own motivations. Do you usually act to benefit yourself
or to glorify God?*

In Sharp Contrast

Eric's passionate explanation is in sharp contrast to a later scene in the
movie, one hour before Harold Abrahams' final race. While his trainer gives
him a rubdown, Abrahams laments to his best friend, "I'm twenty-four and
I've never known contentment. I'm forever in pursuit, and I don't even
know what it is I'm chasing."

*His comment reflects the same attitude we saw in the previous chapter in
Tom, the Florida lawyer. Does it also reflect your attitude?*

If it does, you will eventually discover the same thing Abrahams did.
His experience demonstrates that, without godly motivation for your tasks,
you can even win a gold medal and still not feel content. Liddell, on the
other hand, ran to experience God's pleasure. In the process he not only
won his medal, but also he found lasting contentment.

Describe a specific time when you have felt God's pleasure in what you do.

> **Without godly
> motivation for your
> tasks, you can
> even win a gold
> medal and still not
> feel content.**

---

*Is that a regular, consistent occurrence, or do you usually find that, like
Abrahams, your hard work doesn't really bring any measure of genuine contentment? Explain your answer.*

_____

_____

_____

The Problem

Published surveys indicate that up to 80 percent of working Americans occupy the wrong job. They work at tasks that aren't really suited to their personalities or needs.

Are you in that 80 percent? If so, you probably know the lack of contentment that pervades the American workplace.[2]

Why don't we get what we want from our jobs?

_____

_____

_____

Do you usually act to benefit yourself, or to glorify God?

In hot pursuit of the good life, most men don't find God's pleasure. Instead, they find contentment to be elusive and mysterious. Their "if onlys" betray a general dissatisfaction.

- *"If only* I had gotten that promotion."
- *"If only* that big deal had gone through."
- *"If only* I had married someone else."

What are your "if onlys"?

_____

_____

_____

Men *must* feel a sense of accomplishment and satisfaction in their work if they are to find contentment. If a man is unhappy in his work, *he is unhappy!* His feeling of discontent spills over at home and even at church.

If that's true, then why, in your opinion, do so many men stay at jobs that offer no contentment?

_____

_____

Some men stay on at unfulfilling jobs because they want to maintain a lifestyle, impress other people, win the rat race, please family, build an empire, acquire things, live out their fantasies, or simply because they feel trapped.

Does your job offer you a sense of fulfillment? If not, why are you staying with it?

Is Work a Curse on Man?

Some men who are willing and anxious to do God's will, yet remain unhappy in their employment, simply don't understand God's view of vocation.

You may be surprised to learn that work is not the result of the Fall of man. It is true, of course, that when Satan tempted Adam and Eve and they succumbed, God prescribed that *"through painful toil you will eat of it all the days of your life"* (Genesis 3:17).

We are all familiar with that verse. For most of us, it has affected our attitudes toward work, either consciously or subconsciously. *In your most honest opinion, how has it affected your attitude?*

> **Work is not the result of the Fall of man.**

Now, look up that verse—Genesis 3:17—and read the whole thing very carefully. Notice that God cursed *the ground—not work.*

Work is a holy vocation established by God *before* Adam and Eve sinned. Look up Genesis 2:15 and write it here:

That was *before* the Fall, so it is obvious that God intended work to be a holy vocation. Work is how God intended us to occupy our time in the perfection of His plan for Creation. The holiness of vocation is as close to the fabric of Christianity as dye is to cloth.

How does this alter your perspective regarding your job?

A Substitute for Contentment

In my opinion, the secret of job contentment is not in getting what you want. It's in redefining what you need.

Recently an out-of-town investment partner and I reviewed by phone the terms of a good-sized transaction I was negotiating with a third party. We had been going over the contract terms for over an hour when he said, "Man, I love this!"

"Love what?" I asked.

"The adrenalin. I love the adrenalin! This is what business is all about! This is war; it really is war! I wish I could be there with you to negotiate—I love the rush!"

I assured him I would happily trade places, because the other party was a very tough customer. But perhaps you can relate to him. *Have you ever experienced a feeling similar to that which my partner expressed? Briefly outline the experience and describe its impact on you.*

_____

_____

_____

_____

Most men who like their jobs also like the thrill of the deal or the satisfaction of completing a project. We are made to enjoy the thrill—to feel God's pleasure in our work. But many of us are tempted to become "deal junkies," living to please ourselves (like Abrahams), going from one deal fix to the next in search of contentment. The thrill takes on new meaning when we do it for God.

We can readily admit that there is more to job contentment than shooting up on adrenalin. If you believe that to be true, explain in your own words what you believe is the secret to deep and abiding job contentment.

_____

_____

_____

Redefining Our Ambition

In my opinion, *the secret of job contentment is not in getting what you want. It's in redefining what you need.*

The distinction between wants and needs has always been an integral part of Christian thought. Most men, like Abrahams of *Chariots of Fire*, think only of what they want. The paradox, of course, is that in the process, they find only discontent. Others, like Liddell, redefine their needs and live to please God. They feel His pleasure, and in the process, they find real contentment.

But how does all of this apply to the everyday work world? Stop for a moment and consider your career ambition. Are you aiming to be significant in your industry? Do you want to be an authority figure? Do you hope to make lots of money, to win prestige, to gain respect, to be important, to be "somebody"? Take a moment to write down your ultimate career ambition.

_____

_____

Compare that with what the apostle Paul wrote in 1 Thessalonians 4:1 and 11–12. Write those verses here.

_____

_____

_____

_____

_____

How do Paul's words compare to your own ambition?

_____

_____

_____

Do you sense a need to redefine your ambition? If so, how do you want to reword it?

_____

_____

When God Forces a Redefinition

Sometimes God stops us in our tracks and *forces* us to redefine our career ambition. That's what happened to me.

There was a time when I worked totally for my own ambitions. When I became a Christian, I dedicated myself to Christ and asked Him to bless my ambitions, but they were still my plans rather than God's. He allowed me to bumble along. When I was blocked from a goal, it never occurred to me that God was saying No.

But when the Tax Reform Act of 1986 passed, my ambitions collided with the stark reality of the real estate equity market, or, should I say, the disappearance of the real estate equity market. Literally overnight, equity was a dead topic. No one would talk to me. With many large development projects unfunded, I suddenly realized that what I wanted simply wasn't going to happen.

The result? My ambition collided with God's plan for my life, and the glory days were replaced with agonizing months of working out problems. People had to be laid off, expenses slashed, lenders contacted.

It was a very humbling experience, but through it all, I found that the secret of job contentment truly was not in getting what I wanted, but in redefining what I needed. What I wanted was an ever-expanding business, but what I needed was to crucify my ambition.

I've been a lot more quiet lately, minding my own business and working "hands on," as noted in the Thessalonian verses quoted previously. Because of the "Tax Reform Wars," I decided I'm not making anymore plans for myself. If God wants me to pursue a plan, He will have to show me clearly that it's His ambition for my life, not my own.

It is *possible* to enjoy deep contentment even when the walls are crashing down around you.

Contentment in Hard Times

My experience, and probably yours as well, shows that it is possible to enjoy deep contentment even when the walls are crashing down around you. *Perhaps you have experienced a similar time when God stepped into your life and forced you to redefine your ambition. Describe that time.*

_____

_____

_____

_____

Did you experience contentment in spite of your circumstances? Why or why not?

_____

_____

_____

I was surprised to learn that we can be content in the midst of suffering —not mere inconvenience, but severe, agonizing suffering. The issue, I learned, is that our circumstances don't determine our contentment. Our faith and trust in God do.

Even in my darkest hours, when it seemed the full force of my adversaries and my own sins would crush me completely, there was peace in knowing I was in the center of God's will for my life—not at first, but when I humbled myself, confessed, and redefined my ambition. This peace came even when I was still under the heavy hand of His discipline.

The Holy Spirit is the author of "sweet sorrow." In the midst of calamity, pain, anguish, and suffering, He tells us what we are facing is part of God's plan for our lives (see Romans 8:28). That's why the apostle Paul could say, "For Christ's sake, I delight in weaknesses, in insults, in hardships, in persecutions, in difficulties. For when I am weak, then I am strong" (2 Corinthians 12:10).

If you are experiencing a tough situation now or have in the past, perhaps even a situation that goes beyond inconvenience to the level of real suffering, what does this verse reveal about that situation?

> *". . . for Christ's sake, I delight in weaknesses, in insults, in hardships, in persecutions, in difficulties. For when I am weak, then I am strong."*

_____

_____

_____

_____

_____

Looking Closer in the Mirror:

■ WHO IS BOSS?

The process of redefining our ambitions often requires that we also redefine our roles. Consider, for instance, are you your own boss? If not, are you working toward becoming your own boss?

How can that desire to be independent collide with God's desire? The apostle Paul wrote for a different time, but the principle he explained remains valid. *In the version of the Bible you use most regularly, look up Colossians 3:22–24 and write it here:*

_____

_____

_____

_____

_____

_____

Now, at the beginning of the passage, cross out the word slaves, *or its equivalent in your version, and substitute the word* employees. *Cross out the words* earthly masters, *or their equivalent in your version, and substitute the word* employers. *What is the implication?*

_____

_____

We are to serve our earthly bosses because they hold God's proxy as our employers. But God still owns the company, because He owns everything. What does this imply for your current position or job?

_____

_____

■ *IF YOU OWN YOUR OWN COMPANY*

If you own your own company, you may want to take the same action we did. In 1974, I read a book, *God Owns My Business* by Stanley Tam. My partner read it, too, and was equally excited.

So we made God our senior partner. We endeavored to run our decisions by Him, not perfectly, but we tried. After my partner sold out to me in 1977, I continued with God at the helm. It's His company. He is the boss, and we trust Him to meet our needs. We also work very hard.

What do you expect will happen if you turn your company over to God?

_____

_____

Why do you expect that?

_____

_____

How might it affect your business practices?

_____

_____

How might it affect your relationships with employees?

_____

_____

■ RELINQUISHING CONTROL

In some ways, redefining our relationship to God in terms of His right to be boss can be equated with relinquishing control to Him. This can be illustrated by an experience of a man I know named Steve.

Steve sold his eighty-employee company to a large national concern, but he decided to stay on as a branch manager, even though he didn't have to. Most people never knew there had been a change of ownership, because there was no visible change, but the change in authority structure, reporting relationships, and goals was total and complete. His role changed sharply.

Steve gave up his rights as boss and became an employee. This reflects a similar relationship to that which Jesus described when He said, "Any of you who does not give up everything he has cannot be my disciple" (Luke 14:33). *Describe in your own words what Jesus meant by that.*

God simply does not want to give it to us more than one day at a time.

_____

_____

_____

What is your ambition? Will it survive your physical death? Will it pass the Luke 14:33 test? Explain your answer.

_____

_____

_____

I think we can agree that Jesus didn't necessarily mean we all must sell our possessions and head for China. Instead, I think He meant we are to surrender everything we have to Christ. He will likely leave us in place, hiring us as branch managers.

What area of your life have you not yet surrendered to Christ?

_____

Are you the owner of your career, or the branch manager? Explain your answer.

_____

_____

_____

■ *DAILY SURRENDER*

After many years as a business planner, I am convinced that God simply does not want to give it to us more than one day at a time. When we strive to control the future with our own plans, we choke off God's plans. *James 4:13–15 has a special warning regarding our attempts to control the future. Record those verses here.*

_____

_____

_____

_____

_____

In today's vernacular, perhaps we would paraphrase this passage like this: "Live one day at a time." From your perspective, what will it mean for you to live one day at a time in the manner prescribed by James?

_____

_____

_____

_____

MIRROR WORK

*L*ord Jesus, help me to make You the boss of every aspect of my life. Teach me to redefine my ambition so it's in line with Your plan for my life. Let me feel Your pleasure in what I do. Amen.

In the next chapter . . .

Building on this understanding of the proper place for work, now we will balance that by looking at relationships. Why do men score so low in relationships? We'll try to answer that question together, and then we'll look at what we can do about it.

PART TWO

Solving

Our

Relationship

Problems

Broken Relationships

Happy families are all alike; every unhappy family is unhappy in its own way.

TOLSTOY

Your wife will be like a fruitful vine within your house; your sons will be like olive shoots around your table. / Thus is the man blessed who fears the LORD.

PSALM 128:3–4

Perhaps you remember my comment in an earlier chapter that I didn't know of even ten truly happy marriages. Yet according to Psalm 128:3–4, quoted above, the man who fears the Lord can expect to enjoy a very different situation. *Rewrite those verses in your own words, keeping the main point, but using imagery that represents your family's lifestyle.*

<blockquote>"I was blind as a bat, thinking, 'We've arrived!' 'Yes,' Patsy added, 'but at the wrong place.'"</blockquote>

_____

_____

_____

_____

Families should be considered a blessing from God. But our culture provides such an array of enticing activities that family relationships may, intentionally or unintentionally, fall lower and lower on our list of priorities.

Maybe my experience will awaken memories for you.

Our children were young—one a preschooler and one elementary age. The business finally started to do reasonably well. People who before wouldn't give me the time of day suddenly acted friendly.

The mail started to bring invitations to join organizations and attend functions—community chest groups, societies, dinner parties, service organizations. Money was always involved. I couldn't believe the pressure we felt to join. On what basis should we prioritize our yeses and nos?

For a long time I said yes to just about everything. Then the reality of what we were becoming started to dawn on us. We were about to buy into a network of shallow relationships built on the sole foundation of commercial gain. Time with our kids, who needed us most and whom we love most, was about to go into remission. And the ones who were going to get our time wanted a relationship only as long as we were successful.

Patsy, the proverbial woman of intuition, saw what was happening first, but I was blind as a bat, thinking, "We've arrived!"

"Yes," Patsy added, "but at the wrong place."

One evening, as we reviewed our calendar and a stack of time-consuming opportunities, the thought came, "Why not prioritize everything we do on the basis of who's going to be crying at our funeral?" The results saved our family.

List some of your activities that have a "Come if you have money" or "Come if you have prestige" ring to the invitation.

Many of us are hurting silently in our relationships with our wives and children.

_____

_____

_____

But what about your family? How are they faring in the contest for your time? *Try and list five activities or functions that you have missed with your wife or kids because of wrong priorities.*

_____

_____

_____

_____

The Problem

Let's be honest. Work and its related commitments can be intoxicating. Work features the thrill of the deal. And beyond that, at the office we generally don't have to deal with our wives' occasional unpredictable emotions and our whiny kids. Where do you really experience less stress—at home, or at the office? Many men truly find that work offers a place to escape.

In your own words, explain why many men get so caught up in their careers that they forget to be good husbands and fathers.

_____

_____

_____

Have you found this to be true in your own life? If so, have you found the pursuit of a career to be worth the price you have to pay for success? Explain.

_____

_____

_____

The thrill of a job-related victory may greatly supersede the stress of meeting the demands of family. Yet no amount of success at the office can compensate for failure at home. Many of us are hurting silently in our relationships with our wives and children, and also with our parents and even our friends and business associates. Often, we wound those whom we love most.

Have you recently wounded someone for whom you care deeply? If so, describe the situation.

_____

_____

_____

Perhaps the effect on the other party was obvious, but how did that situation affect you?

_____

_____

_____

How do we hurt ourselves when we wound others?

_____

_____

The simple fact is that, *in pursuit of the good life, many men leave a trail of broken relationships.* Our secular culture has stirred man's natural inclination to pursue fame and fortune into a caldron, creating an unstable mixture of ambition and vision of grandeur. All too often this concoction explodes, scattering what should be our most treasured possessions—our relationships—like the irretrievably shattered fragments of a precious vase, an heirloom that was destined to be the joy of future generations. Somehow the broken shards, like Humpty Dumpty, just cannot be put back together again.

Certainly we need to do what we can to mend our shattered relation-

No amount of success at the office can compensate for failure at home.

ships. But what we need most is a cool resolve to catch the vase, now tumbling through the air, before it bursts into a thousand little bits. *In your own words, what is the advantage to this kind of "preventive medicine" for relationships?*

_____

_____

_____

_____

List some specific steps you can use to implement this "preventive medicine" in your relationships and avoid repeating the kinds of wounds you and those you love have experienced in the past.

_____

_____

_____

_____

Our secular culture has stirred man's natural inclination to pursue fame and fortune into a caldron, creating an unstable mixture of ambition and vision of grandeur.

The Two Greatest Regrets

All of us have regrets when we look back on our lives. Take a few minutes to identify your two greatest regrets.

(1) _____

(2) _____

Now, let's see how your responses compare with the results of my own informal research. As a young businessman, I made it a habit to ask older men about their greatest regrets. I was hoping to glean some wise tips of what to avoid in my own life.

While the responses varied, two showed up on almost every man's list. First, a man would say, "I was so busy taking care of company business that I never put my own financial house in order. Now I'm fifty-five, and I have to do in ten years what I should have done in forty."

Then my contact would add, "I was so busy trying to improve my family's standard of living that, before I knew it, my children were grown and gone, and I never got to know them. Now they are too busy for me."

Perhaps you are among those who still think personal success is worth the price you are extracting from your family. You might not see any problem with your hectic, business-oriented life now. *But when you are the age of these men, how will you feel about the price you paid for running the rat race?*

Why Do Men Score So Low in Relationships?

Given the responses I gained from my question about men's regrets, we must ask ourselves a serious question. Why *do* men tend to score so low in relationships?

Someone has observed that men are generally more task-oriented, while women are generally more relationship-oriented. I have found this to be true in my own experience. When someone calls me for lunch, my first question is, "What do you want to talk about?" I'm usually thinking, "If I can find out what the agenda is, maybe I can handle it with a five-minute call instead of a one-hour lunch."

But when one of my wife's friends calls for lunch no questions are asked. Women will get together just to be together. Men tend to need a reason to meet. Most men seem to work off of agendas.

Why do you think that is true?

_____

_____

_____

> **By having the same attitude as Christ, we can break with the self-interested, secular view of the world.**

I believe that God gave men the natural inclination to be task oriented. We usually refer to this as the *creation mandate* or *cultural mandate*, the mandate to fill, subdue, and rule the earth (see Genesis 1:28). But we must strike the right balance between task and relationship. Only then do we find peace.

A Good Start

Most men don't intend to allow their tasks to overwhelm their relationships. They start chasing the good life with clear thinking and pure motivation.

Our goal? To improve our family's standard of living. The task is simply a means to that end. But we get so involved in the task—and it *can* be exciting—that we lose sight of our reason for working so hard. What was intended to be the means to an end becomes, in reality, the end itself.

Unfortunately, instead of encouraging and nurturing family and relationship values, our society suggests that professional achievement and financial success are the measure of a man.

I will refer to parent/child and husband/wife relationships in greater detail later. For now, keep in mind that *people know if you are for them or not.*

> **We can fabricate an image for our business associates and friends, but when the shades go down, the men we really are come out of the shadows.**

We get so involved in the task—and it can be exciting—that we lose sight of our reason for working so hard.

We can say whatever we want, but people figure out the truth in time. If we tell our wives we love them, but spend Monday night at softball practice, Wednesday night at church, Saturday on the golf course, and the rest of our time watching TV, our wives can tell if we are *really* for them.

For wives and children, time is everything in a relationship. *If you don't have enough time for your family, you can be 100 percent certain you are not following God's will for your life.*

Looking Closer in the Mirror:

I believe that no amount of success at the office can compensate for failure at home. *Do you agree or disagree, and why?*

_____

_____

_____

Think about your own situation for a moment. In the previous chapter we talked about feeling God's pleasure in your employment. Do you also feel God's pleasure when you are with your family? How about when you are with your friends? Describe a specific instance that supports your answer.

_____

_____

_____

When did you last meet a man who, without any prompting, described himself in terms of the impact he is having on his children? I must confess that I have met only one. So I challenge you to think radically. How can you refocus your values enough to describe yourself in terms of the impact you are having on your children? Or on your wife?

_____

_____

_____

■ TAKING AN INTEREST IN OTHERS

Admittedly, the preceding exercise will be a challenge for many of us. We are naturally self-centered, so we tend to gravitate toward the things that build our own images. Developing an interest in the welfare of others is a cultivated skill. Without the power of Christ, only a handful of people would be interested in others.

The apostle Paul made a statement that aptly describes our age: "For everyone looks out for his own interests, not those of Jesus Christ" (Philippians 2:21).

Describe an incident you saw recently that demonstrated this kind of attitude.

_____

_____

_____

_____

In contrast, Philippians 2:4–5 explains what our attitudes should reflect. Look up that passage and record Paul's words.

_____

_____

_____

_____

Of course, not all people who claim to be Christians really model this Scripture. *What would the world be like if everyone ignored this passage and just looked out for his own interests?*

_____

_____

But if we refuse to ignore this passage and choose instead to obey it, how will this affect our relationships?

_____

_____

_____

Thank God for the millions of Christians who *do* look after the interests of others. More of us need to. By having the same attitude as Christ, we can break with the self-interested, secular view of the world. Our score in relationships will improve so much, we might even make the dean's list!

Now it's time for honest self-analysis. On the following scale, with 1 being completely interested in self and 10 showing a completely healthy interest in the well-being of others, put an "X" on the line where you feel you are right now.

| 1 | 2 | 3 | 4 | 5 | 6 | 7 | 8 | 9 | 10 |

Interested in self   Interested in others

Explain why you evaluated yourself that way.

_____

_____

_____

What are some specific steps you can take to move closer to being a "10"?

_____

_____

_____

_____

■ GRUMPY MEN

Describe your communication skills at the office.

_____

_____

How does that compare to your communication skills at home?

_____

_____

_____

How we are behind the closed doors of our own private castle is how we *really* are. We can fabricate an image for our business associates and friends, but when the shades go down, the men we really are come out of the shadows.

If we are honest, most of us will have to admit that we are much more polite at work. In fact, we can be downright grumpy at home. We trap ourselves into thinking our grouchiness and abusiveness is excusable. Our wives and kids just don't understand us. If only they knew what we men put up with in the course of a workday, they would break their necks to make our lives more bearable!

What might be the most common excuses you have heard from men regarding their grumpiness at home?

_____

_____

What are you like behind the closed doors of your own home?

_____

_____

If you had to honestly admit that you are often grumpy, how have you excused it?

_____

_____

Is it a legitimate excuse, or is it just a cover up? Dr. Henry Brandt, a Christian psychologist, says, "Other people don't create your spirit, they only reveal it." That means our wives and kids don't make us grumpy. We simply are grumpy people looking for a place to grump.

In my own situation, when I acknowledged that my wife was not the cause of my anger and frustration, it unlocked the door to her friendship. When I began to include her by sharing my deepest thoughts and hurts with her, instead of taking out my frustrations on her, a new friend started showing up at home every day.

At what level are you sharing with your wife?

_____

_____

How do you think she feels about your level of communication? If you aren't sure, perhaps you should ask her.

_____

_____

Are you satisfied with that level of communication? Why or why not?

_____

_____

List some specific things you can do to improve your communication with your family.

MIRROR WORK

Lord Jesus, help me to see if there is an imbalance in my life between my career and my relationships. Help me to learn the value that You place on people, and to relate with others in the way You want me to. Amen.

In the next chapter . . .

This chapter has dealt with a very important issue. Now it's time to get more precise. Let's examine some specific relationships to see how the rat race is affecting them and what we can do about it.

Children: How to Avoid Regrets

My child arrived just the other day; he came to the world in the usual way. But there were planes to catch and bills to pay; he learned to walk while I was away.

SANDY AND HARRY CHAPIN[1]

Fathers, do not exasperate your children; instead, bring them up in the training and instruction of the Lord.

EPHESIANS 6:4

T*he salmon nearly leaped onto their hooks! That was a far cry from the day before when the four anglers couldn't even seem to catch an old boot.*

Disappointed but not discouraged, they had climbed aboard their small seaplane and skimmed over the Alaskan mountains to a pristine, secluded bar where the fish were sure to bite.

They parked their aircraft and waded upstream, where the water teemed with ready-to-catch salmon. Later that afternoon, when they returned to camp, they were surprised to find the seaplane high and dry. The tides had fluctuated twenty-three feet, and the pontoons rested on a bed of gravel. Since they couldn't fly out till morning, they settled in for the night and enjoyed some of their catch for dinner, then slept in the plane.

In the morning the seaplane was adrift, so they promptly cranked the engine and took off. Too late, they realized one of the pontoons had been punctured and was filled with water. The extra weight threw the plane into a circular pattern. Within moments the seaplane careened into the sea and capsized.

Dr. Phil Littleford determined that everyone was alive, including his twelve-year-old son, Mark. He suggested they pray, which the other two men quickly endorsed. No safety equipment could be found on board—no life vests, no flares, nothing. The plane gurgled and submerged into the blackness of the icy sea. Fortunately, they all had waders, which they inflated. The frigid Alaskan water chilled their breath.

> **"If we are willing to go so far as to die for our children, why is it that we often don't seem willing to live for them?"**

They all began to swim for shore, but the rip-tide countered every stroke. The two men with Phil and Mark were strong swimmers. They both made shore, one just catching the tip of land as the tides pulled them toward the sea.

They last saw Phil and Mark as a disappearing dot on the horizon, swept arm-in-arm out to sea. Phil could have made it to the shoreline, but that would have meant abandoning his son. Their bodies were never found.

What is your emotional response to Phil Littleford's commitment to his son?

Do you think you would do the same thing as Phil if you were in this situation?

What father wouldn't answer yes? What father would not be willing to die for his children? *But why, if we are willing to die for our kids, do we so often seem unwilling to live for them?*

The Problem

In contrast to that story about Phil Littleford, the first quotation at the beginning of this chapter comes from a popular song called "Cat's in the Cradle." Go back and read the words. *Why do you think this song became so popular? Was it because it touched a nerve in our collective unconscience as men? Or was it because so many children responded to these sentiments?*

How much time per day are you spending with your children?

Dr. James Dobson, the respected Christian psychologist, cites research by Dr. Urie Bronfenbrenner. He asked a group of middle-class men to estimate the time spent with their one-year-old children. Their average response—*fifteen to twenty minutes per day.* Yet when Dr. Bronfenbrenner attached microphones to the children's shirts to record actual parental interaction, the average daily time each dad spent with his kids was a mere *thirty-seven seconds.*[2]

That may be a shocking statistic, but stop and think about it for a moment. How much time per day are you spending with your children?

Research indicates the average child watches four to seven hours of TV each day. How does that compare with your children's viewing habits?

Which is having more impact on your kids—you or the TV?

Quality Versus Quantity

Many of us excuse our lack of attention to our kids by saying, "Oh sure, I can't give my kids a lot of time, but hey, it's the quality that counts—not the quantity."

How does it make you feel when someone you admire and respect, someone with whom you have a friendly relationship, is unable to find time for you?

_____

_____

In light of your answer, how do you think it makes your kids feel when you can't find time for them?

_____

_____

A *Fortune* magazine article titled "The Money Society" provides some insight into that issue:

> Psychoanalysts find that many money addicts are children of parents too preoccupied, overworked, or withdrawn to respond with the appropriate oohs and ahs to baby's smiles and antics. The children consequently never stop looking for the withheld applause and pleased response, and money helps them get it—even takes the place of it. . . .
>
> But . . . the ante always goes up because the need is never satisfied. The kid wants a human response. Some of these people . . . end up . . . complaining that their life has no purpose.[3]

It's not exactly a pretty picture, is it? And examining the statistics related to teenagers doesn't make the picture any prettier. Dawson McAllister, specializing in teen ministry, notes that over one million teenage girls become pregnant each year. By the time they graduate from high school, 70 percent of American girls and 80 percent of American boys have lost their virginity.

"Not my kids," you might say. But what are you doing to prevent it? After all, Christian families are not immune to that statistical scenario. And it gets worse, because the pressure experienced by our young people is not limited to sex. It's all adding up and taking its toll.

A 1987 survey, sponsored by the Department of Health and Human Services and health education groups, polled eleven thousand eighth- and tenth-graders. Of those who responded, 42 percent of the girls and 25 percent of the boys have seriously considered suicide. A full 18 percent of the girls and 11 percent of the boys have actually tried to commit suicide.[4]

Perfectionist parents often have trouble letting their kids be kids.

What values are you sharing with your children, be they teenaged or younger, to help them avoid becoming a statistic?

_____

_____

What values would you like to share with your children, but you just haven't had the opportunity to do so yet?

_____

_____

Why haven't you made the opportunity?

_____

_____

What are you going to do about it?

_____

_____

Freedom to Be Kids

Go back and read Ephesians 6:4, quoted at the beginning of this chapter. Let's face it—Paul wouldn't have issued this admonition if fathers never exasperated their children.

Some dads are guilty of this because they are perfectionists. Perfectionist parents often have trouble letting their kids be kids. I once heard a dad screaming at his elementary-aged son. "Why don't you act your age?!?" he asked. Actually, that's exactly what this youngster was doing—acting his age. *What did the father really mean?*

_____

_____

I believe he really meant, "Why don't you act *my* age? Why don't you act like an adult?" It's easy enough to see the folly of this attitude in someone else, but we often don't recognize it in ourselves. I know I didn't.

I'm a perfectionist by nature. I like things to be just so. This doesn't mix well with tiny creatures drooling over everything in sight. Through a pointed comment from my wife, I finally saw what my perfectionist ideals were doing to my kids.

When our two children were toddlers, I was always uptight about the new scratches showing up daily on our coffee table. This was a real point of contention with my wife, who could care less about such matters.

Finally, Patsy couldn't take it anymore and said, "You leave my children alone. I'll not have you ruining a million-dollar child over a three-hundred-dollar coffee table!"

It finally connected with my brain. I was more interested in the table than in the emotional welfare of my kids. I asked Patsy to forgive me and told her, "Let them do whatever they like to anything in the house. When they are grown, we'll buy a whole new houseful of furniture."

Describe a similar situation in your home. How have your children failed to measure up to your adult demands?

_____

_____

_____

Beyond buying your furniture from the thrift store, list some ways you can let your kids be kids in your home.

_____

_____

_____

Another way we fail to let our kids be kids shows up in our responses to their emotional expressions. One day my daughter was crying over some neighborhood spat. I barked out four quick, easy steps to solve the problem. At that point she "boo-hooed" all the louder.

"Dad," she sniffed, "from now on (sniff), when I'm crying (sniff, sniff), would you please not say anything that's logical?"

What if I had responded with a big empathetic hug instead of a brief, action-packed outline designed to correct the situation?

_____

_____

_____

Protection from the World

Not only do we expect our children to behave like adults and respond like adults, but in many ways we also expect them to sift through our

Not only do we expect our children to behave like adults and respond like adults; in many ways we also expect them to sift through our culture like adults.

culture like adults. But because our kids are naive, they are ill-equipped to deal with the realities of our sinful world.

When we allow them to be indiscriminantly exposed to the secular life view, we risk losing their fragile, impressionable minds to secular, non-Christian, and even anti-Christian values.

So much of our society's images of right and wrong invade our homes through the secular media. Yet many parents are shocked when they find out exactly what their children are listening to and viewing.

Popular singer George Michael, for instance, sang on one his records, "I Want Your Sex." He told a whole nation of naive children and teenagers that "sex is natural, sex is fun, sex is best when it's one on one."

Overnight, the record went to number one on the charts. At his Orlando concert the newspaper reported, "During the hit song (his opening number), he thrust his hips and gazed adoringly at girls in the front row . . . mostly 13 to 19 years old."

Put yourself in the place of the parents of those teenaged girls. Perhaps your daughter didn't attend the concert, but you know she owns the album. Or perhaps the song simply comes on the radio while you are driving with her. What would you do?

_____

_____

_____

I'll tell you what we did. We used George Michael's song as a platform to openly contrast our views on sex with the secular view so evident in its lyrics. In fact, we talk openly about everything, because we have found our children already know about everything anyway—sex, AIDS, gays, drugs—so we want them to know our attitudes and viewpoints, and God's attitudes and viewpoints, in addition to those they hear in the world.

How do the results of this approach, emphasizing protection from the world, compare to those experienced by parents who try to insulate their children from the world?

_____

_____

_____

Are you protecting your children, or insulating them? Explain your answer.

_____

_____

_____

Battling the System-Builders

I believe we need to ensure that system-builders in our children's lives —teachers, pastors, movies, TV programs, athletics, and recording stars— stand for the values and beliefs we want our kids to imitate. The fragile minds of young people can't distinguish the merit of values and beliefs presented to them. They tend to adopt whatever they are exposed to, unless *we* intercept the process.

And once they become teenagers, our children's peers exert more influence on them than any other factor, so we need to start early. Teaching our children how to choose friends and placing them in environments where good friends can be found is a gigantic contribution to the stability of their beliefs and values. We need to find out what those young people who remain virgins are doing with their time. And we need to consider how we can encourage our kids to do the same.

> *If we can only learn to control our selfish desires and our tempers, and encourage our kids, we will leave them a great legacy.*

Encourage, Don't Embitter

Society tells us that mothers love and stroke their children, while a father's role is often limited to discipline. When this becomes reality, what is the result?

_____

_____

_____

Maybe that's what Paul had in mind when he wrote in Colossians 3:21, "Fathers, do not embitter your children, or they will become discouraged." Yet angry fathers are everywhere. *If we can only learn to control our selfish desires and our tempers, and encourage our kids, we will leave them a great legacy.*

Gordon McDonald tells a story about Boswell, the famous biographer of Samuel Johnson. Boswell frequently mentioned a childhood memory—a day spent fishing with his dad. Apparently his life had been deeply etched for the better on this single day, for he constantly referred to the many matters he and his father discussed on that one occasion.

Many years later someone stumbled across the following entry in his father's journal. These are the words penned by Boswell's dad: "Gone fishing today with my son; a day wasted."[5]

Whatever the father's feelings at the time, he must have suppressed them. As a result, his son was deeply encouraged by the mundane affair, and the memory became a cornerstone of his entire life. We don't have to be the sweetest guy in the world to have a positive impact on our kids—but we do have to give them time.

If you have a memory of a special time spent with your dad, describe it.

_____

_____

_____

How did it affect you later?

_____

_____

_____

Perhaps you don't have such a memory of time spent with your father. How has the absence of such a relationship affected you?

_____

_____

_____

What have you done, or could you do, to create such a special memory for your son or daughter? List some activities you can enjoy together.

_____

_____

_____

No Replacement for Time

Lee Iacocca once remarked, "I never heard anyone on their deathbed say, 'I wish I had spent more time with my business.'" How does that compare to the two greatest regrets listed in the previous chapter?

_____

_____

Not long ago I was reflecting that my twelve-year-old daughter would be in college at eighteen, so two-thirds of her time with her mom and me is gone. Then it occurred to me that, at twelve, she spends more time with her friends than with her family. That means that really, 85–90 percent of our time together has passed.

It's best to get our time in as early as possible. Don't put it off till next week, because those weeks turn into years faster than a speeding bullet, and then our kids want to spend time with their friends.

L ooking Closer in the Mirror:

How are you communicating your love and acceptance to your children?

_____

_____

How are you balancing that with the need to correct and discipline them?

_____

_____

Children deserve more than a laissez-faire *approach to parenting. A man must provide spiritual leadership in his home. Children need to be guided into the value system we want for them. How does this happen in your home?*

_____

_____

_____

Research indicates that values are caught more than they are taught. What does that imply for your attitudes and behavior as a father?

_____

_____

_____

So much of our secular society's images of right and wrong invade our homes through the access of the secular media. *Do you know and understand the music your children listen to and the TV programs or movies that they watch?* *List their two favorite musicians:*

(1) _____

(2) _____

List their two all-time favorite movies:

(1) _____

(2) _____

List their two favorite, regularly scheduled TV shows:

(1) _____

(2) _____

(Note: If you need to, ask them. They will appreciate your interest.)

What kinds of values undergird your child's favorite means of entertainment?

_____

_____

Our children's values and beliefs are influenced by us, teachers, pastors, athletes, music, movies, and television. How active have you been in monitoring these influences? What should you change?

_____

_____

Once our children become teenagers, their peers become a primary influence in their lives. What can we do before they reach that stage to prepare them for the teen years?

_____

_____

What can we do while they are teenagers to help them through these rough years?

_____

_____

■ GUARDIANSHIP THROUGH PRAYER

In a Denver crusade, Billy Graham spoke about a scriptural promise—"Believe in the Lord Jesus, and you will be saved—you and your household" (Acts 16:31). He said statistics indicate that in 60 percent of the homes where fathers came to faith in Christ first, the entire family also came to Christ. When wives came to Christ first, that number dropped to 40–50 percent. And when children came to Christ first, only 25 percent of them saw their entire families become Christians.

That indicates that fathers have tremendous spiritual influence on the family. How are you using that influence to build a spirit of prayer in your home?

_____

_____

_____

_____

Over the years, I have developed a regimen of prayer subjects for my children. It's an eclectic assortment from many sources, including Scripture, and my own desires for my kids to be spared some of the anguish I have borne.

I can't think of anything in the world more important for my children than placing their faith in Jesus Christ and finding His plan for their lives. Naturally, my prayer list for my children begins with a request for their salvation and continuing nurture. But I also pray that they will have these things:

- That there will never be time they don't walk with God,
- A saving faith (thanksgiving if already Christian),
- A growing faith,
- An independent faith (as they grow up),
- Persevering faith,
- To be strong and healthy in mind, body, and spirit,
- A sense of destiny (purpose),
- A desire for integrity,
- A call to excellence,
- To understand their spiritual gifts,
- To understand the ministry God has for them,
- Values, beliefs, and a Christian worldview,
- To tithe 10 percent and save 10 percent of all earnings,
- To set and work toward realistic goals, as revealed by the Lord,
- That I will set aside times to spend with them,
- To acquire wisdom,
- Protection from drugs, alcohol, tobacco, premarital sex, rape, and AIDS,
- The mate God has for them (alive somewhere, needing prayer),
- To do daily devotions,
- Forgiveness and be filled with the Holy Spirit,
- Glorify the Lord in everything,
- Any personal requests or matters in discussion with their mother.

List some subject areas in which you are praying for your children.

_____

_____

Perhaps you will want to add to that list. I invite you to use some of the items from my list, or to find your own items to add. Now, take some time to write out a specific prayer for each of your children. If there's not enough room on this page, use another sheet of paper.

MIRROR WORK

*D*ear Heavenly Father, Help me to be the kind of father to my kids that You are to me. Help me to love them and to give them the place You want them to have on my list of priorities. Help me to be willing to die for them, but also to live for them. Amen.

In the next chapter . . .

Many couples live together more as roommates than as partners. Their social and sexual needs are met, but they never really develop any intimacy. But our relationships with our wives don't have to be that way. Keep reading, and we'll discover together how to develop that intimacy and move to a new level of happiness in our marriages.

Wives: How to Be Happily Married

Let the wife make the husband glad to come home, and let him make her sorry to see him leave.

MARTIN LUTHER

Husbands, in the same way be considerate as you live with your wives, and treat them with respect as the weaker partner and as heirs with you of the gracious gift of life, so that nothing will hinder your prayers.

1 PETER 3:7

You've seen them at restaurants. In a strange way, they look a little alike. His eyes are distant. She never looks up from her food. The only words they speak are to the waiter.

They've been married thirty years, but they scarcely know each other. As the children were growing up, ball games and school plays kept everyone on the run. Now they have time on their hands—time to enjoy each other—but they don't really have a personal relationship. They don't even know *how* to talk.

When you read that description, who among your friends or acquaintances comes to mind?

> **Every marriage needs a balance between listening and talking. . . . There cannot be a meeting of the minds if the minds never meet.**

_____

_____

Perhaps you don't know anyone whose relationship is that stilted, but you do know some couples that seem to be headed in that direction. List them, and describe how you know they may have trouble communicating with each other.

_____

_____

What about your own marriage? Do you see any warning signs indicating that you and your wife might be experiencing this empty kind of relationship, or that you might be headed in this direction? List them.

_____

_____

_____

_____

The Problem

[Your wife] has a right to expect to be treated by you in the same way that she is treated by Christ.

If a husband isn't careful, his relationship with his wife can degenerate to this point without his being aware of it. He isn't *unhappy* with his wife. He just knows he isn't really enjoying her. He has problems *feeling and expressing love.*

Have you found this to be true among the men you know?

_____ Yes   _____ No   _____ Don't know.

In case you had problems answering, let me assure you that, in a written survey I conducted, I found that the inability to feel and express love troubles men deeply. *In your opinion, why is that true?*

_____

_____

A man needs a friend he can let his hair down with, someone he can really trust—and that friend ought to be his wife.

When all is said and done, marriage is hard work. It's the exacting kind of work in which all the little blemishes become noticeable—but often, only to your wife.

And let's face it—women can be hard to understand. Freud, the father of psychoanalysis, posed this interesting question: "Despite my thirty years of research into the feminine soul, I have not yet been able to answer . . . the great question . . . *What does a woman want?*"

Unfortunately, Christian men are not necessarily any better at answering this than are their nonbelieving counterparts. Wouldn't it be great if, when men became Christians, God blessed them with a supernatural gift that enabled them to understand their wives?

And so, for most men, the easier road is to throw themselves into their jobs. We can hide behind our game face at work. That way, we don't have to figure out our wives, nor do we have to let them in on our weaknesses and fears.

In this situation, many couples live together more as roommates than as partners. Their social and sexual needs are met, but their intimacy as friends never develops. A man needs a friend he can let his hair down with, someone he can really trust—and that friend ought to be his wife.

The Role of the Wife

One of a man's deepest needs is to be respected. Problems in a marriage often arise when a man doesn't feel he is respected by his wife.

Sam, for instance, intuitively knew his wife held him in low esteem. He had not achieved the same station in life that her father held, and though she never said anything, Sam sensed her contemptuous pity.

How do women communicate disrespect, even contempt, for the men in their lives?

_____

_____

The importance of respect is highlighted in a scriptural passage that touches on how wives are to treat their husbands. In Ephesians 5:33, Paul wrote, "The wife must respect her husband." What should be the attitude of a Christian wife?

_____

Earlier, in Ephesians 5:22, Paul wrote, "Wives, submit to your husbands as to the Lord." According to that, what is the primary way Christian wives can show respect to their husbands?

_____

Given the fact that many women, like Sam's wife, don't talk about their lack of respect for their husbands, how does your wife indicate that she respects you or doesn't respect you?

_____

_____

A person can be forced to obey someone else, but he can't be forced to submit, because true submission is nearly impossible without respect.

As we already noted in the Ephesians passage, Scripture requires your wife to submit to you in the same way that she submits to the Lord. This implies, of course, that she has a right to expect to be treated by you in the same way that she is treated by Christ. *How does Jesus relate to your wife? What conditions must she meet in order to gain His acceptance?*

_____

The answer, of course, is that Jesus' acceptance is unconditional. How close do you come to reaching that high standard?

Some women take exception to this concept of submission. To many, it seems archaic. The word *submit* translates from Greek into English as "to subordinate, obey, or submit oneself to." The goal of this instruction is not to reduce women to the level of servants or doormats, but to provide an authority structure to support and enhance the marriage relationship.

The opposite of submission is resistance. What are the consequences of resistance in any organization?

The affect on marriages is similar. When marriage doesn't run according to God's authority structure—regardless of whose fault that is—morale and productivity automatically go down.

Figure 9.1

THE ROLE OF THE WIFE

SUBMIT ├──────────────────┼──────────────────┤ RESIST

Figure 9.1 shows a continuum between submitting and resisting. *Put an "X" on the continuum at the place that you think best represents your wife. Explain why you chose that place.*

If she is not a submitting wife, how has your "management style" contributed to her morale? Have you promoted good relationships at home? How?

_____

_____

_____

The Role of the Husband

If the wife's role is to submit and operate under an authority structure, then the husband's responsibility is to create an environment that will foster a good relationship. This means being honest with each other, even on issues related to our feelings.

Don hid deep feelings of guilt from his wife. He couldn't tell her he loved her, because he didn't *feel* any love toward her. And his integrity was too high to lie about something so important, so he said nothing at all.

How do you think this affected his wife?

_____

_____

How important is it that men "feel" love for their wives?

_____

_____

Look up Ephesians 5:25–28 and write it here:

_____

_____

_____

_____

That passage notes that husbands are to love their wives as Christ loved the Church. How did Christ love the Church?

_____

_____

The Greek word used to describe how men are to love their wives is the same word God used to describe His own love for the world. It's also the same love we are to have for God, as used in the command, "*Love* the Lord your God with all your heart and with all your soul and with all your mind" (Matthew 22:37, italics added).

This is *volitional* love rather than *emotional*. This is *agapao* love. It is a deliberate act of the *will* as a matter of principle, duty and propriety. Biblical love is a decision and a responsibility. When faithfully given, feelings will follow.

Remember Don? If he really understood this principle, how would it free him to demonstrate his love to his wife?

_____

_____

What kind of response would he get if he showed this kind of love to his wife?

_____

_____

Unfortunately, the English word *heart* does not communicate the full weight of its intended meaning. The heart, the inner self, is composed of three parts, shown in figure 9.2.

Figure 9.2

THE HEART

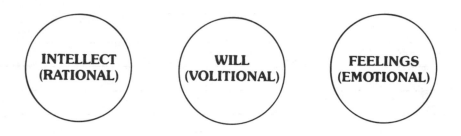

The *intellect* is the *rational* man, the *will* is the *volitional* man, and the *feelings* are the *emotional* man. We are to love our wives volitionally, as an act of the will by choice.

We are not instructed to *feel in love* with our wives. Love is not a feeling. We are to love our wives first as an act of the will, and amazingly, when we do that, feelings will come—but they will also go. In fact, they will come and go regularly, but we can maintain a balance in this tidal wave of feeling if we remember that biblical love is a *decision,* not a feeling.

Figure 9.3

THE ROLE OF THE HUSBAND

LOVE |————————————+————————————| HATE

Figure 9.3 shows a continuum similar to the one we used regarding the role of the wife. On this one, regarding the role of the husband, love sits at one end and hate at the other. Hate in its worst form could be called "indifference."

Given the information in the previous section, place an "X" on the contin-uum at the place you think best represents your success in loving your wife. Explain your answer.

———

———

———

Four Types of Marriages

If a woman can submit or resist, and a man can love or hate, then how many marriage combinations can we come up with? The answer, of course, is four.

Naturally, these are only meant to be useful working generalizations. An infinite number of shades and degrees is possible, depending on where each partner puts the "X" on the continuum, but most marriages can be placed in one of the four following categories:

- Love and Submit
- Hate and Submit
- Love and Resist
- Hate and Resist

Figure 9.4

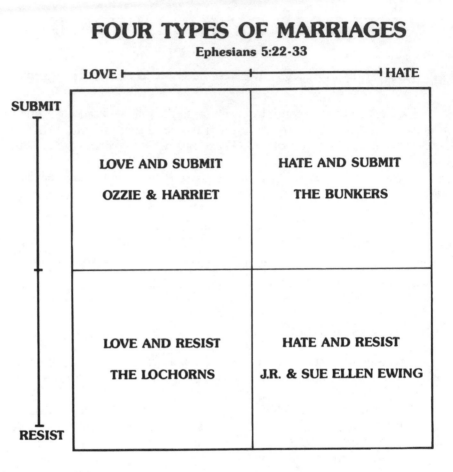

FOUR TYPES OF MARRIAGES
Ephesians 5:22-33

The Hate and Resist Marriage

The worst possible marriage is one in which both partners are unhappy, and both aim for their own selfish way. Perhaps the most prominent example of a Hate and Resist marriage occurred in the 1980s in the television couple of J. R. and Sue Ellen Ewing. Eventually, Sue Ellen locked J. R. out of the bedroom, and he was keeping several girlfriends around town.

In the Hate and Resist marriage, the wife nags her husband and contends with his authority. The husband treats his wife sharply and doesn't consider her feelings when making family decisions. Animosity and disrespect characterize their attitudes toward each other.

If your marriage falls short of the ideal, and you're still together, it's unlikely that it is truly a Hate and Resist marriage. In today's world, you probably would already have divorced if your marriage were a true Hate and Resist marriage.

The Hate and Submit Marriage

Edith and Archie Bunker provide a caricature of the Hate and Submit marriage: Archie, the opinionated, domineering emperor of his row house, and Edith, the submissive attendant to Archie's belligerent demands.

Sometimes the Archie Bunkers of this world show up in a Christian disguise. My wife married me because I convinced her I was a Christian. But within weeks of our wedding day, it was crystal clear that our definitions of what makes a Christian were drastically different.

Although I said I was a Christian, there was no correlation in my thought life, my speech, or my actions. I didn't nourish or care for Patsy in any way. On the contrary, I expected her to wait on my every whim.

I was fortunate. Patsy continued to submit to me, regardless of my response. The Bible suggests a wife can win her husband by godly behavior. That's exactly what happened in our home. She continued to respect me, to manage our home, and to pray for me. Within six months I surrendered my life to the Lord.

If the Hate and Submit marriage sounds like yours, then you have the most common form of marriage that is not working. This area of life is so overrun by Satan that we need to look at several biblical commands and internalize them.

Look at 1 Peter 3:7, quoted at the beginning of this chapter. What does that verse say to the husband in any marriage? How is he to treat his wife?

_____

_____

If he refuses to obey this injunction, what does this passage say will happen to his relationship with God?

_____

_____

Now, look up Colossians 3:19 and write it here:

_____

And 1 Timothy 5:8:

> **The husband's responsibility is to create an environment that will foster a good relationship.**

_____

_____

_____

Now, transfer those three passages to index cards, and also Ephesians 5:28–29, which you transcribed earlier in this chapter. Take them with you throughout the day, and commit them to memory. As you internalize the words, ask God to help you apply them to your marriage. Then do it!

The Love and Resist Marriage

The feminist movement has fueled the Love and Resist marriage syndrome, which cartoonists have depicted by showing a wimpy, little guy dominated by a screechy-voiced battle-axe of a woman.

Today, unfortunately, the feminist movement seems to make women uncomfortable with their traditional roles as wife and mother. Several years ago my wife started feeling inadequate because she was "*just a housewife and mother.*" After some discussion, we realized she was being influenced in her thinking by the editorial bias of certain women's magazines. She promptly canceled her subscriptions.

Biblical love is a decision and a responsibility.

The husband in a Love and Resist marriage should continue to love, regardless of his wife's response. Since a husband's love is to be a decision rather than a feeling, through self-discipline he can continue to cherish and show consideration and respect to his wife. It's not easy, I grant you, but it *is* possible through true submission to the Holy Spirit.

The Bible is clear on this issue. Write 1 Corinthians 7:11 and 19–20:

_____

_____

_____

_____

_____

If you have a resistant wife, list some practical steps you can take, in accordance with this passage, to thwart Satan's effort to destroy your marriage.

_____

_____

_____

Perhaps you are not married to a resistant wife, but you have a friend who is. How can you minister to him?

_____

_____

How can Christians in general minister to men whose resistant wives have divorced them, perhaps even in spite of their loving and nurturing actions?

_____

_____

The Love and Submit Marriage

After you get past the facade of wanting to appear that life is wonderful, most men will confess that their marriage is not working as it's supposed to. In short, they don't have a Love and Submit marriage.

Actually, even the Bible has few examples of marriages that work right. Notable exceptions are Abraham and Sarah, and Joseph and Mary, two prominent examples characterized by love and submission.

With the information already given, list some key factors that build a Love and Submit marriage.

_____

_____

_____

Which category best describes your marriage? Explain.

_____

_____

_____

Now, the question is, *do you want to improve?* In the remainder of the chapter, I will offer some specific suggestions to help you and your wife move toward a Love and Submit marriage.

Time Together

How much time do you spend with your wife on a daily basis? Every marriage needs a balance between listening and talking. Harmony about family goals and problems comes from spending time fleshing out our differences about them. There cannot be a meeting of the minds if the minds never meet.

Several years ago my wife and I started a tradition of staying at the table for twenty minutes or so after dinner. The kids race off to practice guitar and do homework, so we spend some time talking about each other's day. It's not a law that we have to do it, but we almost always do. This time investment tells her I care, and the impact is that we have become best friends.

What can you and your wife do to set aside daily time for each other?

_____

_____

_____

Shared Responsibility

When I was in college, my roommate and I split the housekeeping duties. As the months rolled by, I really got steamed because I felt I was doing most of the work.

"Steve!" I exploded. "You're taking advantage of our relationship. I'm the only one who ever changes the empty roll of toilet paper, I always have to do the vacuuming, and you hardly ever wash the dishes."

"Me?" came his surprised yelp. "You're the one who isn't pulling his share of the load. I'm the only one who ever mops the kitchen floor, and you have never taken out the garbage!"

> **We are to love our wives volitionally, as an act of the will by choice.**

We looked at each other in astonishment, and suddenly it dawned on us at the same time—we had each inventoried the other's shortcomings and our own strengths.

In the end we decided that, if we were going to be successful roommates, we needed to make the relationship *90–10, Both Ways.* In other words, we realized that *if we both felt as though we were giving 90 percent and only receiving 10 percent, then we would probably end up at about 50–50.*

In my opinion, marriages work better if we apply, by mutual agreement with our wives, the *90–10, Both Ways* principle. *What about you? What has your wife been saying about your role in shared responsibilities?*

_____

_____

How have you reacted to her statements?

_____

_____

How would the 90–10, Both Ways principle help your relationship with your wife?

_____

_____

How Do Marriages Get into Trouble?

Marriages get into trouble for a variety of reasons. Some people marry for the wrong reasons. More often, though, we marry with the best of intentions, but temptations hit us immediately.

•**Critical spirits**—My wife observes that most marriages begin to break down because partners are critical of one another. When you are criticized, you naturally defend yourself, building walls around your self-image which eventually will barricade you from your partner.

•**Unyielded rights**—Power struggles doom a marriage. The presumed right to tell the other person what to do shows a lack of respect and sensitivity. Since we don't own our partners, we should at least show them the same level of courtesy and respect we would show to a stranger.

•**Self-centeredness**—Self-centeredness in either partner can cause big problems. When I married, I pictured my wife serving my varied interests with doting affection. When it dawned on me that she wanted to be a teammate and not a slave, I became angry—both at her for not capitulating, and at myself for being so foolish.

The presumed right to tell the other person what to do shows a lack of respect and sensitivity.

Sex!

Beyond the temptations listed in the previous section, no temptation causes more trouble for men than sex.

One day I made the mistake of boasting to a friend that lust is "a temptation the Lord has delivered me from; it's something I just don't struggle with anymore."

Later I decided to share a cab with some people. I found myself shoe-horned into the taxi next to a very lovely, warm woman. I could feel her, starting at my shoulder, running down my side, along the outside of my thigh, all the way to my ankle. That was the longest twenty-minute cab ride of my life. Within moments of thinking I had arrived, the Lord reminded me of just how weak I am.

I know that's true of almost all men. Whether it's an issue of not enough, unfaithfulness, or a troublesome thought life, our sexual drive is an Achilles' heel to every one of us. But it's not impossible to deal with.

List some steps you can take to reduce the intensity of sexual temptation in your own life.

Each of us must be commited to love his wife, and her alone, without reserve. Beyond that, a man and his wife must be at least as committed to the institution of marriage as they are to each other. If the institution itself is not highly esteemed, sooner or later, when one partner starts to feel unloving, there is no moral framework to motivate him or her to work through the problem.

Money

If sex is the impulsive marriage assassin, money is the killer that slowly strangles. One Gallup Poll indicated that 56 percent of families consider economic problems to be the biggest problems they face. No wonder money issues are a root cause in the majority of divorces. That's why we'll devote two chapters to money.

Communication

If sex is the impulsive marriage assassin, money is the killer that slowly strangles.

With all of these problems tearing at the fabric of marriage, how can couples hope to remain together at all, let alone be *happy* together?

Do you remember the childhood game in which you would form a circle, and someone would whisper a phrase in the ear of the person next to them? Then each person would repeat the phrase to the person next to them, all the way around the circle, and the last person would repeat it out loud. Do you remember how different it would invariably be from the original? That's the misunderstanding that takes place when we are talking.

The answer is in communication and dialogue. But because men and women are cognitively different in so many ways, communication between spouses frequently transmits on different wavelengths. The inevitable result of communication is misunderstanding, because we assume the receiver picks up the same transmission we send. But the receiver always has a separate agenda. Only through *dialogue* can we be certain we are being understood.

◣ Looking Closer in the Mirror:

Since we now understand the crucial need for dialogue to gain and maintain health in marriages, I suggest that you and your wife spend twenty minutes or so together each day. Make it a habit. This will allow you to begin communicating with one another. To get started, perhaps you would like to discuss the following questions. If not, work through them on your own so you'll have a head start in your communication process.

What are three to five things about me that you really like?

_____

_____

Name two things I do that you wish I would stop doing, or I would change.

_____

_____

Where are you on your personal spiritual pilgrimage?

_____

_____

What do you think is your purpose in life? What is our purpose in life together? Why did God bring us together?

_____

_____

What activity do we both enjoy that we could do together in our spare time?

_____

_____

Name a place you've always dreamed of visiting. What kind of trip have you always wanted to take?

_____

_____

What are your greatest regrets about life? What has been your greatest disappointment?

_____

_____

How do you feel about how our kids are turning out (or have turned out)?

_____

_____

What one thing about your life would you change if you could?

_____

If you had no one to answer to, what would you like to be doing in five years?

_____

_____

Tell me one way I can better express my love/respect to you.

_____

_____

Put an "X" on the continuum where you think you are and your partner is:
For men: Love   ├──────────────┼──────────────┤ Hate
For women: Submit ├──────────────┼──────────────┤ Resist
Discuss your answers. Why are they different? How can you change? Are you willing to do so?

_____

_____

_____

Circle which of the four types of marriage listed in this chapter yours is.

Love and Submit   Hate and Submit

Love and Resist   Hate and Resist

What practical steps could I/you take to have a "Love and Submit" marriage?

_____

_____

_____

Husband: Read 1 Corinthians 13 aloud to your wife. Confess to her the areas where you have failed and ask her forgiveness.
Wife: Repeat.
(Note: To continue the process of bringing down the barriers between you,

read together my book *Marriage Without Walls* [September 1994 release] from Thomas Nelson Publishers.)

MIRROR WORK

Lord Jesus, I want to be a good husband. I want to love my wife in the way that You intended—in the way that You love the Church. Help me to purpose to show her how much I love her, and help us both to move toward the Love and Submit marriage that you intend for us to share. Amen.

In the next chapter . . .

Most men have a friendship "deficit." Their balance sheets are empty when it comes to friends. Most men don't know how to go about developing a true friendship, and they don't know how to be a true friend. Keep reading, and together we'll explore the ins and outs of gaining and maintaining true friendships.

10 Friends: Risks and Rewards

Five years from now you will be pretty much the same as you are today except for two things: the books you read and the people you get close to.

CHARLES JONES[1]

Jonathan said to David, "Whatever you want me to do, I'll do for you."

1 SAMUEL 20:4

"Most men live with that paradox —we sincerely want to have close friends, but we fear the transparency that it requires."

*I*f you were to receive notice today that your next paycheck would be your last with your present company, who, besides your wife, would you call? Is that person your best friend? Or is he a pastor, small group leader, or counselor?

When I faced a situation like that, I turned to a friend, and he made me an offer that I found downright embarrassing, but in the process he revealed what it means to be, or to have, a true friend.

The recession brought the pressure of negative cash flow, and I was at my wit's end when I turned to Robert. We had been friends for a dozen years, so it was natural to visit him when my business problems were bigger than my own ingenuity.

Maybe I thought Robert would give me advice that would magically turn around the business. Or maybe I was seeking some other type of encouragement. But what he said caught me completely off guard. "I don't have any answers, but if the worst comes to pass," he said, "I've got enough money for the both of us to live on. Whatever I have is yours."

Of course, I could never take Robert's offer, but his act of true friendship reminded me of the God who owns the cattle on a thousand hills. Suddenly the problems seemed minuscule, for I knew God would provide for me. By being my friend, Robert had shown me how much God loved me, and I knew I would be all right.

The Problem

Robert's reaction reminds me of Jonathan in the Old Testament. As quoted at the beginning of this chapter, Jonathan told David, "Whatever you want me to do, I'll do for you."

Do you have that kind of a friend? Not just someone to call for lunch, but a genuinely close friend like you had in college or high school—someone you could let your hair down with.

Whatever happened to that kind of friend? Why do adult men find it difficult to develop friendships that have those same transparent, vulnerable qualities as the friendships of youth?

After we tear out the calendar pages of school, we get down to the tasks of establishing careers, choosing life mates, building our kingdoms, and accumulating things. Sometimes we just don't find time to develop relationships. And, frankly, a lot of times we don't perceive the need—our new wives and children meet many of our relationship needs.

What relationships we do enjoy outside of our homes and families often are organized around our careers. We work all day with other men on common tasks, and those common goals create a level of fellowship and a kindred spirit. But work relationships rarely develop into personal interest.

Describe your relationships with specific people at work.

In our mobile society, work relationships frequently are broken by transfers and moves. Have you been able to make and keep any truly personal friends on the job?

Friends Versus Acquaintances

In my experience, most men are surrounded by many acquaintances, and we may even mistake them for friends. But when times are tough, we really don't have anyone who is willing to listen, to pray with us, and to offer wise advice.

Describe the difference between a friend and an acquaintance.

When we talk to a friend, we are forced to organize our thoughts into coherent sentences.

Once I boasted to an acquaintance that I had hundreds of friends. Without a pause, he countered, "No, you don't. You may have met hundreds of people, but there's no way you can really know more than a handful of people. You'd be lucky if you had three real friends." At first I was offended, but as I reflected on what he said, I realized he was right. I had a thousand acquaintances, but at that moment not even three genuine friends.

Too Close for Comfort

Of course, we must admit that pursuing genuine friendship brings certain risks. *List some of them.*

Pursuing genuine friendship opens us up to rejection, betrayal, embarrassment, and even hurt. In a nutshell, you could say that friendships can bring other people too close for comfort. Most men live with that paradox—we sincerely want to have close friends, but we fear the transparency that it requires.

Real friends are worth the risk.

John understood that, because he was leading a secret thought life, and it was far different from the image he projected. He was never more aware of this than when he had lunch with his friend Bill. When Bill asked how things were going, John felt like Bill somehow peered into his mind. The longer they were friends, the more "naked" his thoughts seemed.

In reality, he disguised himself completely and had Bill totally fooled. Still, he started to cancel out on lunches at the last minute, finally giving up the friendship altogether.

Why did John pull back when he had Bill so completely fooled?

One price of friendship is personal vulnerability. But we may unconsciously stiff-arm a friend when he gets too close. What do you see in your own life that may indicate you are stiff-arming a friend?

_____

_____

What are some symptoms that would indicate that your friend is stiff-arming you?

_____

_____

Bill and John's experience points out one very real problem with friendship. As we become closer to another person, we really want to share our secrets with them. We want to know that, even though that person knows our bad points, he still likes and accepts us. But we also find another force at work, urging us to keep our distance so we won't get burned.

Betrayed!

Some of us have broken off a relationship because the person we thought was a friend has betrayed us. And because of the hurt, we have hesitated to open ourselves up to more betrayal.

Of course, Jesus knew what it meant to be betrayed—He experienced the ultimate betrayal from a close friend. Other historical characters experienced similar situations.

Julius Caesar, for instance, trusted Marcus Junius Brutus implicitly. They had shared great ideas, but they had also shared their secrets. When Caesar entered the Roman Senate on the Ides of March, 44 B.C., he was greeted by assassins. He struggled to escape, clashing with the conspirators. Then he saw Brutus!—approaching with drawn dagger, ready to strike.

Stung by betrayal, Caesar abandoned his resistance. He pulled his robe over his face and uttered that famous, haunting question, "Et tu, Brute?" or "You, too, Brutus?" He went without further protest to his death.

I haven't experienced anything this drastic, but I *have* been betrayed. I can identify with the psalmist. *Look up his words in Psalm 55:12–14 and record them here.*

_____

_____

_____

How do those verses play out in everyday life? Well, suppose Fred always greets me like an agitated porcupine, and I come away pulling spikes

Why do adult men find it difficult to develop friendships that have those same transparent, vulnerable qualities as the friendships of youth?

out of my hide. I tell my friend Jim in confidence how I struggle to like Fred. I just need to talk it through with someone.

Two weeks later, a mutual friend approaches me. "I know what you mean about Fred," he says. "I have the same struggle!"

Betrayed! Although the results were not as catastrophic as those in King David's case, or in Caesar's case, or in Jesus' case, the trust level may be difficult to repair.

Describe a time when you experienced a similar situation.

_____

_____

How did you feel?

_____

_____

How has it affected your willingness to build other friendships?

_____

_____

Unfortunately, friends often unintentionally betray each other through gossip. In fact, lower-natured gossip often disguises itself as "Christian concern." Benjamin Franklin captured the idea when he said, "Three people can keep a secret, as long as two of them are dead."

Describe some ground rules you can establish for times when you want to share something with another person.

_____

_____

_____

The Purposes of Friendship

Based on what I've shared so far, you might conclude that friendship just isn't worth the effort. Thankfully, that's not true. The bottom line is that real friends are worth the risk. Here are a few reasons why:

Friends Are There When You Need Them

Solomon put it more eloquently than I can. *Look up his explanation in Ecclesiastes 4:9–10, and write it here:*

_____

_____

_____

_____

Everyone falls down once in awhile. Who helps us up? Friends do—in a multitude of ways. A friend can help us chisel the truth in our thinking. A friend can help us defend ourselves against the enemy we cannot see. Ecclesiastes 4:12 tells us, "Though one may be overpowered, two can defend on themselves." No one can sneak up behind two men fighting back-to-back. Two men fighting back-to-back can cover all the angles.

A Friend Keeps Us on Track

It frightens me to recognize how quickly I can go off on a tangent. I think most of us have the capacity to rationalize ourselves into believing our theories and ideas are always right.

Some years ago a bank turned down the first loan I had ever applied for. For three years I had banked with them. Was I ever hot! I told everyone who would listen what a terrible deed those bankers had done to me.

A friend pulled me up short and said, "Pat, in life, if you like what you see, tell your friends. If you don't like what you see, tell them."

I realized what a fool I was to tell everyone except someone who could do something about it. The bank's executive vice-president agreed to see me. I shared what my friend had said and that I had come to set things right. He made the loan.

My friend's advice is the perfect example of a scriptural counsel given in Proverbs 27:6. Look it up and write it here:

_____

_____

Who has provided this kind of reality check for you? What was the situation which that friend addressed?

_____

_____

What were the results?

_____

_____

A Friend Helps Us Crystallize Our Thinking

"I just need someone to talk to," he said.

"Come on by," I replied.

For an hour and a half he went on and on. Then, without a moment's notice, he said, "Thank you, you have no idea how much this has meant to me," and he abruptly left. All I did was say "hello" and "good-bye."

Our minds play tricks on us, but a friend can help by acting as a "sounding board." When we talk to a friend, we are forced to organize our thoughts into coherent sentences. Talking through a matter helps us crystallize our thinking as no other method of reasoning can. There's a certain discipline in speaking that doesn't exist in thinking.

Proverbs 27:17 explains it this way: "As iron sharpens iron, so one man sharpens another." Name someone who has provided this type of ministry to you, and describe a time in your life when that person became the "iron that sharpened iron."

Often what we need is not wise counsel, but wise empathy. No words—just compassion.

A Friend Will Listen

Trustworthy people who have the potential to be good friends are not limited to certain demographic categories.

Sometimes we don't need a solution to our problem—we just need someone to feel our pain.

I found this after a deal I was working on fell through. When Sid's voice came on the other end of the line, my hands trembled. The deal was off. Somehow, I knew it was useless to try to change his mind. I would just become a pitiful beggar.

He continued to drone on, but my thoughts raced ahead—"cash flow, lay offs, all that wasted time . . . *I wonder if Patsy has left the house yet?*"

I finally got to call Patsy. The phone rang four times—my palms started to sweat. She always ate lunch with her sister on Mondays. I guessed she had already left. A sea of anguish swept over me at the thought of not being able to talk to my best friend-wife Patsy right away. Then she answered—relief.

As only a friend will do, she canceled her plans. When we met at the restaurant parking lot, seeing her was like a warm ray of sunshine on a rainy day, consoling my downcast spirit.

She listened. That's all she needed to do. What I wanted most was just someone to listen—listen without having to give advice. Often what we need is not wise counsel, but wise empathy. No words—just compassion.

Do you have a friend who will just listen? Someone who will "feel" for you without giving a big lecture? Write that person's name here, and thank God for that unique gift of friendship. Purpose in your heart to thank that friend as well.

L ooking Closer in the Mirror:

Now it's time for some honest self-assessment. Perhaps you have several close friends, or maybe you have none. More likely, you know many men, but you're not sure how deep the waters run. Reflect on these questions.

1. When things go sour and you feel really lousy, do you have a friend you can tell?
   _____ Yes   _____ No

2. Do you have a friend you can express any honest thought to without fear of appearing foolish?
   _____ Yes   _____ No

3. Do you have a friend who will let you talk through a problem without giving you advice? A friend who will just be a "sounding board"?
   _____ Yes   _____ No

4. Will your friend risk your disapproval to suggest you may be getting off track with your priorities?
   _____ Yes   _____ No

5. Do you have a friend who will take the risk to tell you that you are sinning? Or using poor judgment?
   _____ Yes   _____ No

6. If you had a moral failure, do you know that your friend would stand with you?
   _____ Yes   _____ No

7. Is there a friend with whom you feel you are facing life together? A friend to talk over the struggles of life which are unique to men?
   _____ Yes   _____ No

8. Do you have a friend you believe you can trust, that if you share confidential thoughts, they will stay confidential?
   _____ Yes   _____ No

9. When you are vulnerable and transparent with your friend, are you convinced he will not think less of you?
   _____ Yes   _____ No

10. Do you meet with a friend weekly or bi-weekly for fellowship and prayer and possibly for accountability?
    _____ Yes   _____ No

What goal would you set for yourself, based on your answers to those 10 questions?

List three action steps you can take to meet that goal.

1. _____

2. _____

3. _____

Now, begin to take the risk—develop a few close friendships. It's worth the risk, *if your time and energy are invested in developing this depth of relationship with trustworthy people.*

The Bible provides two key reasons why *trustworthy* friends are so valuable. *First, a friend loves at all times, and a brother is born for adversity* (Proverbs 17:17). And second, *there is a friend who sticks closer than a brother* (Proverbs 18:24).

List three people with whom you think you can develop this kind of true friendship.

1. _____

2. _____

3. _____

■ *DON'T LIMIT YOURSELF*

Trustworthy people who have the potential to be good friends are not limited to certain demographic categories. Over fifteen years ago I asked a man thirty years my senior if he would like to meet weekly for fellowship, prayer, and accountability. He responded with an enthusiastic, "Yes!" We still meet.

Maybe you've only been thinking of men in your own age category when considering whom to try to attract as a friend. Broadening your age group of men to consider, who might you approach?

■ *"TRUE BLUE" OR "FAIR WEATHER"?*

Look up Proverbs 19:4 and write it in the space provided.

How do you know if a friend is "true blue," or if he will turn out to be a "fair weather" friend if you really have problems?

_____

_____

Perhaps you have suffered from fair weather friendships, but perhaps
you are also guilty of being a fair weather friend. *List some reasons why you
have broken off existing friendships or hesitated to build new ones.*

_____

_____

_____

■ *THE NEED FOR RECONCILIATION*

*Earlier in this chapter I asked you to describe a time when a friend betrayed
you. Now, consider carefully. Have you ever betrayed a friend? If so, how did it
make you feel? How have you tried to repair the breach of trust that resulted?*

_____

_____

_____

Look up Matthew 5:23–24 and write it here:

_____

_____

_____

_____

In this passage, Jesus said if we bring a gift to the altar and then remember
someone has something against us, we ought to be reconciled before we continue
our worship. *Does He mention who is right and who is wrong in the relationship?*

_____

*What does this imply regarding loving confrontation when we know we have
hurt someone, intentionally or unintentionally?*

_____

_____

MIRROR WORK

Lord Jesus, I don't want to be the kind of friend that Judas was to You. And I don't want to be hurt by that kind of friend either. Give me Your wisdom as I branch out to develop more true friendships, that I might choose trustworthy men who can best help me fulfill the potential for which You created me, and that I might be the friend who can best help them do the same. Amen.

In the next chapter . . .

Now that we have finished our discussion on relationships, we'll move to another area that gives men headaches—migraines, in fact. MONEY. We'll look at just exactly what the Bible says about finances, and together we'll see how to apply those principles to put our personal financial houses in tip-top order.

PART THREE

Solving

Our

Money

Problems

Money: A Biblical Point of View

The problem with money is that it makes you do things you don't want to do.

WALL STREET, THE MOVIE

A faithful man will be richly blessed.

PROVERBS 28:20

I'm sure you've heard it said many times, "Money is the root of all evil." Those who say it are convinced that's what the Bible says. What does the Bible really say in 1 Timothy 6:10?

> **"He began to envision himself holding his money gently in his open palm, offering to take care of it, but aware God had entrusted it to him for a reason."**

Howard Dayton, author and founder of Crown Ministries, a financial training ministry, has counted about five hundred verses in the Bible on prayer, but over 2,350 verses on how to handle money and possessions. The entire Scriptures have to be combed to have a total grasp of what they say.

Knowing that, how would you rate your biblical I.Q. on money?

It can be dangerous if we don't really understand and act on the true biblical principles of money management. Let me illustrate.

For several months Todd felt the mounting pressure of his debts. He loved the good life and followed the advice of magazine and TV ads. But his lifestyle put a strain on his family and weighed heavily on his mind.

His wife, Judy, patiently supported him, but she felt helpless. From out of nowhere thoughts of divorce would pop into her mind, but she would immediately dismiss them. Still, she wondered if Todd would ever stop chasing the rainbow.

One day Todd noticed the neighbors on every side had swimming pools. Todd talked to a pool contractor, who agreed to drop by after dinner.

Todd wondered how he could afford a new pool. "How are people supposed to make important financial decisions?" he queried to no one in particular.

How would you answer Todd's question?

The Problem

Recently I asked eighty men if they were having financial problems. All of them answered yes. In fact, one man told me, "I don't have any problems money can't solve." Does that sound familiar?

And as I already noted, Scripture is full of injunctions regarding financial questions. By winking at Scriptures we don't like—and "cherry picking" those we do—we create our own tidy little theology about God and money. The result is a personal perspective that often suits the desire of our private wish-world, rather than one carefully chiseled by a search for truth.

The bottom-line problem is best summed up by Jesus. *Write Matthew 6:24 and memorize it:*

There is no choice; we can serve only one master. We are either a slave to God or a slave to money.

The word *serve* in that verse means "to be a slave to, literally or figuratively, voluntarily or involuntarily."

The truth spoken by Jesus is not a matter of *advisability,* "You *should not* serve both God and money." That would be a priority choice. Nor is it a matter of *accountability,* "You *must not* serve both God and money." That would be a moral choice.

Rather, it is a matter of *impossibility,* "You *cannot* serve both God and money." *There is no choice;* we can serve only one master. We are either a slave to God or a slave to money.

Not Merely the Weak

Frankly, this principle is hard to accept. I used to think, "This must certainly apply only to weak people. I can see how it would apply to someone of less self-discipline and intelligence. But I am different. I think I can serve God just fine and still pursue my plans to acquire wealth." My failure to handle money biblically is my best qualification to write on this subject.

If God were to ask you directly, "How do you rate yourself regarding your pursuit of money versus your pursuit of Me?" what would you tell Him?

_____

_____

In His parable about the sower who went out to sow, Jesus describes the different reactions individuals have to the Word of God. *Read Mark 4:3–20 and describe how verses 18 and 19 could be true of people today.*

_____

_____

Put bluntly, money is intoxicating. It's an opiate that addicts as easily and completely as alcohol and narcotics. Its power to change us is similar to that even of Jesus Christ. Money has power to rule our lives, not for good and forever, as Christ, but to lure us, like a moth, too close to the flame until, finally, our wings are set ablaze.

Why is money so addictive and destructive?

_____

_____

_____

The Power of Money

Let me illustrate. Perhaps you remember the 1976 "I Found It" campaign, which saturated communities with media coverage. "I Found It" bumper stickers were everywhere! People who asked about them learned what had been found: "New life in Christ."

Sandy, the "I Found It" director at a wealthy Florida coastal town, found that the farther people lived from the water, the greater their interest in the gospel. Wealthy people lived in the condominiums closest to the water, while the service help lived in mobile home parks farthest away.

Jesus illustrated this same principle, related to wealth and spiritual interest, in His parable of the sower. Transcribe Matthew 13:22:

_____

_____

_____

Recall a time when you've seen this operating in your life.

The Test of a Man's True Character

No test of a man's character is more conclusive than how he spends his time and money. If you want to know what's important to him, you can ask him, and he will give you his best guess. But what shows up in his checkbook?

If I were to audit your checkbook for what is important to you, what would I find?

If I were to check your calendar, what would appear to have been most important to you in the last two weeks?

> **Money has power to rule our lives, not for good and forever, as Christ; but to lure us, like a moth, too close to the flame until, finally, our wings are set ablaze.**

Is it possible you've been running the risk of letting "the worries of this life and the deceitfulness of wealth" choke out true meaning in your life?

Out of Control

A cover story of *Fortune* magazine in the late seventies summed up the social malady of our time with its title, "The Money Society." The article read like this in part:

Money, money, money is the incantation of today. Bewitched by an epidemic of money enchantment, Americans in the Eighties wriggle in a St. Vitus's dance of materialism unseen since the Gilded Age or the Roaring Twenties. Under the blazing sun of money, all other values shine palely. . . .

"I think people are being measured again by money rather than by how good a journalist or social activist or lawyer they are," says an investment banker. . . .

As a result, this banker is continually comparing himself with others to make sure he's okay. He schmoozes about compensation to try to determine if he makes more or less than the person he's talking to. But such conversations can be inconclusive, so when he visits friends or business acquaintances he's continually sizing up the towels, the cars, the silver, with practically an auctioneer's eye, to see what he's worth by comparison. . . .

"It frightens me to be sensitive to the idea that my neighbor just got a big-screen TV that's three inches bigger than mine," says the banker. "But that's something I look at. Or I know the guy got $ _____ more in his compensation packages last year than I did. Why should that bother me? Can I spend it? Do I need it? Do I want it? Only because I want to make more than he makes. I think the stress and internal turmoil that creates in most of us is unhealthy."[1]

For many men, this is more than just a little unhealthy. It's out of control! We have become a society of pretenders, bent on portraying an image of financial success whether or not there is any substance to it. And there is little marginal difference between the way Christians and non-Christians handle their money in our secularized culture.

What evidence do you see in your household that you may be a pretender?

_____

_____

Write Philippians 4:19.

_____

_____

According to this verse, do you need to be a pretender? Why or why not?

_____

_____

Since God has promised to meet all of our needs (as determined by Him, not us) if we are faithful and obedient to Him, we can conclude that feeling "out of control" is self-inflicted pain. It results from serving money instead of God.

Can you be satisfied with what God determines to be your needs and then provides for you?

Is It Money or Me?

How would you describe money? What are its qualities?

_____

_____

Money is morally neutral, just like a handgun. Put a pistol in the hand of a policeman and it's a tool of justice, but in the hand of a criminal it's an instrument of evil.

Money is simply a commodity, a medium of exchange, an inert means to other ends. We get money in four ways. *Check off the way or ways in which you acquire most of your money:*

_____ *I exchange my labor for it.*
_____ *I rent it to others.*
_____ *I hire others and earn a profit on their labor.*
_____ *I take risks calculated to earn money.*

Whether rich or poor, everyone needs money. The more money we have, the more we need. Solomon said, "As goods increase, so do those who consume them" (Ecclesiastes 5:11). More money only brings more responsibilities. In fact, you could say that the poor sometimes have an advantage over the rich—they can still cling to the illusion that money will make them happy.

Three Perspectives of Prosperity

The three prevailing theological views about prosperity are *poverty theology, stewardship theology,* and *prosperity theology.* The last one is sometimes championed as the *prosperity gospel.*

According to what you already know, describe them.

(1) *Poverty theology* _____

_____

(2) *Stewardship theology* _____

_____

(3) *Prosperity theology* _____

_____

Which perspective best fits your personal attitudes?

_____

Each of these views has Christian followers, because a case for each can be built from the Bible. Yet God did not intend for us to have a menu of options, depending on individual tastes and preferences. Most of us decide what we want to do, and then look for evidence to support it. We like to "cherry pick" the Bible—looking for verses we like and ignoring those we would rather not have there. We also kid, trick, and fool ourselves, letting our powerful self-wills persuade us simply to ignore a truth.

Three Perspectives of Prosperity

Figure 11.1 shows the range of these theological perspectives which are so commonplace today. They are represented on a continuum, because an endless number of perspectives can be covered if you talk to enough people.

Figure 11.1

RANGE OF THEOLOGICAL PERSPECTIVES OF PROSPERITY

| Poverty Theology | Stewardship Theology | Prosperity Theology |

Poverty Theology

This position holds that possessions are a curse. It rejects materialism in any form. Disciples have a strong bias toward helping the poor, but they have few resources to actually do anything.

What elements of this theology merit our attention?

Prosperity Theology

This position holds that you have not because you ask not. Disciples often have learned about tithing and have experienced the material blessings available by following the tithing principle. Because of their success with this, they tend to develop a preoccupation with money. They tend to explain the experience of others' not enjoying God's financial blessing as a lack of faith. Other dimensions of a relationship with God become, somehow, less significant.

How does prosperity theology manifest itself in Christian society today?

_____

_____

Who tends to be overlooked, even derided, by people most strongly committed to this theology?

_____

Stewardship Theology

Stewards believe God owns and controls everything. Possessions are a privilege rather than a right. The steward understands Scripture to say possessions are a trust given in varying proportions, depending on his innate, God-given abilities, and his faithful obedience to follow biblical principles. His preoccupation is not with accumulating wealth or renouncing it, but with being wise in the conduct of his affairs.

What tends to motivate the person living in accordance with this theology?

_____

_____

Figure 11.2

THREE PERSPECTIVES CONTRASTED

	POVERTY	PROSPERITY	STEWARDSHIP
View of Prosperity	Non-materialistic, disdain for possessions	Prosperity is the reward of the righteous	Possessions are a trust given in varying proportions
In a Word, Possessions Are	a curse	a right	a privilege
Scriptural Reference	Lk. 18:18-22 sell, give to poor (rich young ruler)	Mt. 7:7,8 ask, seek, knock	Mt. 25:14-30 parable of talents
Mitigation	Pr. 21:20 In house of wise are stores of choice food & oil, but a foolish man devours all he has.	Pr. 23:4,5 Don't wear yourself out to get rich.	None
Needs Met By	"carefree attitude" don't worry - seek kingdom 1st Mt. 6:25-34	"transaction" tithe for a blessing Mal. 3:10	"faithful administration" I Cor. 4:2 Mt. 25:21,23
Concept	Rejecter	Owner	Steward
Attitude Toward Poor	We are	We owe	We care
Preoccupation	Daily needs	Money	Wisdom
Attitude	Carefree (Pr. 3:5,6)	Driven (Pr. 10:17)	Faithful (Lk. 16:10,11)

Leaks in the Dike

Prosperity theology doesn't hold water because it contends you can "give" to "get." The theory is that you can create a binding transaction on God in which He is obligated to *bless* you. This view disregards your motives, whether you are living in sin, and what God's plan is for your life.

When I was a young businessman, I heard about the idea of pledging a tithe of a certain amount to God and then, by faith, claiming the income level to support that amount. So I figured out a nice, round six-figure income that I secretly desired, and I pledged to give God 10 percent of that amount.

All of a sudden, my income was clobbered. I had the worst year imaginable. I tried to buy God, and He chastened me severely and taught me a lesson I have never forgotten. *You'll find it in Proverbs 10:22. Look it up and transcribe it in the space provided.*

_____

_____

Poverty theology is equally full of holes. The person who thinks you must be poor to be humble is mistaken. He doesn't understand God's mandate to be industrious and to make full use of his abilities, in whatever proportion they have been given.

Poverty theology carries the presumption that anyone doing well financially must be doing something dishonest. It forgets what we read in Proverbs 22:2. Write that verse here.

_____

_____

How do disciples of poverty theology sometimes display an elitist attitude?

_____

_____

We have become a society of pretenders, bent on portraying an image of financial success whether or not there is any substance to it.

A good illustration of this came one year when we invited a prominent Christian speaker to a leadership conference. We opted to host a luncheon for lawyers and judges as well. I announced the conference and the special luncheon at our church on Sunday.

After the service I was accosted by a disciple of poverty theology. This man, who holds extensive postgraduate degrees, was earning his living as a substitute schoolteacher, barely making ends meet.

"I don't guess I will be able to come to your conference," came his acerbic greeting.

"Oh, I am sorry to hear that!" I replied.

"Yeah, since I wouldn't be welcome at your elitist luncheon, I am not interested in your message, whatever it is."

The message, at the "elitist" luncheon and the conference, centered on the importance of building relationships between haves and have-nots, rich and poor, powerful and powerless. His presuppositions kept him from a significant blessing.

God wants the message of reconciliation distributed to all classes and segments of society. Lawyers have as much right and need for God's message as any group.

The Best of All Three

Stewardship theology weaves the virtues of prosperity and poverty theology together with the balance of God's Word about money and possessions. In other words, much of poverty and prosperity theology is sound, but making it a total point of view breeds error. Stewardship theology would be impotent if it did not include the beautiful promises of God's blessings and the admonitions to care for the poor.

We could list hundreds of Scriptures to illustrate stewardship theology but, in the end, all we would possess is a long list of rules and regulations. Being a steward is more of an attitude, a way of looking at life as a caretaker. It's watching out not only for our own interests, but also for the interests of others.

> *Being a steward is more of an attitude, a way of looking at life as a caretaker. It's watching out not only for our own interests, but also for the interests of others.*

 ## *L* ooking Closer in the Mirror:

We've already decided that money is a neutral commodity. If that's true, then the problem with money must really be a problem with men. The Bible says so much about money because God knew it would be His main competitor for our affections.

What evidence do you see in yourself or your family members of this competition for our affections?

_____

_____

_____

Money represents different things to each of us. What are the reasons you want money?

_____ *Symbol of achievement*   _____ *Measure of self-worth*
_____ *Buy things*   _____ *Improve standard of living*
_____ *Provide for family*   _____ *Financial independence*
_____ *Ambition*   _____ *Fear of the future*
_____ *Other (Explain):* _____

People have reacted to that kind of pressure by deciding how they want to handle money, and then searching for Scriptures that support that decision. As we noted, some have adopted prosperity theology, while others have moved toward poverty theology.

Based on the information in this chapter, describe prosperity theology.

_____

In a nutshell, you could say that prosperity theology invites people to bribe God. List some ways you have tried to buy God's favor:

_____

_____

Describe poverty theology.

_____

_____

List two attitudes of poverty theology that don't make sense to you biblically.

1. _____

2. _____

Now, look up 1 Corinthians 4:1–2. Describe stewardship theology in light of this passage.

_____

_____

Which of the three theological viewpoints is most sound, when you take into consideration the entirety of Scripture? _____ Prosperity _____ Poverty _____ Stewardship

■ WHAT ABOUT YOUR THEOLOGY?

Assess the attitude you have had toward money and material possessions.

_____

_____

_____

What financial decisions have you made as you worked through this chapter?

_____

_____

_____

How will you make sure you stick to them?

_____

_____

_____

■ *REMEMBER TODD AND JUDY?*

Let me follow up on the story about Todd and Judy from the beginning of this chapter. They saw their folly when Todd asked a true friend for advice about financing that new pool. That friend challenged him about his material appetites, and Todd responded.

He started reading the book of Proverbs, and he was overwhelmed by the advice those thin, crinkly pages contained about money. Since there are thirty-one chapters in Proverbs, he decided to read the whole book through once a month—a chapter a day. He also purposed to seek God first. He began to tithe, even going above the tithe for special needs at his church. Although paying off the balances of his cut-up credit cards came first, he started planning for a savings account.

He recognized his own habit had been to wrap his hand tightly around his money. He began to envision himself holding his money gently in his open palm, offering to take care of it, but aware God had entrusted it to him for a reason.

MIRROR WORK

Todd and Judy made some commitments to God that shaped their attitudes toward money. I invite you to do the same.

Read through Psalm 112, concentrating on verses 3–5 and 9–10. Then write out as a prayer your own commitment to God in respect to your finances:

_____

_____

_____

_____

In the next chapter . . .

Now that we have drawn a theological blueprint for financial matters, let's move on a little further. Let's look at how we can build a sound financial house on the four biblical pillars of financial strength.

12 The Four Pillars of Financial Strength

Entrepreneur's credo: A dollar borrowed is a dollar earned, a dollar refinanced is a dollar saved, and a dollar paid back is gone forever!

TED MILLER

He who gathers money little by little makes it grow.

PROVERBS 13:11

"Save 10 percent, share 10 percent or more, and steer clear of debt."

In the previous chapter I introduced you to Todd and Judy. They were looking for ideas to help them be financially responsible. Now, in this chapter, I will present four ideas that I would suggest to them. In fact, I would suggest them to anybody. Even if we try nothing else, these four "pillars of financial strength" will revolutionize our lives and help us become more faithful stewards of what God has given us.

Pillar #1—Earnings: "Little by Little"

Chuck asked members of his Bible study to pray for his business. The tension in his face and voice communicated the gravity of his request. "I must sell five boats this month or I won't make it," he explained.

The group prayed faithfully. At the end of the month Chuck reported, "You'll never believe what happened! We didn't sell a single boat. But we sold enough batteries, skis, ropes, anchors, and other accessories to give us a pretty good month. And now the boat shoppers are starting to come by the showroom."

Chuck was astounded. "I can't believe how God works!" he said. "He answered our prayers, but in a way totally different from what I expected. He did it *little by little!*"

Look at Proverbs 13:11, quoted at the beginning of this chapter. In your opinion, why do so few people pay attention to the principle of this verse?

Most of us would like to rake in money hand over fist. We may even look disparagingly at the "little by little" principle. I know I did, until my friend Ed taught me a huge lesson.

Ed's goal was to own enough rental property to cover his desired annual income. He planned to buy houses that would throw off cash of $25 to $100 each per month.

I distinctly remember thinking how unambitious his scheme sounded. My ambition was to make it big by selling large properties and knocking down huge commissions that would make his rent checks pale by comparison. Five years later I was still a slave to closing that elusive big deal, while Ed earned all of his income while he slept.

Are you like Ed or like me? Why?

If you decided you are more like me, let me recommend that you become more like Ed. His experience shows that the "little by little" principle is valid, even in our fast-paced culture.

Pillar #2—Saving: "Little by Little" Too

The "little by little" principle applies to saving as well as to earning. Scripture supports the concept clearly.

For example, look up Proverbs 21:20 and write it here:

What principle is expressed in that verse, and how does it apply to the financial questions we face today?

When we spend up to the limits of our income (and beyond), we just dare our car to break down or the water heater to leak and ruin the carpet. Only the person who has learned to save *little by little* has something for a "rainy day." And since all of us, if we live long enough, will encounter at least one proverbial rainy day, it is only wise to prepare for it.

Write 1 Timothy 5:8:

_____

_____

_____

> *If we take that verse seriously, what are the implications if we don't prepare for rainy days, and then rely on the government or charitable organizations to provide for our families?*

_____

_____

_____

Unfortunately, men in their fifties often realize they were so busy taking care of their company's affairs, they didn't put their own financial houses in order. Then they must do in ten years what they should have done over a forty-year career.

This brings incredible stress. Many succumb to the pressure to make high-risk investments. A few go sour, adding to the stress of preparing for retirement. Even Christians are not immune to the temptation to skim a little off the company expense account. How can we avoid this? We need to build a "nest egg" for retirement.

Only the person who has learned to save little by little *has* something for a "rainy day."

The Nest Egg Principle

What if someone told you that you can actually choose the annual retirement income you want? Would you believe him?

Well, you can. Pick any income level you want, and then follow this simple plan: Each year of your forty-year career, save 10 percent of your desired annual retirement income, put it into a qualified retirement plan, and you can extend your targeted income in perpetuity.

Let me illustrate:

• Desired Annual Income at Retirement	$40,000
• Amount to Save Each Year	$ 4,000
• Required Average Annual Earnings Rate	6.2%
• Number of Years	40

Here are the results at retirement:

• The Nest Egg (Capital Accumulated)	$651,000
• Yield Required to Produce Desired Income	6.2%
• Annual Retirement Income	$ 40,000

(Note: Tax and inflation consequences are not considered. Money saved can be sheltered through proper tax planning, and retirement income can be protected through lower tax rate and tax-exempt income instruments such as municipal bonds.)

How does your retirement plan compare to this?

I call this the "nest egg" principle. It's also called compounding. Each year, interest is earned on all of the initial funds saved, as well as on all of the interest earned to that date. You achieve true exponential growth.

Too Little Too Late?

Maybe you're saying, "Dream on! There's no way I can put away that much on my income. I'll get started when I've moved a few rungs up the ladder and am getting a better salary."

This is faulty thinking. Suppose you're past your twenties—maybe well past your twenties—before you get started building your nest egg. Then you will need to catch up, either by saving more or by earning a higher interest rate. Here are the interest rates you would have to earn for shorter periods to produce the same income:

	30 years	20 years	10 years
Yield needed	8.3%	12.8%	27.0%
Capital accumulated	$479,000	$316,000	$147,000

As you can see, the requirement to earn a higher yield goes up disproportionately as the window of time narrows. That's because the money is not available to compound over a longer period of time. Obviously the chances of making double-digit returns require high risk. People under that kind of pressure are most likely to fall for "get rich quick" investment scams, often losing all their money.

If you are still young enough to really benefit from the "little by little" approach to building a nest egg, what steps can you take to involve the whole family?

If you are not-so-young, what will you have to do in order to prepare adequately for retirement?

> *The "Nest Egg Principle" personifies the character qualities of that different way of life: quietness, diligence, industry, prudence, patience.*

If you can't take advantage of the Nest Egg Principle because you've waited too long, then at least teach the principle to your children or grand-children. Teach them the habit of saving. Very few financial pointers will be as helpful.

What specific steps can you take to teach the Nest Egg Principle to others?

Be Willing to Get Help

If you need help to sort through the issues related to your particular situation, ask a certified financial counselor to help you determine where you are today and what you need to do to retire successfully. And keep in mind that I believe a permanent life insurance program should be the foundation of every investment strategy. Excellent yields are attainable if you stick with the top ten mutual companies.

As a self-check, list the insurance programs you have invested in, including all life insurances, mortgage insurance, accident or disability, etc.

Remembering 1 Timothy 5:8, which you looked up earlier, do you have adequate insurance to protect and provide for your family if you were removed as a breadwinner?

Christianity is a way of life—a different way of life. The Nest Egg Principle personifies the character qualities of that different way of life: quietness, diligence, industry, prudence, patience. And we do it all "little by little."

Pillar #3—Sharing: Where to Store Your Money

Several years ago, when we began to earn more money than we needed to live in the manner to which we were accustomed, I began to make plans to move. That's what people do when they can afford it, isn't it?

I knew that people and relationships are more important than possessions, but the social pressure to buy a bigger house preoccupied my mind. The image of having money, and making sure everyone else knows it, pulls like a tug-of-war against the Christian life view.

In my case, it tugged so hard that I overlooked an important family dynamic as I cast about for a better house. We live in a neighborhood where our children are happy, secure, and settled. My wife likes the convenient location and the neighbors. One of my daughter's very best friends lives two doors down from us. No dogs bark in the middle of the night, and no expressway drowns out conversation when we cook in our backyard.

So one day I noticed I was the only family member pressing to move. That got me thinking. Finally I yielded my ambition to move to that bigger house, and I allowed God to work. We stayed where we were, and simply redecorated.

What could have happened to our family's sense of well-being if I had insisted on moving?

_____

_____

How should men respond to family needs and desires when they are making major decisions?

_____

_____

Capping Our Standard of Living

Over the years, my family and I have begun to understand the warning implicit in Proverbs 11:28. Briefly paraphrase that passage to show its implication for our current society's view of acquisition.

_____

_____

_____

_____

So how are Christians supposed to handle the siren song of financial gain? Where should we store our money? Look up Matthew 6:19–21 and transcribe it in the space provided:

_____

_____

_____

_____

_____

_____

My family has responded to those principles by forming the belief that God wanted us to put a cap on our standard of living. However much He blesses us over and above that standard, He wants us to invest in helping to fulfill His purposes. Now everything that God entrusts to us over and above what we need to live and save for retirement, we give to His work.

The Right Way to Give

As I read the Bible, I believe each of us should give to the Lord a percentage of every dollar earned. This establishes that we give in direct proportion to the way God has blessed us. I believe the minimum for that amount should be 10 percent. This is a "tithe." This money should be set aside as it is earned. For those of us who own businesses or are in sales, I believe we can deduct normal business expenses from the top line before calculating the 10–percent minimum.

Assuming that you agree, does your giving reflect this pattern? Why or why not?

_____

_____

_____

Where Should We Give?

I believe the money you give is to be used in the work of the Church. The Church is both the congregation to which you belong and the larger Body of Christ worldwide. Each local church has its own recommendations, and you should follow them if they agree with your conscience. Many worthwhile organizations without church affiliations would welcome your support, if after you pray, you believe God has directed you that way.

How Should We Give?

Scripture not only advises an amount for our giving and a place for our giving, but it also offers criteria regarding *how* we should give. I summarize it like this:

1. Your giving should be done in secret to guard against any temptation to be proud.
2. Give your gifts as an offering to God, not to men. Don't seek the approval of men, and don't look for a blessing from specific people or churches or organizations to whom you give. God will bless you for cheerful, anonymous giving, though the blessing may be spiritual rather than material.
3. Develop regularity in your giving. God doesn't need endowments. And systematic giving is good discipline.
4. Don't give only out of your abundance. The highest form of giving is sacrificial. Some people call it "giving till it hurts."

Pillar #4—Debt: The Ability to Pretend

Consumerism, the economic theory that a progressively greater consumption of goods is beneficial, depends on a constant sparking of our desire to buy. The strategy is to keep the image of the beautiful, wrinkle-free life ever before us. Those who are successful in doing that become successful entrepreneurs.

Is the idea of being in debt really attractive? Why or why not?

_____

_____

Most of us say no. The idea of being in debt is not attractive. And so, in order to make debt attractive, our consumer-oriented marketers play to our hidden needs for love, approval, companionship, significance, and relief from anxiety. They lure us to accumulate "things" to meet those needs.

Yet Scripture gives a stern warning regarding this type of lifestyle. *Look up Proverbs 12:9 and 13:7. Write them in the space provided.*

_____

_____

Just as our savings earn a wage through compounding our interest, debt has a hidden cost in the interest we pay on the loan. Debt is a costly venture.

Despite the warnings, many of us succumb to the need to be something we are not. We wear false faces before the world by acquiring things. And there are only two ways to accumulate—income and debt. What happens when the lure of Madison Avenue supersedes our income? Many of us choose to borrow.

Charles Lamb said, "The human species, according to the best theory I can form of it, is composed of two distinct races, the men who borrow, and the men who lend. Men either earn interest or pay interest." Just as our savings earn a wage through compounding our interest, debt has a hidden cost in the interest we pay on the loan. Debt is a costly venture.

Debt is also addictive. Once we discover how to get things by going into debt, we drink up more and more of it, as if it were sweet wine. But the frustration of how to repay the debt produces an acid that eats at the lining of our guts like the torch of a welder cutting steel.

Analyze your own debt picture. Is it causing anxiety? How do you know?

Is debt addictive to you? How do you know?

The Bible has no prohibition against going into debt. Yet most of the Scriptures that do relate to debt are cautionary. Or they may deal with solving problems created by debt.

A Debtor Nation

Debt obviously affects individuals, but in many ways it also affects nations. Consider what it has done to the United States.

Financial author Howard Dayton sent me a shocking graph which is reproduced as Figure 12.1. Please look at the graph before reading on.

Figure 12.1

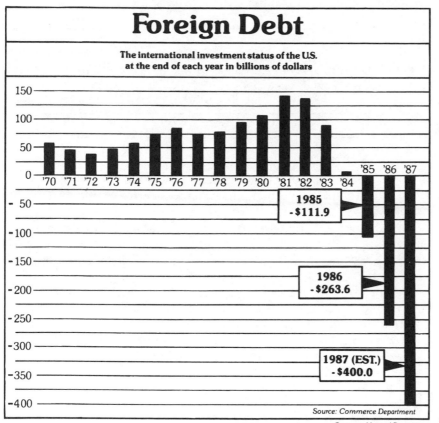

As you can see from the graph, America was a net lender nation through 1984. Then our unbridled spending habits turned us into a debtor nation in 1985, and in succeeding years we have borrowed increasingly large amounts of money from other nations.

Look up Deuteronomy 15:4–6. According to this passage, what happens to a nation that lives in obedience to God?

_____

_____

Now look up Deuteronomy 28:43–46. According to this passage, what happens to a nation in disobedience to God?

_____

_____

What conclusions can you draw regarding the United States?

_____

_____

Can these verses apply to individuals as well as nations? Why or why not? If you answered yes, how do they apply?

_____

_____

The possible implications of the chilling scenario offered in those passages and that graph provide ample reason to steer clear of debt. But there are contemporary as well as biblical reasons to avoid debt.

The eighties and nineties have been tumultuous—deregulation, tax reform, the stock market crash, all in addition to the growing national debt. These were accompanied by a transfer to an information-based economy, lay-offs in nearly every industry, and spiraling consumer debt.

In light of these problems, I suggest that you do your best to become financially secure. Give the ideas in this chapter a try. Save 10 percent, share 10 percent or more, and steer clear of debt.

How simple! In fact, it's so simple, we may be tempted to scoff. But if we follow these principles, we are virtually guaranteed a promotion to a new job—the job of faithful steward.

Looking Closer in the Mirror:

The Nest Egg Principle shows how simple it would be for all people to retire in financial security. *Why do most people end up financially strapped?*

_____

_____

How much money is enough for you? Why?

_____

_____

Consider the warning issued in 1 Timothy 6:17–19. To whom is the warning addressed?

_____

What are the specific details of the warning?

_____

_____

_____

This passage doesn't say wealth is bad, but it says there is no eternal hope in wealth. *If that's true, how are we to measure our riches? What are we to be rich in?*

_____

If we heed this warning and become rich in our good deeds, what will be the end result?

_____

_____

That warning echoes Jesus' words in Matthew 6:19–21, which you looked up earlier. Based on that passage, where would you say your heart has been set in recent years?

_____

Where would you like for your heart to be set? You can take positive action in that regard. Figure your expenses, including your retirement planning. Discuss your figures with your family to determine if your expenses are within God's will. Then set a cap for what you and your family consider to be a reasonable standard of living.

_____

_____

_____

_____

_____

_____

Now, with your family, list some specific Christian laborers, organizations, or church projects you would like to help financially once you have established your standard of living.

Keep in mind the value of sacrificial giving. According to Matthew 6:19–20, when you give more than the comfortable-to-part-with-amount, you actually are sending it ahead to be stored where moth and rust don't destroy. *In light of that, where is the best place to store money?*

Regarding debt, would you say that most men owe too much money to other people and institutions? Explain your answer.

As an individual, are you a borrower or a lender?

Look up Proverbs 22:7. What caution does it offer?

Perhaps you still think debt doesn't really matter. But when you are a servant to someone other than God, how does it affect your relationship with Him?

Several years ago Bob, a family man with five children, visited the Philippines, where he felt God leading him to return and share Christ with the peasants in the hill country. He obeyed, and when he returned for a furlough after four years, he reported that 10,000 people had been led to a saving faith in Jesus Christ, and that he had been instrumental in the planting of 27 churches.

Picture the loss for the Kingdom of God if his debts had forced him to say, "No, I want to go, but I can't."

What encumbrances would prevent you from responding to God's call for specific service in His Kingdom?

What action steps would you be willing to take this week to help put you in the position of saving 10 percent, sharing 10 percent, and getting out of debt?

_____

_____

_____

MIRROR WORK

*H*eavenly Father, I want to be a good steward of what You have given me. I want to build my family's financial house on the foundation of Your Kingdom principles. Help me to learn how to save a tenth, give a tenth, and avoid debt. Help me to involve my family in this process, so we can enjoy the unity of purpose in following You. Amen.

In the next chapter . . .

We've already said you can judge your own character and priorities by how you spend your money and your time.
We've looked at our money problems.
Now let's move to our time problems.
Keep reading, and we'll discover how to beat the clock.

PART FOUR

Solving

Our

Time

Problems

Decisions: How to Make the Right Choice

Once—many, many years ago—I thought I made a wrong decision. Of course, it turned out that I had been right all along. But I was wrong to have thought that I was wrong.

JOHN FOSTER DULLES

Elijah went before the people and said, "How long will you waver between two opinions? If the Lord is God, follow him; but if Baal is God, follow him." But the people said nothing.

1 KINGS 18:21

Some time ago I was victimized by my inability to make up my mind about how to spend my evenings. I'm a morning person. By evening I'm just too tired to do much other than vegetate in front of the TV. To at least partly redeem the time, I rode a stationary cycle while I watched, but even that was boring. I wanted to spend more time with the Lord, but I was married to the television—and to the wrong thoughts it stimulated.

The best time of day for me is early morning. So finally the big idea hit me: Why not go to bed an hour earlier! That would accomplish several objectives. I could exercise in the morning when rested, and by using an optional reading stand, read the Bible at the same time. Best of all, I could go to bed when I was really tired. The trade: an hour of television for extra time with the Lord. And I could eliminate a source of temptation for my thought life.

Yet, as ingenious and productive as the idea seemed, I couldn't quite make the *decision* to change. I knew it was the right idea, but twelve years of inertia encumbered me. After I had the idea, months went by, but nothing happened until finally, I *decided* to make the change.

We all do exactly what we decide to do. *We are the sum of our decisions. Do you agree or disagree? Explain your answer.*

❝Decision making determines who and what we are more than any other aspect of our lives.❞

Even not making a decision is a decision in itself. If your daughter's school play starts at 11:30 A.M., and at 11:35 A.M. you're still on the phone to the home office, then a decision has been made.

The Problem

We are branded by our decisions. Decision making determines who and what we are more than any other aspect of our lives.

If our decisions are so crucial, then it's important that we understand how we make them. How do you make decisions?

Unfortunately, the world has not produced a common set of factors, traits, or processes among leaders to help us through the process of making decisions.

Consider, for instance, research cited in *Stodgill's Handbook of Leadership: A Survey of Theory and Research.* After examining more than five thousand research studies and monographs on decision-making among leaders, researchers were unable to isolate the decision-making qualities that identified effective leadership.[1]

The chief executive officer of a Fortune 500 company put it this way: "I'll be darned if I understand how we make some of our most important decisions around here."[2]

If most men have this degree of difficulty making good decisions, should we expect our decision-making to be any easier? *Despite the overwhelming evidence to the contrary, does a set of principles exist which we can follow?*

The Priority/Moral Distinction

Happily, the answer to that question is yes. And the principles begin with understanding that decisions can be divided into two categories: *priority* decisions and *moral* decisions. Aside from minor choices—no-brainers, such as which way we will drive home from work—decisions tend to fall into those two general categories. They represent our choices about how we will allocate our time and our money.

Deciding whether to take your wife to dinner or to play ball in the city league tonight is a priority decision. Working on Saturday mornings versus spending time with the family is a priority decision. Investing in the stock market or staying liquid is a priority choice between two acceptable alternatives.

The only imperative in making a priority decision is to be wise. *A*

A priority decision involves choosing between right *and* right.

In contrast, moral decisions are choices between right *and* wrong.

priority decision involves choosing between right and right. In other words, two or more choices can be made, either of which would be morally right. List some priority decisions you are facing right now.

In contrast, moral decisions are choices between *right* and *wrong*. There is the morally correct choice and the morally incorrect choice. To make the wrong choice is sin. The decision whether to report overcharges to a customer is a moral choice. The decision whether to engage in mental adultery with a young beauty at the office is a moral decision.

Find James 1:5–7. According to this Scripture, how do we gain the wisdom and power to make morally correct decisions?

The power to make correct moral decisions results from a desire to have integrity and to trust in the power of God.

Decisions that have both moral and priority implications are not merely decisions about how to spend time or money. They carry with them the full weight of God's principles.

The purchase of a new car, for instance, is simply a priority decision when transportation is the consideration for the purchase. But the decision to buy a luxury car we covet may steal money from higher priorities, such as savings for college tuition or tithing. This takes on the added dimension of a moral issue—a choice between right and wrong.

What is the most difficult moral decision you are facing right now?

How Not to Make a Wrong Decision

Perhaps you haven't given much thought to the question immediately before this section. Or perhaps you didn't have to give much thought to it—perhaps you knew immediately what you wanted to write down as your answer. Perhaps that decision has been nagging you for a long time.

Let me encourage you. *The best insurance for making the right decision is to know how not to make the wrong decision.*

Admittedly, this isn't always easy. In fact, Peter Drucker, in an article in *Harvard Business Review* titled "Getting Things Done: How to Make People Decisions," notes that even highly paid executives sometimes make the wrong decisions. "By and large," he notes, "executives make poor promotion and staffing decisions. By all accounts their batting average is no better than .333: at most one third of such decisions turn out right."[3]

The first principle for effective decision making is *to* live by the Word of God.

But Jesus batted 1.000. He always made the right choices. Scripture outlines His model for decision-making in the story of His temptation in the desert. Satan presented Him with some alluring opportunities. If He had made the wrong decisions, He would have ended up just another sinner like us. He would not be an innocent lamb to die as a sacrifice for our sins, and today we'd *still* be waiting for the Messiah.

Yet because He did not make the wrong decisions, we read this about Him in Hebrews 4:15:

> We do not have a high priest who is unable to sympathize with our weaknesses, but we have one who has been tempted in every way, just as we are—yet was without sin.

How Jesus Decided

You might already be very familiar with the story of Jesus' temptation in the desert. Let's review it. *Look up Matthew 4:1–3. Based on that passage, what was Jesus' first decision?*

_____

_____

Was it an easy decision? Why or why not?

_____

_____

Jesus' decision not to turn stones into food was, in fact, a decision not to rebel against God's plan for His life. And no, it wasn't easy. After all, Jesus hadn't eaten for forty days. But His response to Satan's temptation at the level of physical appetite, a tactic that had won for Satan with Adam and Eve, gives us the first principle of effective decision-making.

Look up Matthew 4:4 and write it here:

_____

_____

The first principle for effective decision making, based on that verse, is to *live by the Word of God.*

Jesus faced His second decision in Matthew 4:5–6. What decision did Satan hold before Him?

_____

_____

In choosing not to jump off the roof of the Temple, Jesus actually chose not to test God. He refused to put God in a position that required God to save Him from the consequences of a foolish decision.

Can you identify a situation where you made a decision that tested God? Describe it here.

_____

_____

In Jesus' case, Satan even used Scripture to entice Him. But Jesus prevailed. *Look up His answer in Matthew 4:7 and write it:*

_____

_____

The second principle of effective decision making is *not to put God to a test.*

I imagine that for those first two temptations, Satan probably disguised himself as a friend, maneuvering himself into a position of trust. But when his first two temptations failed, he decided to go for it all.

Jesus faced His third decision in Matthew 4:8–9. Based on that passage, what choice did Satan offer Him?

_____

_____

Jesus' third decision occurred when Satan tried to trick Jesus into worshiping him. In reality, Jesus faced a choice of whether to renounce the Fatherhood of God to serve other gods.

How do people in our contemporary culture "jump the tracks" and set out to serve other gods? What gods do we choose over God the Father?

_____

_____

How is this the result of our decisions?

_____

_____

Matthew 4:10 records how Jesus decided this issue. Look up His answer in that verse and write it here:

_____

_____

_____

The third principle of effective decision making is *always to worship God and serve Him only.*

Now, let's review. Go back and re-read the three principles of decision making found in Jesus' temptation in the desert. Record them here:

(1) _____

(2) _____

(3) _____

How can you incorporate those three principles into your decision-making process?

_____

_____

_____

_____

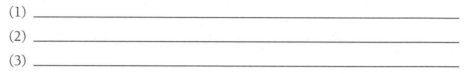

The second principle of effective decision making is not to put God to a test.

Because of our humanness—to paraphrase a great philosopher, it *is* human to err—these three principles will not guarantee that we will always make the right decisions. But they will give us the highest probability of *not* making the *wrong* decision. They are *risk-management principles*—ideas to keep us close to God's plan and purpose for our lives.

Jesus referred to God's Word each time He faced a difficult decision. He knew man's inner strength isn't enough. We need a citadel of truth to give us moral backbone. A man who lives by God's Word will make the right choices, and in the end, he will prosper in all his ways.

Consequences

Every decision has consequences. At a minimum, they are *spiritual* and *financial.* Christ's announcement that a man "cannot serve both God and money" contemplates the spiritual and financial aspects of every decision we make.

Paul advised Timothy of this same principle. Turn in your Bible to 1 Timo-

thy 6:6–10. What are the consequences of ignoring this principle according to Paul?

_____

_____

Now, let me show you how that principle works. A man received an unsolicited job offer that required him to work fifty hours a week instead of the forty he worked now. He didn't need the money, but took the offer anyway. Something in his schedule had to go, so he stopped reading his Bible and coaching his son's Little League team.

Identify the potential spiritual and family consequences of his decision.

_____

_____

What if you are in sales, and you decide to coach your son's Little League team? How will that reduce your selling time in the field? How will that affect your income?

_____

_____

When you follow Christ in your business practices, your saving habits and charitable generosity will often change sharply, and those decisions, too, have financial consequences.

Forgiven, but Still in Jail

One of our greatest hopes and promises is that our sins are forgiven. God patiently waits for us to confess and renounce our sins, and then He grants us all the rights of a co-heir with Christ.

However, a huge difference exists between receiving *forgiveness* and receiving a *pardon*. If a man robs a convenience store and then becomes a Christian and confesses his sin, he is still *guilty* of the crime. His verdict may be influenced by his contrition, and he can be certain that he is forgiven by God, but he still must bear the *consequences* of his actions—he probably will go to jail.

And so, we really are the sum of our decisions. Consider the case of David in 2 Samuel 12. I'm sure you remember the story of his adulterous affair with Bathsheba, and his planning for the death of her husband.

Bathsheba became pregnant and bore David a son. But God, angered by David's sin, confronted him through the prophet Nathan. David repented and exclaimed, "I have sinned against the Lord."

The third principle of effective decision making is always to worship God and serve Him only.

Case closed, right? Not according to Nathan. Look up his answer in 2 Samuel 12:13–14. David was forgiven, but forgiveness didn't eliminate the consequences of his decision. What were the consequences?

_____

_____

List some examples from contemporary society that demonstrate that forgiveness doesn't necessarily erase the consequences of sin.

_____

_____

_____

Life in the Fast Lane

Jim is among the many who have borne the consequences of sin. He spent eight years in prison for murder; he was a drug dealer. In prison, Jim found a second chance in Christ. Now a minister, he often speaks to high school students about the decision to take drugs.

We all face the choice of doing things that look like fun, but will result in a life of pain.

"Don't let anyone kid you," he tells them. "Drugs are fun, drugs make you feel good, and getting high is fun. You know the beginning of drugs. But I know the end of drugs. . . ." Then Jim tells them about the decisions that nearly ruined his life.

While most of us will never self-destruct the way Jim did, we all face the choice of doing things that look like fun, but will result in a life of pain. Just when we think we have gotten away with it, the consequences catch up with us. Adulterers get divorced, drug users get hooked, dishonest men lose their jobs, smokers get cancer—not every single time, but it's the rule.

A lot of this comes from "living in the fast lane." Yet, life in the fast lane isn't all it's cracked up to be. Many men at the close of the twentieth century have gone full-speed-ahead, and now they're running out of gas. They're worn out, fatigued, and overcommitted. Do you find it hard to keep up with all your responsibilities? The man with a full resume always pays a price to get it. Everyone has the same 168 hours to work with, so something has to suffer when we are an elder, a businessman, a civic leader, and a sportsman. The family usually pays the price. I believe that every man has some priority that competes with putting God first.

If you are in the fast lane, and you decide to get out, God will help you through the decisions you need to make. He is not as much interested in where you are as He is in where you are going. If you have the courage to decide to stay out or get out of the fast lane, He will bless the direction you are moving. He will empower you to make the adjustment—to find an exit.

If you were speeding down an interstate highway in your car, list the steps you would take to exit safely from the road.

_____

_____

_____

_____

I assume you wouldn't swerve sharply without warning. First, you would notice whether or not the road is crowded. You probably have a lot of company in the passing lane. You would turn on your blinker and start to work your way over to the exit lane. Even then, you would have to wait until you found an exit ramp.

What does this imply in a figurative sense if you want to "get out of life's fast lane"?

_____

_____

_____

Looking Closer in the Mirror:

In what area do you have the most difficulty making decisions? Prioritize the following list by putting a "1" by your most difficult area, a "2" by the next most difficult area, and so on until you have completed this list.

_____ *In relation to parents*
_____ *In relation to your wife*
_____ *In relation to your children*
_____ *In relation to entertainment*
_____ *In relation to television viewing*
_____ *In relation to job situations*
_____ *In relation to time with God*
_____ *In relation to major purchases*
_____ *Other* _____

Look at the top three most difficult areas for you. What aspects of these areas make them difficult?

_____

_____

What is your batting average for making good decisions on the big issues? Explain your answer.

_____

_____

Describe one very good decision you have made. What factors in your decision contributed to its success?

_____

_____

Describe one "lousy" decision you have made. What caused you to make this decision? What consequences have you had to bear because of it? Would you make a different decision if you had to do it over again?

_____

_____

What key decision are you facing that will have financial consequences?

_____

What key decision are you facing that will have spiritual consequences?

_____

How will the passage in 1 Timothy 6:6–10, which you looked up earlier in this section, affect those decisions?

_____

_____

_____

Describe the difference between receiving forgiveness and receiving pardon.

_____

How should this understanding affect our decision making?

_____

We all do exactly what we decide to do. Admittedly, we can decide with or without God's help, but He promises to always help if we trust Him. Look up His promise in Philippians 2:13 and write it here:

_____

_____

_____

I encourage you to memorize that verse. Now, what do you want God to "will" and to "act upon" in your life?

_____

_____

MIRROR WORK

Lord Jesus, I understand that in many ways I am defined by my decisions. I want those decisions to be in line with Your vision and purpose for me. Fill me with Your Holy Spirit. Give me the mind of Christ, that I might come as close as possible to batting 1.000 in my decisions. Amen.

In the next chapter . . .

How do you spend your Saturday mornings? How you answer that question says a lot about your priorities. Stick with me, and in the next chapter we'll go beyond basic decision making. We'll learn how to decide what's really important.

14 | Priorities: How to Decide What's Important

The constant desire to have still more things and a still
better life and the struggle to obtain them imprints many
Western faces with worry and even depression, though it
is customary to conceal such feelings.

ALEKSANDR SOLZHENITSYN

"Teacher, which is the greatest commandment in the
Law?" Jesus replied: "'Love the Lord your God with all
your heart and with all your soul and with all your
mind.' This is the first and greatest commandment."

MATTHEW 22:36–38

> **❝ The man in the mirror can do nothing better than to look intently into the Word of God that gives freedom, and discover the principles, precepts, and guidelines offered. ❞**

Almost everyone has gone grocery shopping on an empty stomach
and without a shopping list. Everything that tastes good ends up
in your cart, so you take home too much junk food and not
enough nutritious food. When the cashier rings up the total and announces
your bill, you're shocked at the cost of your unplanned spree. And the worst
part may be explaining to your wife how you spent so much money and still
didn't get what your family needed.

The Problem

Setting priorities helps us allocate our limited amounts of time and
money to the places where God directs. According to *Webster's Dictionary,* a
priority is something we give precedence to by assigning a degree of ur-
gency or importance to it. To have any control over our lives, we must
decide in advance what activities and relationships are important enough for
us to invest our time, energy, and money in them.

Unfortunately, we often choose our priorities with the same foresight
that we gave to our earlier trip to the grocery store. *Most men have not settled
the issue of what their priorities should be. And among those who do know the
right priorities, too few live accordingly.*

A Neighborhood Illustration

In previous chapters you have looked up Matthew 6:19–21. Re-read it now. According to verse 21, how can you tell where a person has placed his priorities?

_____

_____

In practical experience, I don't have to look any further than my own neighborhood on a Saturday morning to see how many different priorities men have set for themselves. One man rises early; another sleeps until ten o'clock. One plays golf every week; another watches his son's soccer game. One does yard work, but his neighbor goes to the office to catch up on paperwork. Another washes his car and cleans the garage; his neighbor shoots baskets with several kids from the block. One relaxes with the newspaper; another reads his Bible. One takes his family out to breakfast; another eats breakfast in bed.

Perhaps no time of the week reveals more about us than Saturday morning. We discharge our work Monday through Friday, and Sunday is the Lord's day, but Saturday is the day we decide for ourselves. Saturday is like the discretionary income in our paycheck. Most of the paycheck goes to essentials, but the amount left over can be spent any way we want. Most of the week goes to essentials, but the amount left over—Saturday—can be spent any way we want.

List your regular Saturday activities.

_____

_____

Do they reflect priorities for which you would like to be remembered? Explain your answer.

_____

_____

Establishing What Is Important

Has God already made out a "shopping list" for our lives? Has He prioritized things for us at all? If so, what are God's priorities for a man's life?

_____

_____

_____

Setting priorities helps us allocate our limited amounts of time and money to the places where God directs.

I believe God's priorities rest on four questions:

- What does God want me to *be* and *do*?
- How does God want me to use my *time* and *money*?
- What *character* and *conduct* traits does God desire in me?
- What *relationships* and *tasks* does God want me to emphasize?

At the risk of stating the obvious, secular values lead to secular priorities, and biblical values lead to biblical priorities. Based on what you've already learned in this book, evaluate your value system. Do you live by a Christian life view, or do you see secular values occasionally cropping up in your life view? Explain and give specifics.

_____

_____

_____

_____

When we say yes to the Christian life view, we must also adopt biblical priorities. They will be a flashlight in a dark world, illuminating the way for how we spend our time and money. They will be a method for us to determine the people, events, and activities to which we should give precedence.

The American writer Gertrude Stein owned two Picassos. She used to tell her friend, "If the house were on fire and I could only take one picture, it would be those two." Choosing between two or more competing priorities is tough, but it's where we see in a tangible way how the interior life has progressed.

Our Top Priority

According to what we have already discussed, what would you say is God's top priority for individuals?

_____

_____

One day an expert in God's law tested Christ with that exact question. "Teacher," he asked, "which is the greatest commandment in the Law?" Jesus replied by quoting from the scroll we know as the book of Deuteronomy. *Look up his answer in Matthew 22:37–38 and write it here:*

_____

_____

_____

What does this imply in terms of your own priority list?

_____

_____

How will this affect your use of time and money? Give an example.

_____

_____

_____

If we penetrate the full scope of this great commandment, if we saturate our minds with the Word of God and devote every ounce of our strength to loving God, then our lives will take on a new dimension—a softness will begin to appear. "He will quiet you with his love," Scripture promises in Zephaniah 3:17.

This is the essence of our being, for our most important work is to love Him. Whatever task He gives provides an opportunity to demonstrate our love and gratitude to Him in a tangible way.

Most of us are familiar with John 3:16. At the very least we've seen it on signs at sporting events. If possible, write that verse from memory here. If you can't do that, go ahead and look it up, record it here, and then memorize it.

_____

_____

_____

Now look up Romans 5:6–8 and write it here:

_____

_____

_____

_____

_____

_____

_____

_____

_____

After reading that passage, how do you feel about God's action toward you? How do you want to respond?

_____

_____

Implementation

The obvious answer to the previous question is that we want to respond to God's love by loving Him in return. But how do we do that? Jesus answered that in John 14:15, 21, and 23. Turn to those verses and transcribe them in the space provided.

_____

_____

_____

_____

_____

_____

What is the relationship between loving and obeying God?

_____

_____

The man in the mirror can do nothing better than to look intently into the Word of God which gives freedom, and discover the principles, precepts, and guidelines offered. Read and meditate on the Word, pray (talk) with Him constantly; worship Him with your praise, your time, and your money; and share His Word through your witness and through enabling others to share their witness.

Priority Number Two

At the same time that Christ answered the "lawyer" about the greatest commandment, He also noted a second commandment found in Leviticus. He said this one is the second most important. *You'll find His answer in Matthew 22:39. Record that verse in the space provided:*

_____

_____

Our relationship priorities distill to these two great truths: Love God, and love others. If we could change ourselves in these two areas alone, we would have demonstrated more of the gospel of Christ than any generation before us.

Too often we see the errors of the other fellow, but don't pay enough attention to our own need for change. Tolstoy put it well when he said, "Everybody thinks of changing humanity, and no one thinks of changing himself." Our relationship priorities are the place to start moving toward change.

> *Saturday is like the discretionary income in our paycheck.*

Priority Number Three—Learning to Rest

A priority that is often treated like an orphan in our fast-paced world is *rest*. Everywhere I go these days I see tired men. In fact, they're just plain exhausted.

Admittedly, there are two kinds of tired. Sometimes when I go home I'm "good" tired. You know the feeling—you've spent yourself in a worthy cause. You're tired, but you feel great.

Theodore Roosevelt described it like this:

The credit belongs to the man who is actually in the arena; whose face is marred by dust and sweat and blood; who strives valiantly. Who errs and comes short again and again; who knows the great enthusiasms, the great devotions. Who spends himself in a worthy cause. Who at the best knows in the end the triumph of high achievement; and who at the worst, if he fails, at least fails while daring greatly so that his place will never be with those timid souls who know neither victory nor defeat.

What worthy cause leaves you with that "good" tired feeling?

If you are not part of such a worthy cause, what are some causes you could pray about and get involved in?

_____

_____

What would you have to eliminate from your schedule to do that?

_____

That simple exercise required you to establish priorities. And that's very important in this issue, because I find that most men these days aren't really "good" tired. They're just "worn-out" tired.

One of the greatest Christian fallacies is that we aren't doing enough for the Lord. It's not that we're not doing enough, but we're doing too much of the wrong things.

The areas in which God wants our help are evangelism, disciple making, and caring for the poor and needy.

As a young Christian, I didn't have a clue about God's priorities for my life. I lacked the self-confidence to say no because I honestly didn't know where the boundaries were.

One fall I went to a men's retreat just to get a break. Tom Skinner, the primary speaker, completely stunned me with his teachings about biblical priorities. I was so impressed, we invited Tom to come to Orlando to share his understanding of the Scripture with some worn-out friends. Tears of relief flowed from several Christian "workaholics" who attended.

Look at your schedule carefully. What do you find on there that might fit into the category of the "wrong things" we discussed earlier in this section?

_____

_____

Listing your activities, would you classify yourself as a workaholic Christian? Explain your answer.

_____

_____

Priority Number Four—Work

Work is where we men tend to find our significance. It's where we believe we can make a contribution. And that is true, for at the very beginning of creation, God prescribed work as the way we would occupy our days.

According to our earlier discussion in the chapter titled "The Secret of Job Contentment," what is the purpose of work, from God's perspective?

_____

The purpose of work is to glorify God with the abilities He has given us. By pursuing excellence, we demonstrate to a world weary of Christian "talky-talk" that Christ can make a difference in a man's life here and now. Since I already spent a whole chapter on this issue, I won't go into detail here. Just let me note that work is one of the five overarching areas in which God wants us to prioritize our lives.

Priority Number Five—Good Works

To have faith without good works is to have no faith at all. Faith, not good works, allows us to enter into relationship with God. But our deeds are still important, *as Paul teaches in Ephesians 2:10. Look up that passage and record it here:*

_____

_____

In other words, Jesus has a will, a purpose, and a plan for every man, which includes some good work He had in mind for us before we even knew Him. In fact, He was preparing us for it even when we were totally unaware of it.

The areas in which God wants our help are evangelism, disciple making, and caring for the poor and needy. *Identify how you are contributing to God's agenda in those three areas:*

(1) Introducing others to Him _____

_____

(2) Helping others to learn about and become like Him _____

_____

(3) Caring for the poor and needy _____

_____

Trying to keep up with all of our responsibilities, like an old farmer said, is like trying to put two tons of fertilizer in a one-ton truck.

This is God's agenda. We try to make it more complicated, but these are the three tasks God wants us to help Him with. Different men can contribute to these areas in different ways, depending on their temporal and spiritual gifts. Each of us must make an honest assessment of how we are endowed: in intelligence, wisdom, acquired competencies, and innate abilities. I'll help you get started on that in the section titled "Looking Closer in the Mirror."

Now, recapping, list the five areas of importance to God under which we are to prioritize our lives.

(1) _____

(2) _____

(3) _____

(4) _____

(5) _____

To be a biblical Christian is to have these five priorities in balance. If they aren't in balance in your life, you can do something about it. The Holy Spirit is very willing to help you prioritize your life.

The Competition with God's Priorities

Trying to keep up with all of our responsibilities, like an old farmer said, is like trying to put two tons of fertilizer in a one-ton truck. We need to sort out what is competing with God's priorities.

The Bible gives us the attitude we are to have in the midst of this competition. It is recorded in 1 John 2:15–17. Please turn to that passage and write those verses here:

_____

_____

_____

_____

The primary thing that competes against our establishing God's priorities in our lives is identified in 1 Timothy 6:10, where Paul noted, "Some people, eager for money, have wandered from the faith and pierced themselves with many griefs."

An acquaintance of mine wanted to be rich. He also wanted to be a Christian. Unfortunately, Bible study interfered with selling time, and church came when he needed to recover from the exhaustion of the week. In the end, money was more important to him, and he walked away from God. He illustrated the power of the world and money as it competes against God's priorities.

God knows we face choices more numerous than our time and money resources. That's why He has so clearly outlined His agenda to us and has shown us what our priorities should be.

Men frequently pine for God's direction, saying, "If only I knew God's will for my life." We need to look in the Bible—it has the answers.

Looking Closer in the Mirror:

■ PRIORITY NUMBER ONE—LOVING GOD

There are at least four specific areas in which our obedience can demonstrate our love for God. Describe how you are showing your love through obedience in:

(1) Bible Study _____

_____

(2) Prayer _____

_____

(3) Worship _____

_____

(4) Sharing your blessings _____

_____

What one area of those four are you not doing all that you should?

_____

Name one practical thing you can do to improve that.

_____

■ PRIORITY NUMBER TWO—LOVING PEOPLE

We've already discussed our relationships with our wives, children, and friends, but let's put them, and other relationships, in the context of demonstrating our love to God. *How are you showing your love for Him in your relationships with:*

(1) Your wife _____

(2) Your children _____

(3) Your employer or employees, or your work associates _____

_____

(4) Your associates at church _____

(5) Your neighbors _____

(6) *Your friends* _____

(7) *Your enemies* _____

(8) *Strangers* _____

(9) *Rich people* _____

(10) *Poor people* _____

Read John 15:12–14. Regarding your demonstration of God's love in your relationships, who would you be willing to die for, and why?

_____

_____

■ PRIORITY NUMBER THREE—REST

Do you feel guilty when you relax? _____ Yes   _____ No
The simple fact is that you don't have to feel guilty about resting. Look up Matthew 11:28–29 and write it here:

_____

_____

_____

_____

What is Jesus' attitude toward rest?

_____

Whose "yoke" have you taken—Jesus' yoke, or the yoke of expectations originating with you or with others? Explain.

_____

_____

How can you find rest for your soul? What does it mean in practical experience to take up Jesus' yoke and learn from Him?

_____

_____

■ *PRIORITY NUMBER FOUR—WORK*

If you still have trouble with this one, go back and review the chapter on job contentment.

■ *PRIORITY NUMBER FIVE—GOOD WORKS*

The spiritual gifts we most frequently think of are serving others, teaching, encouraging, contributing to the needs of others, leadership (including the gift of administration), showing mercy, and preaching.

Several passages of Scripture give inventories of different spiritual gifts God gives to men. Look up these passages and list the gifts that are mentioned.

(1) *1 Peter 4:10–11* _____

_____

(2) *Romans 12:4–8* _____

_____

(3) *Ephesians 4:11–12* _____

_____

(4) *1 Corinthians 12:1–12* _____

_____

_____

Now, spend a moment in prayer and ask God to show you how He has gifted you for good works. In what areas do you believe you are gifted?

_____

_____

_____

MIRROR WORK

Lord Jesus, I want my priorities to be in line with what You've said in Your Word. Show me the areas where I need to pull them back into line, to re-prioritize my life. Then, help me to live in a way that demonstrates those priorities. Amen.

In the next chapter . . .

Ecclesiastes tells us there's a time for everything. Yet do you really know anyone who thinks he has enough time to accomplish everything on his schedule? In the next chapter we'll take a look at how proper time management is a primary facet of doing God's will.

Time Management: Doing God's Will

15

One of the greatest reasons people cannot mobilize themselves is that they try to accomplish great things. Most worthwhile achievements are the result of many little things done in a single direction.

NIDO QUEBIN

There is a time for everything, and a season for every activity under heaven.

ECCLESIASTES 3:1

W ith what you now know about the importance of managing time and prioritizing activities, evaluate how you spent the last week. If you had the opportunity to live that week over again, what would you change?

_____

_____

> **❝Instead of wasting time by making plans without God's direction and approval, why don't we just go to Him first?❞**

Imagine that you are the chief executive officer of a global corporation with 15,000 employees. You are constantly on the go, speaking and meeting key people who have the power to make substantial financial commitments to your organization. What would be your number-one priority in terms of time management?

_____

_____

Now let that imaginary person become flesh and blood. In my experience, this person actually is Dr. Bill Bright, founder and president of Campus Crusade for Christ. I heard him address a national conference of Executive Ministries of Campus Crusade for Christ. In his opening remarks, he said, "I try to prioritize everything I do in light of the Great Commission."

When he said that, I pictured him accomplishing this through his ministry to huge groups. I saw him preaching to hundreds—even thousands. I visualized him sharing the Gospel with important heads of state.

Then came the time for the banquet. One of Patsy's best friends from college lived in the city where we held our conference. She was a Christian, but her husband, Tom, had walked away from the Lord many years before. Their marriage had just enough gas left to go about two more weeks. We asked them if they would be our guests at the banquet, and they said yes.

During the banquet, Nancy DeMoss told Dr. Bright about our friend Tom. But about one hundred well-heeled people wanted to say hello to Dr. Bright that night after his address. I didn't think I had a chance of introducing him to Tom. After all, these people had big bucks! So I naturally presumed Dr. Bright would visit with potential financial supporters when the dinner broke up.

I was wrong. He made a beeline for Tom.

For the next hour and fifteen minutes he shared and listened to Tom, and he helped Tom commit his life to Christ. By the time they finished talking, only six of us were left in the room—Bill and Vonette, his wife, Tom and his wife, and Patsy and me. So much for valuable contacts!

When Bill Bright said he tried to prioritize everything he did in light of the Great Commission, *I had no idea he meant one person at a time.* Since then, I have repeatedly seen him leave a crowd to minister to one individual.

Bill Bright did not become a great leader by doing great things, but by doing many little things in a single direction. I'm certain if he had set out to be *great,* he would have fallen flat on his face. Instead he set out to be *faithful.*

Most of us think we have to do great things to become great leaders. What did you learn about time management for success in the example of Bill Bright?

> **God always provides enough time to accomplish God's plans. . . . We need to stop always going for the "long bomb" and run more dependable short yardage plays.**

_____

_____

Now look back at the quote from Nido Quebin with which I began this chapter. How does Bill Bright's time management decision reflect the principle of that quote?

_____

_____

The Problem

We all have the same amount of time to work with as do Bill Bright and Billy Graham, as well as men from the past like Martin Luther and Abraham Lincoln. It's exactly 168 hours each week. Then why don't we get the same results?

The time management problem is less a *tips and techniques* problem than it is a *strategic* problem. The issue is not so much memorizing twenty clever ideas to help accomplish every item on our "to do" list, though tips and techniques are helpful. Rather, the issue is a clear understanding of God's *purpose* for our lives, living by biblical *priorities,* and making *plans* that reflect God's will for our lives.

In this chapter we want to examine the strategic aspects of time management. We want to consider the larger perspective—what we give our time to in the first place. Then we want to examine how we can convert our priorities into a plan of action.

Even though God forgives, we must bear the consequences of our decisions.

From Purpose . . . to Time Management

Bill Bright closes his letters, "Yours for fulfilling the Great Commission in this generation." I imagine that comes as close to a Written Life Purpose Statement as we'll ever find (see Matthew 28:19–20). Dr. Bright knows his life purpose. And that makes setting his priorities and managing his time a lot easier.

Look back at the Life Purpose Statement you wrote for yourself at the end of Chapter 5. How will it help you to prioritize your activities so you can manage your time more effectively?

_____

_____

_____

A couple traveling through the countryside was lost. Spotting an old man beside the road, they asked, "Where are we?"

"Where are you going?" came his reply.

"We don't know," they said.

"Then it doesn't matter."

When we don't have a sense of where we are going, where we are now isn't that important. Only when we know our purpose—where we are going —can we make heads or tails out of how to use our time.

People like Dr. Bright demonstrate that our purpose helps us prioritize. Time management, then, is based on this progression: from *purpose* to *priorities* to *plans* and *goals.*

Use that progression to prioritize your current activities in the following exercise.

Your purpose: _____

_____

Your priorities: _____

_____

Your plans: _____

_____

Your goals: _____

_____

Perhaps you aren't ready yet to complete all those statements. That's no problem—you can come back to them later.

As you work on this exercise, your list may seem very challenging. "Where will I find the time?" may creep into your thinking before you even get started.

God always provides enough time to accomplish God's plans. We just need to use it more productively. We need to stop always going for the "long bomb" and run more dependable short yardage plays. We need to block and tackle better. If we do, we will have all the time we need. If we don't, we'll have to punt. "Little things done in a single direction"—that's the way.

Describe a time when you had to punt because you failed to run the "short yardage plays" well.

_____

_____

_____

Can you identify one area in which you may be tempted to "go for the long bomb"—to accomplish too much too fast? How can you mobilize yourself to do many little things in a single direction, and do them faithfully?

_____

_____

_____

Discerning God's Will

The greatest time waster in my life has been the time I've had to spend undoing that which ought not to have been done in the first place. It is a question of whether to pursue our own will or God's will. Pursuing our own will can cost us a world of wasted time. The secret to time management, in my opinion, begins with discerning God's will. *Describe the process you go through to know and do God's will.*

I wonder if your experience in figuring out what God wants you to do is anything like mine. I seem to go through five stages before I finally agree to march in step with God's will.

Step One: I Tell God What I'm Going to Do

Solomon had a pretty good idea of what goes on with me when he wrote, "To man belong the plans of the heart" (Proverbs 16:1a).

Why do we make our own plans rather than asking for God's guidance right from the start?

I don't know about you, but there are many situations that I don't like to bother God with unless I have to. I know He has a lot on His mind: wars in the Middle East, droughts in North America, famines in Africa, earthquakes in Central America. Rather than take up His valuable time, I frequently make plans without consulting God, intending to bring Him in on them later.

I remember one time we decided to open an office in Tampa, Florida. Only later did I mention it to the Lord. Instead of asking His advice, I told Him what I was going to do. "Oh, by the way," I said, "we have decided to open a branch office in Tampa. Please bless us."

How would you rate our chances of success?

Have you taken action on something recently without consulting God? Describe your action.

Describe the results.

Step Two: God Responds

Thankfully, we haven't finished that verse in Proverbs that we mentioned in the previous section. The second half goes like this: "but from the LORD comes the reply of the tongue" (Proverbs 16:1b).

Concerning the Tampa office, that verse worked out this way: A few months after we opened that facility, the new operation was in the weeds. The anchor tenant in our building became insolvent, and our office was spending money like it grew on trees. Only then did it dawn on me that I had run ahead of God, and my plan did not have His stamp of approval.

Look up Proverbs 19:21 and record it here:

_____

_____

What does that verse mean in terms of present-day, practical experience?

_____

_____

Have you seen this principle at work in your life? If so, when and how?

_____

_____

Step Three: I Beg God to Let Me Do It Anyway

In my situation, even though God had now responded and made it entirely clear that I ran ahead of Him, my financial, emotional, and time investments were pretty substantial. So I pleaded my case before Him in prayer, begging Him to change His mind and allow us to succeed in Tampa.

We've already looked at Proverbs 16:1. Now look up the next verse, Proverbs 16:2, and transcribe it here:

_____

_____

How did that verse apply to my situation?

_____

_____

Sometimes God does change His mind (or so it seems to us) and lets us have our own way. You may have a half-dozen situations where prayer resulted in God's changing His mind. I know it happens. In Tampa, though, it didn't. He brought His painful discipline into our lives, putting the brakes on our ambitious plans.

Identify an experience in your own life that can only be described as "painful discipline" designed to set you back on the right track.

_____

_____

Step Four: Finally, I Humble Myself and Listen

After I have realized I'm unable to persuade God to do things my way, I usually go off and pout for a little while. Eventually, I come to my senses and get still before the powerful God who wants to guide me in the use of my time.

In Proverbs 16:3, God promises us something. Write out that verse here.

_____

_____

What is the promise mentioned?

_____

What does it mean to "commit your works to the Lord"?

_____

Step Five: God Tells Me What He Is Going to Do

Now, go one last step in that passage in Proverbs 16. Look up Proverbs 16:4 and write it here.

_____

_____

What does that say about God's sovereignty?

_____

_____

When we have listened for God's leading for a time, perhaps a long time, and a sense of His desire starts to take shape in our minds, He sometimes leaves us alone with our thoughts, perhaps for years, causing us to trust in Him and Him alone.

Efficiency is doing the job right. Effectiveness is doing the right job.

We had to shut down our Tampa office at a major, major financial loss. Even though God forgives, we must bear the consequences of our decisions.

This experience moved me to put God in charge of my life in a new, deeper way. My former plans became despised memories. I now pray to God, "I crucify those plans, and I purpose to not make anymore plans for myself. However I spend my time from this day forward will only be how You direct me, and only after a period of patient listening."

The Most Effective Time Management Strategy

Most of us think only in terms of wasted time and money when we pursue our own will and God has to rein us in. But there usually is a third area of loss as well, and this probably is the most costly of all. Usually our relationships suffer.

Remember the Old Testament stories about King Saul and the prophet Samuel? Read part of their story in 1 Samuel 13:1–14. This passage describes the result of a situation where Saul ran ahead of God. What happened when he refused to wait for Samuel?

_____

_____

_____

It's obvious, then, that in order to avoid loss on all three fronts—time, money, and relationships—the most effective time management strategy is to eliminate the first three of the five steps I said I usually go through before I end up where God wants me to be.

Instead of wasting time by making plans without God's direction and approval, why don't we just go to Him first? We should begin by listening for Him. When we don't hear His voice, we should wait patiently for Him to act—after all, His timing is always perfect. This is *strategic* time management, not mere *tactics*.

Unfortunately, in today's fast-paced society, listening is not a skill we actively seek or cultivate. List some ways we can listen for God's voice.

_____

_____

_____

When a goal, plan, or idea begins to form, that's when to consult with God. We should pray over our plans before our minds are made up.

A mind made-up is almost impossible to change. Before we take any action, we should pray and seek the counsel of godly men. This is the most strategic way to manage our time.

Efficiency Versus Effectiveness

Define efficiency.

_____

Define effectiveness.

_____

What is the real difference between those two terms?

_____

_____

How are efficiency and effectiveness demonstrated at work?

_____

_____

The way I would answer those questions is by providing an illustration.

Three junior executives were as different as earth, wind, and fire.

The first rarely checked with his boss. He set his own priorities, but frequently had to redo his work, or worse, he found he had just completed a project no one really cared about. His skills were sloppy. His boss usually found errors in his calculations, so they had to be refigured. He was both inefficient—the work he did was wrong—and ineffective—he worked on the wrong projects.

The second junior executive was a planner. He mapped out his plans and kept his boss informed by memos. He never asked if he was on the right track, or if his boss had any suggestions, but at least he kept his boss informed. He was very efficient—he did good work. But he was ineffective, because he often wasn't working on the right projects.

The third junior executive was wise indeed. When a project took shape in his mind, he would present it to his boss. Then he would listen carefully to the voice of experience. Adjustments would be made, and sometimes project ideas would be abandoned altogether. When he finally tackled his work, he breezed through the task. He was efficient—he did the job right; and he was effective—he did the right job.

And that is the bottom-line difference between the two terms. *Efficiency is doing the job right. Effectiveness is doing the right job.* And we all know that there is no cigar for doing the wrong job in the right way.

Why are some men unwilling to take the necessary steps to be both efficient and effective?

_____

_____

How does this difference in the terms apply to our spiritual lives?

_____

_____

When we become a tractable piece of clay in the Potter's hands, He will mold and shape us into effective time managers.

In our spiritual pilgrimage, we may execute all the spiritual disciplines efficiently—Bible reading, Scripture memory, prayer, church attendance, tithing, etc.—but if we don't translate them to our daily living, we doom ourselves to an ineffective spiritual life.

Hard Work Versus a Balanced Schedule

While it is certainly true that no success will come to a lazy man, it is not conversely true that hard work assures success. God's blessing determines a man's lot in life. Our part is to be faithful—to be diligent, industrious, and creative. God's part is to provide the increase as He sees fit.

Compare the following examples.

A gift store owner arrived at his store at 7:00 A.M. Monday through Saturday. He was there till 9:30 P.M. every night—thirty minutes after closing. After fifteen years he still lived from week to week, with few reserves to fall back on if business went bad. Because he worked so hard and still did not seem to get ahead, he was bitter. His customers sensed his tension and hostility, so repeat business was slow.

On the other hand, the owner of an insurance agency refused to work nights and weekends. His theory was, "If it can't be done before 6:00 P.M., then I don't need the money." Since his home life was balanced, he was warm and concerned about his customers. They always felt they were important. He found time to play golf once a week and contributed to community life through involvement with the local university.

Why did one fail and the other succeed?

_____

_____

Which kind of person are you? Explain your answer.

_____

_____

Would you like to change, and if so, how will you plan to do that?

_____

_____

Things That Last

There is a thin, delicate line representing the threshold between this world and the next. That line is physical death.

Part of effective time management is wrapped up in understanding the significance of crossing that line. When we understand that life is forever, we begin to look for activities that have the potential to last forever.

Have you ever noticed how someone who has enjoyed an elegant dining experience tells everyone he meets about his discovery? That a man who has stopped smoking tries to convert everyone he meets into a non-smoker?

Yet those of us who know Christ have the most mind-boggling news of all. We have a far different eternal destiny from those who don't know Christ.

With what percentage of the people you meet would you be willing to discuss the question "Where are you on your spiritual pilgrimage?"

_____

_____

In what kinds of situations do you meet other men where this question could be asked naturally?

_____

_____

Describe the most recent time you engaged in conversation with someone regarding his or her eternal destiny.

_____

_____

My own experience is that virtually every man wants to discuss the important question. Asking it consistently is part of managing your time with eternity in mind.

The Road to Greatness

Don't you marvel at the accomplishments of some men? How do they ever get so much out of their time?

The apostle Paul was such a man. But when you analyze his life, you find he didn't do great things. He did small, obedient things of which, when totaled, their sum was great. Even then, he wasn't considered great in his own generation. He was even despised. His many small contributions were seen as great only in retrospect.

When Paul arrived in Corinth he divided his time between making tents and speaking in the synagogue on the Sabbath. Later, friends joined him there, and he was able to devote all his time to preaching. When the Jews became abusive, he started preaching exclusively to the Gentiles. He just kept plugging away, using his time to do what was at hand.

Paul's life was not glamorous. He had no international organization raising funds and encouraging him. He had just a few friends who stood by him. But he understood that God always includes enough time to accomplish God's plans.

I challenge you to manage your time by God's priorities, making your decisions under the premise that all of life is spiritual. When we become a tractable piece of clay in the Potter's hands, He will mold and shape us into effective time managers, and He will show us what He wants us to do for the long-term and for the short-term.

ooking Closer in the Mirror:

Go back to the beginning of this chapter and read the quote from Nido Quebin. Now, can you give an example where you have tackled a project so big that you could never get it off the ground? What factors kept you from success?

_____

_____

_____

What is the best way to make progess?

_____

Read Ecclesiastes 3:1–8. So many of us are pushing hard all the time. According to this passage, though, we can see that a sovereign God is in control of an ordered world. *Do we have enough time to do everything God wants us to do? How should we approach our days if that is true?*

_____

_____

_____

Name an area where you have been pushing too hard. What changes could you make to acknowledge and better enjoy God's plan for your life in that area?

_____

_____

_____

Re-read Proverbs 16:2–3. How do you deceive yourself into thinking God owes you a positive answer on plans that you have "hatched" without His counsel?

_____

_____

_____

What do you think it really means to "commit to the Lord whatever you do, and your plans will succeed"?

_____

_____

_____

Look up Ecclesiastes 11:6. You are probably not a farmer, so you can't necessarily relate "sowing seed" to your lifestyle. Paraphrase this verse in terms of your specific business or employment.

_____

_____

_____

Look up Proverbs 23:4–5 and write it here:

_____

_____

_____

According to that passage, what happens when we set riches, or any other temporal goal, as our priority, and then manage our time accordingly?

_____

List the activities you are involved in that have eternal potential.

_____

_____

_____

MIRROR WORK

*L*ord Jesus, I want to accomplish great things for You, but I understand that I can do that only by effectively managing my time. Help me to block and tackle better. Help me learn to depend on short yardage plays and avoid the long bomb. Help me to build on the priorities You have begun establishing in my heart, and make wise decisions regarding where I will invest my time. Amen.

In the next chapter . . .

"I am the greatest," Muhammed Ali told the world. Many of us laughed, but if we were completely honest, we'd have to admit we are guilty of the same feeling about ourselves. Pride is the first of the temperament problems we'll examine as we move into the next section.

PART FIVE

Solving

Our

Temperament

Problems

Pride

16

I am the greatest. Not only do I knock 'em out, I pick the round!

MUHAMMAD ALI

God opposes the proud but gives grace to the humble.

JAMES 4:6

W hen I go out for breakfast, I'm usually in a good mood. After all, morning is my best time of the day.

Nothing gets my day off to a worse start, though, than being served by a surly waitress. You know the kind I mean. Without a trace of a smile she slams the coffee cup down and splashes coffee on your new white shirt. Watch out! Here comes the silverware! *Clunk!*

You have ordered eggs over lightly, but they come back charbroiled. By now you have confirmed that all waitresses resent men and are bitter about their station in life. You think, "With an attitude like that, no wonder she's *just a waitress.*"

Contrast how men would treat that waitress as opposed to how they would treat a peer or boss with a similar attitude.

> **The key to developing this proper kind of pride is not to compare ourselves with others.**

_____

_____

What makes the difference?

_____

_____

The Problem

Men want to feel good about themselves. Is it wrong to enjoy recognition and to feel good when you receive a compliment? Explain your answer.

_____

_____

When does being proud of our position or accomplishments become sin?

Pride is a sin of comparison. We compare our strengths to the other fellow's weaknesses. To make ourselves feel better, we put other people down, sometimes verbally, but always mentally.

Two Types of Pride

The Bible tells of two types of pride. *Pride Type 1 is found in Galatians 6:4. Look up that verse and record it here.*

The key to developing this proper kind of pride is not to compare ourselves with others. Rather than testing our self-worth by comparison to others, we are encouraged to use the Bible as our yardstick for self-examination.

What happens when we measure ourselves against Scripture?

Pride Type 2 is a spurious feeling of superiority that stalks Christians, especially those who feel they are above normal in their spirituality. C. S. Lewis once said, "A proud man is always looking down on things and people; and, of course, as long as you're looking down, you can't see something that's above you."

What is the subtle danger of this type of pride?

Jesus told a story about a man who had this kind of pride. What does He have to say about this man in Luke 18:9–14?

By comparing himself to the tax collector, the religious leader elevated himself at another's expense, comparing himself to a weak man rather than a strong God.

In the same way, why do we tend to compare ourselves to the man who isn't a loving husband, or to the fellow who travels too much and doesn't spend as much time with his kids? Or to a colleague who doesn't have the same mental software we do?

Is the sin of pride easy or hard to self-diagnose? Why?

Two Types of Humility

Just as there are two types of pride, there are also two types of humility. *In Romans 12:3 we can confirm the right type of pride, Pride Type 1, and we can learn how to define the right type of humility, Humility Type 1. Record that verse here:*

According to that verse, Humility Type 1 is simply defined as "not thinking more highly of yourself than you ought to." This affirms the cliché, "Humility is not thinking little of yourself, but rather, it's simply not thinking of yourself."

On the basis of Romans 12:3, is it possible to be both proud and humble? If so, how?

At the same time, many men suffer from the wrong kind of humility. Humility Type 2 is the opposite of Pride Type 2. If I compare my weaknesses to your strengths, I will end up with a negative self-image. Self-depreciation is a grueling, harmful poison to spirit and mind.

In other words, thinking too lowly of yourself is just as dangerous as thinking too highly of yourself. *How does a negative self-image interfere with your relationship with God?*

_____

_____

Keeping the Right Balance

Have you ever watched a gymnast perform on the balance beam at the Olympics? The gymnast must move confidently, but still exercise caution not to fall off one side or the other.

Refer to Figure 16.1. How does that image of the gymnast apply to our attempt to balance Pride Type 1 and Humility Type 1?

_____

_____

Figure 16.1

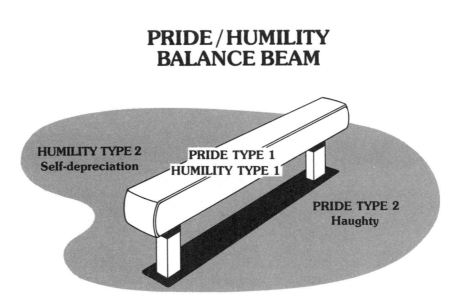

PRIDE / HUMILITY BALANCE BEAM

If we begin to think more highly of ourselves than we ought, we slip and fall off the beam into Pride Type 2. Or if we begin to think self-defeating thoughts, we slip off the other side into Humility Type 2.

Let's look at this another way, using a contemporary lexicon:

- Pride Type 1 + Humility Type 1   = I'm O.K., you're O.K.
- Pride Type 2   = I'm O.K, you're not O.K.
- Humility Type 2   = I'm not O.K., you're O.K.

My Own Foolish Pride

Now that we've established that foundation, let's admit that Pride Type 2 can cause us to do some foolish things.

My greatest desire during my first year after college, working in the business world, was to own an American Express card. That small green card seemed to be a proxy for success which would announce to the world that I was somebody.

Now, what is the real product of the American Express company? If you called the vice president for marketing at American Express and asked him, do you think he would tell you, "That's easy. Our product is a plastic card that will enable you to purchase just about anything just about anywhere"? No, he would tell you that his product is *prestige.*

What was my problem, if prestige was my only motivation for getting this credit card?

> *One of the most fertile soils for pride is smug self-satisfaction regarding how God has blessed us.*

Well, my problem showed up several years later. You see, when the American Express Gold Card became popular, I didn't want one. Since it signified only a $5,000 credit line, I reasoned it would actually be a step back in prestige for me to have one.

But when the *Platinum* Card came out—that was a different story. To qualify, you must have spent a minimum of $10,000 on your card in the previous year. *That's* prestige.

Now you can see my problem. I had spent nowhere near the required amount, so even before the Platinum Card officially debuted, I began to put everything on my American Express Green Card. And, of course, that's exactly what the company wanted.

Finally I realized that my reason for having a Platinum Card was not for the extra benefits and conveniences. It was to make me feel more important than men who didn't have one. I was permitting myself to be pressed into the world's mold.

I happily carry a Green Card again (better a little prestige than none at all.) Describe a situation from your own life in which you have pursued prestige or power to make you feel more important than someone else.

Too Much of a Good Thing

Beyond our being shaped by worldly definitions of success, one of the most fertile soils for pride is smug self-satisfaction regarding how God has blessed us. At one time God had blessed my business career with abundance, prosperity, and honor. As I mused with a friend about why He had done so, when other men of far greater talent struggled, he responded, "God is blessing you because He trusts you."

I grew proud, not in arrogance, but in subtly looking down on others, commending myself for superior accomplishment. But God got my attention. He put my business on its back, and it was the best education I ever had. It also was the most spiritually rewarding time of my life. I would gladly do it again.

Why does God sometimes have to do something drastic to get our attention before we realize that pride has invaded and taken over our lives?

_____

_____

_____

God spoke to this problem of pride when He gave Israel the words that were to prepare them for entry into Canaan. We read them in Deuteronomy 8:12–14. Look up that passage and paraphrase it. Put it into common, everyday, twentieth-century language.

_____

_____

_____

_____

Why is it so difficult to remain internally humble before the Lord, who has blessed us so abundantly?

_____

_____

No Permissive Parent or Tyrant

Another cause of Pride Type 2 is an absence of the fear of God. To fear the Lord is to hate evil, to be consumed with reverence for God. God is love, but He is also holy and just.

How does Scripture describe our God in Hebrews 12:29?

If God were not just, describe how He could become like an overly permissive parent.

_____

_____

How could He become like a tyrant?

_____

_____

To fear an oppressive tyrant is to fear injustice. In other words, we fear *getting what we don't deserve*. But the fear of God is the reverence we give to Almighty God because He has the power and authority to give us what we *do* deserve.

Read Psalm 36:1–2 and describe the man who doesn't fear God.

_____

_____

According to that passage, what will happen to that man?

_____

_____

The Fragile Male Ego

Do you use your wife's hairspray? Probably not. Have you ever noticed that men's hairspray comes in black cans, while women's comes in white ones? There is, of course, no difference in the actual hairspray. *The ingredients are the same, but the cans are different. Why?*

_____

The answer is male ego. Black is a macho color. The Mafia drive black cars. Dark suits project a strong image. Black leather jackets are the classic icon of the tough guy. So if you want men to do something traditionally done only by women, appeal to male ego, and make the can black.

That's just one example of what men go through to preserve the image we have of ourselves. List some other things we do to protect our "Male Ego."

_____

_____

Is there anything wrong with "ego"? Explain your answer.

_____

_____

Our Greatest Strength Is Our Greatest Weakness

I guess the answer to that previous question is "No, not really, unless . . ." I say that because, as we strive to protect our egos, we concentrate on the areas where we are strongest. The paradox of that is that our greatest strengths often can be our greatest weaknesses as well.

Let me explain. At the office I am very analytical and logical. My precise, incisive way of looking at problems has been one of my greatest strengths.

One day I walked into the house only to be greeted by my wife's long face.

"What's the matter, honey?" I asked.

She hadn't really wanted me to solve her problem. She just wanted someone to listen.

She unfolded a typical neighborhood spat that all kids go through. But these weren't just any kids—these were our kids. The day had been particularly hard on her, and her nerves were totally frazzled. I listened carefully and then counseled her with three easy steps to patch things up.

My wife broke down in tears. I was astonished, figuring I had said something wrong. Further inquiry revealed she hadn't really wanted me to solve her problem. She just wanted someone to listen. My strength had become my weakness.

What is your greatest strength?

_____

Describe how it has been or could become a weakness.

_____

_____

In the same way, when we become confident in our Christianity, that strength can become a weakness if we compare ourselves to others. Pride Type 2 actually tends to be a greater temptation to Christians than to unbelievers. How? Because of our pursuit of moral living, we can see how our morality is superior to those around us. The more self-righteous we become, the greater the potential for us to become proud.

Remember the story of the Pharisee and the Publican? Which attitude does God prefer, and why?

_____

_____

No Runts, No Pecking Orders

My daughter has two hamsters, one of which is the runt of his litter. Every litter has a runt. He's the little guy who has to work extra hard for his share of the food. In the world of chickens, he's the little one at the bottom of the "pecking order." The rule is survival of the fittest.

Unfortunately, we humans also tend to organize society into pecking orders and runts. But God doesn't have any runts. Christ came to usher in a new order. He requires that we love our neighbors as ourselves—without even thinking about the pecking order.

How can you help God usher in the new order where there are no "runts"?

_____

_____

Remember the waitress I talked about at the beginning of this chapter? Talk to your waitress sometimes. The younger ones, divorced and lonely, often support young children on what's lunch money to many men. The older ones often work because their husbands died and made no provision for them.

Should we peck away at them? Or should we make an effort to cheer them up and let them know there are Christians who don't look down on them because of their position?

Who is the "waitress" in your life? It can be anyone you know who has ended up on the bottom of life's pecking order.

_____

What will you do to help encourage them to find their real position in Christ?

_____

_____

_____

Pride: A Sin of Transition

Look up Proverbs 6:16–19. Pride is the first of the seven cardinal sins listed in this passage. It is a fountainhead for other sins. What does pride lead to?

_____

_____

Among other things, pride can lead to discord, jealousy, conceit, haughtiness, boasting, fits of rage, envy, arrogance, an independent spirit, hatred, self-righteousness, a judgmental attitude, and a sanctimonious spirit.

Are any of those sins evident in your life? Explain your answer, and describe how you came to the conclusion that you have a problem with that particular sin.

_____

_____

_____

The Sin of a Blind Man

Jesus called the Pharisees "blind guides." No sin more conclusively violated the new command He gave—to love one another—than the pride of the blind guides.

Unfortunately, we still have blind guides. When you look at other people, do you see the anger of men as a cry for help, or as a provocation for counterattack? Do you differentiate between classes of people with a pecking order you have devised? Are you listening to radio programs and watching television shows that arouse hatred or anger against other groups in society?

Look up James 2:1–13. What can we learn from this passage regarding God's attitude toward the pride inherent in partiality?

_____

_____

_____

What does James indicate is God's judgment on those who show partiality?

_____

_____

With God, there is no favoritism. If we are His children, we should reflect that attitude. We should not show partiality. Christ's example was humility, and we should have that same attitude.

Pride Type 2 eliminates the possibility of our having that attitude of humility. Pride Type 2 also leads us down the pathway toward hard times. Before a man's downfall, his heart is proud. The Lord detests all men who are proud, and they will not go unpunished. Disgrace is the by-product of pride.

Unfortunately, Pride Type 2 often defies detection. It cloaks itself with shadows. When you lose your temper with your wife or dwell on women in your secret thought life, you are engaging in high-awareness sins. Pride is more subtle. Frankly, all of us are guilty of pride and should ask God to make us humble so we won't suffer pride's consequences. This may sound unpleasant, but only radical surgery will remove this soul-destroying disease.

We are all proud to some degree. Some of us are just more humble about it than others.

> *All of us are guilty of pride and should ask God to make us humble so we won't suffer pride's consequences.*

⧉ *L ooking Closer in the Mirror:*

■ *THE PRICE OF JUDGING OTHERS*

We often tend to judge other men's spiritual condition on the basis of outward appearance. We constantly critique others. We editorialize about why different people are successful and others are not. We put down Christian men who aren't successful by worldly standards, or we are suspicious of those who are.

How is this propensity to judge linked to pride?

_____

_____

List some other ways we reveal our judgmental attitude and spiritual pride through our treatment of others—especially other Christians.

_____

_____

_____

Look up Matthew 7:1–3 and paraphrase it. What does Jesus really mean in common, contemporary language?

How does Jesus feel about the activity of judging others?

According to this passage, when I am harsh in judging others, they will be harsh with me. How does this principle work in real life?

Describe a time that you were the victim of harsh judgment, and explain how it made you feel.

Describe a time when you were guilty of harshly judging someone else. How did it make you feel? What did you do about it?

MIRROR WORK

Heavenly Father, I know that pride is difficult to detect, even with self-examination. If I am guilty of considering myself more highly or more lowly than I should, please show me, and then empower me to change. I trust You to make me more and more like Your Son, who humbled Himself and became a Servant. Amen.

In the next chapter . . .

What are you afraid of? Do you have the job jitters? Do you think a pink slip may be in the wind? Suppose you have just found out you have a disabling illness. How will you provide for your family? Are you afraid to die? Keep reading—we're about to discover the cure for fear.

17 Fear

The only thing we have to fear is fear itself.

FRANKLIN DELANO ROOSEVELT

Take courage! It is I. Don't be afraid.

JESUS, MATTHEW 14:27

"Fear is the agitated state of mind that cripples us from looking any further than the hardship itself."

Franklin Delano Roosevelt had served as a state senator and Assistant Secretary of the Navy when tragedy struck. He fell victim to a severe case of polio. The dark days that followed left him in twisted physical pain. But a determined Roosevelt, whose career many observers thought to be over, summoned the depths of his personal courage, regained the use of his hands, and learned to walk with braces.

During his convalescence, a fear of fire tormented Roosevelt. He feared that he would be trapped in a burning building. His life already devastated, who would blame him if he spent the rest of his days wallowing in self-pity? Instead, he struggled to overcome his handicap and conquer his fears.

Eight short years later, he became governor of New York. And just eleven years after he was paralyzed, after enduring countless months of severe pain, after being urged to retire, Franklin Roosevelt—man of fear, man of courage —was sworn in as the thirty-second President of the United States of America.

As he took the oath of office, the country was in the depths of the Great Depression. Perhaps you lived through this dark time, or perhaps you have just heard stories about it. List some details you know about that period of American history.

During that time, one in four men were unemployed. Many had no money for food for their families, and many lost their homes. This great nation was driven to its knees. God humbled America.

Our country, like Roosevelt himself, was crippled by fear. Imagine one out of every four men in your neighborhood jobless. The men on either side of you have been foreclosed. You have lost all your savings through a bank failure. Where do you turn?

It was against this backdrop that FDR scuffled to the microphone and delivered this century's most riveting inaugural address, "The only thing we have to fear is fear itself."

Who in your circle of acquaintances reminds you of FDR? Who has struggled against seemingly insurmountable odds, refusing to give in to fear, and has been victorious as a result?

The Problem

The person you just listed echoes Roosevelt's statement regarding fear. But what about you? What are you afraid of?

Put an "X" beside the items in the following list that fill you with dread.

_____ *Business deals hanging by a thread*
_____ *A disabling illness*
_____ *The threat of a pink slip*
_____ *A son or daughter on drugs*
_____ *Lack of direction in your life*
_____ *Fear of violence*
_____ *What may happen in the office today*
_____ *That your secret affair will be exposed*
_____ *That your wife may act on her threat to leave*
_____ *Other (Please identify)* _____

Some of us are consumed by the problems this day brings to our doorstep. "I don't have any problem with eternal life and salvation and all that—it's these next twenty-four hours I'm worried about!"

Every man struggles with the emotion of fear. Fear of failure, fear of rejection, fear of sudden disaster, fear of men—fears of all sorts elbow their way into our streams of conscious thought. While some fears are constructive—many heroes are born by their reaction to a life threat—most fears are handicaps.

Fear and courage are opposites. *Webster's Dictionary* defines courage as the state of mind that enables us to face hardship or disaster with confidence and resolution. Fear is the agitated state of mind that cripples us from looking any further than the hardship itself.

When Jesus spoke, He often began with, "Fear not." On what basis could He make this statement? Refer to Psalm 27:1–3 if you need help.

Look up 2 Timothy 1:7 and write it here:

_____

_____

Look up 1 John 4:18 and write it here:

_____

_____

_____

According to those verses, what does fear actually represent?

_____

_____

What do these verses say to people who live in a constant pattern of fear?

_____

_____

If you are struggling with fear, I suggest that you memorize those verses, and others to which I will refer in this chapter. They will help you to become confident and courageous in your faith, and that will transform your entire life.

Why Am I Afraid?

To be afraid is essentially to not *fully* trust God. He instructs us not to be afraid. *Look up 1 Peter 5:7 and write it here.*

_____

What is God's attitude toward us?

_____

Why should that fact calm our fears?

_____

But many of us still are fearful. Why? Let me list three problems that I believe Satan uses to cause us to be afraid rather than trust God.

I've Been Lied to All My Life

I remember being suspicious that my high school girlfriend had gone out with another fellow. When I confronted her, she vehemently denied it. Later I picked a fight with the senior (I was a mere junior) whom I suspected was her "other" knight in shining armor. My fears were true, and the price I paid to confirm her lie was a bloody nose.

Identify a lie that deeply hurt you. What did you do about it?

_____

_____

List situations where someone's lies rocked your faith in man's ability to tell the truth.

_____

_____

_____

Do you know any sin more prevalent than the white lie? In reality, I'm a liar, you're a liar, my wife is a liar. My parents lie. My business colleagues lie. My children lie.

And all of those same people have been *lied to*. In fact, we *all* have been lied to many times, by everyone we know.

How does that affect our ability to believe what we read in the Bible?

_____

_____

How does it affect our ability to trust the Bible's author, God?

_____

_____

There Is No Such Thing as a Free Lunch

The Bible promises that if we trust God with our lives, He will meet all of our needs and direct all of our paths. If we confess our weaknesses and sins, God will not only forgive us, but He will cleanse us from our unrighteousness. In other words, *God will give us everything we've ever wanted, in exchange for everything we've ever wanted to get rid of.*

Do you know any sin more prevalent than the white lie?

To most men, that sounds like a "free lunch"—especially if we add that if we confess our sins and follow God, He will also give us love, joy, peace, patience, kindness, goodness, faithfulness, gentleness, and self-control. In essence, He'll help us live out all of our New Year's resolutions.

For this "free lunch," all we have to do is allow Him to blot out the memory of everything we have ever done wrong.

But the most unbelievable statement of all is found in Romans 8:1–2. In the version of the Bible that you use most regularly, look up that passage and copy it here.

_____

_____

_____

Why do so many men have trouble believing that statement?

_____

_____

We Really Are Guilty

The third reason we don't trust God revolves around our moral guilt. We know we have been guilty of moral depravity in our thought lives, our speech, and our actions. We find our sins contemptible. We despise our unrighteousness.

Yes, we really are guilty. We really do deserve God's punishment and wrath. We really should be afraid of God, who has the power to give us what we justly deserve.

But in God's hard-to-fathom love, He withheld His punishment from us and brought it on the Lord Jesus Christ instead.

When men do not accept God's forgiveness for their moral guilt, they have not been "made perfect in love," and the fear of their guilt remains with them. How can we help them deal with that guilt?

_____

_____

_____

The Cycle of Fear

I believe a cycle of fear is evident in Matthew 14:22–31. Look up that passage and see if you can identify the cycle as displayed by the disciples, and particularly by Peter.

_____

_____

_____

I believe the cycle goes something like this:

The disciples' boat was caught in a fierce storm while crossing a lake. Jesus came walking toward them—on the water. They were terrified, but Jesus said, "Take courage! It is I. Don't be afraid." Peter responded, "Lord, if it's you, tell me to come to you on the water." Astonishingly, Peter got out of the boat and he, too, began walking on the water.

Just as Peter was on his way to becoming a hero, Scripture says, *"He saw the wind."* Suddenly he realized the crazy thing he was doing—he was walking on water.

Reality

The first step in the Cycle of Fear is *REALITY*—we see the wind.

Perhaps you can relate to Peter's sense of being overwhelmed. In what experience did you recently "see the wind"?

_____

_____

Then Peter was no longer interested in the original goal of being like Jesus. Instead, when he saw the wind, "he was afraid."

Response

The second step of the Cycle of Fear is our *RESPONSE.*

In the business world, it may look like this. Our minds dreamed of the glory of owning our own company. But when reality set in, and the sales were not enough to cover the costs, our *response* was fear.

What was your response in the situation you described above when you saw the wind?

_____

_____

Once fear seized Peter he found himself "beginning to sink." His faith had kept him afloat, but when he chose *fear* over continuing in *faith*, he started to sink.

Result

The third step in the Cycle of Fear is the *RESULT*.

Our faith kept us afloat in the "owning our own company" example just mentioned, but when the winds came up and buffeted our business, we soon saw that our faith was too small and we began to sink.

In your own situation when you "saw the wind" and "were afraid," how did you "begin to sink"?

_____

_____

Now, Peter was no fool. When he began to sink, he had the presence of mind to call out for help (which is more than some of us do). He cried out, *"Lord, save me!"*

Return

This simple prayer is the fourth step of the Cycle of Fear—the *RE-TURN*.

Peter returned to his source. He wisely acknowledged that he needed help, and he returned to his source of power, Jesus.

Did you take this fourth step when you were caught in the Cycle of Fear? If not, will you do it now and if so, how?

_____

_____

How did Jesus respond to Peter's brief prayer? He could have been filled with disgust; He could have given a sanctimonious discourse. Instead He simply reached out His hand and caught Peter.

Rescue

Jesus gave the fifth and final step in the Cycle of Fear—the RESCUE.

That's the wonderful ending of the Cycle of Fear—Jesus promises to rescue us. He doesn't promise to save your business, get your son off drugs, bring your wife to salvation, or keep you from losing your job. But He *does* promise to rescue *you*.

Now, let's review the Cycle of Fear. I'll give the principle. In the space provided, write how that principle was revealed in the story about Peter's attempt to walk on water:

- *Reality:* _____
- *Response:* _____

- *Result:* _____
- *Return:* _____
- *Rescue or Recovery:* _____

Everyone struggles with the Cycle of Fear. No "once for all" cure exists. But you can improve the amount of time you spend, following the charge by Jesus, "Take courage! It is I. Don't be afraid."

From Cliff to Cliff

In our story about Peter walking on the water, Jesus expressed great patience and saved Peter from the Cycle of Fear. But can a man move past the Cycle of Fear, and even overcome his fears?

We often find ourselves standing on a Cliff of Fear peering across a wide, deep chasm to a Cliff of Courage, where we wish we could stand. But how do we get there? Figure 17.1 illustrates the dilemma. Jesus gives the answer.

Right after Jesus saved Peter He said, "You of little faith. Why did you doubt?" Faith is how we traverse from the one cliff to the other. We cross from the Cliff of Fear to the Cliff of Courage on the Bridge of Faith. Figure 17.2 shows how faith bridges the gorge between fear and courage.

Figure 17.1

THE CLIFFS OF FEAR AND COURAGE

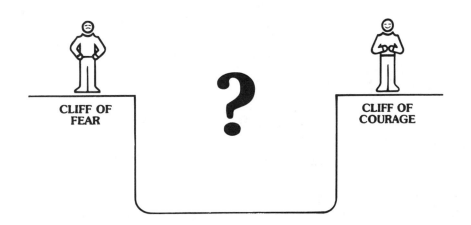

CLIFF OF FEAR   CLIFF OF COURAGE

Figure 17.2

THE BRIDGE OF FAITH

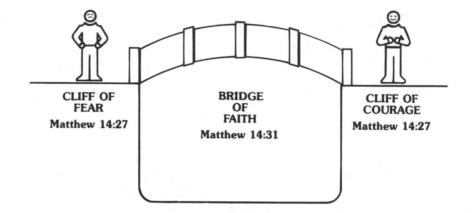

CLIFF OF
FEAR
Matthew 14:27

BRIDGE
OF
FAITH
Matthew 14:31

CLIFF OF
COURAGE
Matthew 14:27

But if we are to move across that bridge, we must understand what faith is. The writer of Hebrews provided our answer. *Look up Hebrews 11:1 and write it here:*

_____

_____

Faith is always oriented toward the future. Why is that?

_____

_____

An old saying sums it up, "We don't know what the future holds, but we know who holds the future." Many times I have heard Dr. Bill Bright add, "Faith is like a muscle. The more you exercise it, the bigger it grows."

Godly Fear Versus Secular Fear

I remember my first really big deal. The commission was six figures—was I excited! At the closing, the buyer ranted and raved and threatened not to close unless I took a cut in commission. A neophyte, I crumbled at the thought of no closing and settled for one-sixth of the earned fee.

We fear men because they have the power to give us what we *don't* deserve and to withhold from us what we *do* deserve. Men have the capacity to do the wrong thing. *How have you experienced this?*

_____

_____

_____

We should fear God for an equally practical reason. God has the power to give us what we *do* deserve. But God *does not* have the capacity to do the wrong thing. Let me ask you a question. Would you, at the end of any day, *really* want God to give you "exactly" what you deserve?

What do we deserve from God?

_____

What do we receive instead?

_____

God has genuine power. He has the power of life and death, the power to judge our sins. But He offers mercy. Look up Romans 8:28. What does that verse promise to you?

_____

A little later in that same chapter, in Romans 8:37, Paul says God will make us "more than conquerors." So who are we better off fearing—God or man?

_____

The wise King Solomon noted this same principle in Proverbs 29:25. Look up that verse and write it here.

_____

How have you experienced this contrast?

_____

_____

The Basis for Hope

Was Jesus ever afraid? No—He wasn't. That fact offers us hope. He was tempted to fear, but He never succumbed.

If ever a situation merited fear, it was the one Jesus faced on the Mount of Olives. He knew the temptation to be afraid. He told His disciples, "Pray that you will not fall into temptation."

Then Jesus withdrew and prayed His well-known prayer, "Father, if you are willing, take this cup from me; yet not my will but yours be done." For Jesus to ask God to change His mind is our first clue to the inner torture He was experiencing. He knew He would die the next day. He was tempted to fear.

Just then an angel was sent to strengthen Him, because His agony had reached its peak—He had begun to sweat drops of blood. This medically documented phenomenon, *hematidrosis*, only occurs in rare instances of extreme anxiety.

Unbundling Our Emotions

Describe the difference between fear and other emotions of anxiety and dread.

_____

_____

_____

> *We fear men because they have the power to give us what we don't deserve and to withhold from us what we do deserve.*

The Bible describes Jesus' condition as one of *agonia*, which translates as agony or anguish as a result of a struggle. According to *Strong's Exhaustive Concordance of the Bible,* this is the only time *agonia* is used in the Bible. I think we can say conclusively that Jesus underwent the most terrifying temptation ever encountered. Yet He remained sinless.

God did not remove the source of His agony. His *circumstances* did not change. But God *did* strengthen Jesus so that He did not become afraid. Agony—yes. Fear—no. That's our hope.

Looking Closer in the Mirror:

Take a look at Psalm 23:4. Perhaps you can't identify with some of the things David was afraid of. Paraphrase this passage by substituting the things you fear, and remind yourself that God is still in control of all those details.

_____

_____

_____

_____

What are you currently struggling with that has you afraid? How can you overcome your fear? The following is a list of the steps in the Cycle of Fear. Note how far you have come in the Cycle, and how you intend to see it through to the end.

- *Reality:* _____
- *Response:* _____
- *Result:* _____
- *Return:* _____
- *Recovery:* _____

Why can't we overcome our fear in one fell swoop? Why do we have to wrestle with it day to day? Read Matthew 6:34.

_____

_____

Courage and fear are opposites (see Matthew 14:27). What makes you feel courageous? What is the biblical way to courage? (Read Mark 4:40 and refer to Figure 17.2 in this chapter.)

_____

_____

_____

Look up Joshua 1:5–9. How many times does God tell Joshua to be "strong and courageous" in this passage? _____
Verse 5 explains why God could require that of this man who was facing such great odds. Joshua truly had reason to fear. Not only was he preparing to enter a battle zone, but he also was trying to fill the shoes of the previous commander-in-chief—Moses, himself. God said, "As I was with Moses, so I will be with you; I will never leave you nor forsake you." What does that imply for your life?

_____

_____

Describe the difference between secular fear (fear of man) and godly fear. Read Proverbs 8:13 and 1 Peter 3:10–14.

_____

_____

When you have done everything you can do, and things still don't seem to be working out, how are you to respond? For ideas, read 1 Peter 4:12–19 and 5:6–7, 10.

_____

_____

MIRROR WORK

Lord Jesus, I want to be strong and courageous. I claim Your promise that You won't leave me or forsake me. Help me to learn confidence by developing my faith. Amen.

In the next chapter . . .

Anger destroys. It destroys our families, our homes, our reputations, our health. And once released, angry words can never be erased—forgiven, maybe, but never erased. Together, let's look at how we can learn to control our anger.

Anger

18

"I lose my temper, but it's all over in a minute," said the student. "So is the hydrogen bomb," I replied. "But think of the damage it produces!"

GEORGE SWEETING

My dear brothers, take note of this: Everyone should be quick to listen, slow to speak and slow to become angry, for man's anger does not bring about the righteous life that God desires.

JAMES 1:19–20

D an and his wife, Shirley, were driving home from a welcomed night out for dinner. The Baltimore streets were crowded. As Dan slowed for a traffic light, a cab driver swerved into the narrow space in front of Dan's car.

Dan leaned on the horn and yelled expletives at the cabby. But the light turned green, and the driver took off. Dan decided to teach this cabby a lesson and began to chase him down the street, honking and screaming and waving his hands out the window.

Finally, the cab driver caught a red light, and Dan pulled alongside the passenger door of the cab. He ranted and raved, but the cab's window was rolled up. After thirty seconds or so, the cab driver leaned over, rolled down the window, and dryly asked Dan, "What do you want me to do, buddy—drop dead?"

Name something that really gets under your skin—perhaps even causes you to act as Dan did.

❝But the truth is that 99 percent of the time we become angry because we are selfish *and* impatient.❞

Not long ago I came out of a large mall and saw a man tongue-lashing his seven-year-old son. His timid wife, holding an infant, looked on—her demure face frozen in apprehension. Without warning, the father slugged his son in the face.

The boy began to cry, the mother became hysterical, and I flushed with the rage of injustice. Nothing makes me angrier than to see a father strike his child with a closed fist.

Now look at your answer to that question about what gets under your skin. I wonder if, like me, you thought of an instance when righteous anger boiled within you, or if you remembered a time when you got angry because you didn't get your own way?

Occasionally we become angry for a righteous cause, and righteous anger tends to flatter us; the other kind makes us look foolish. But the truth is that 99 percent of the time we become angry because we are *selfish* and *impatient.*

Is anger a problem for you? _____ Yes _____ No

If so, how often? _____

The Problem

When anger pierces the soul of the home, the lifeblood of the family starts to drain away.

Anger resides behind the closed doors of most of our homes. Personally, I have never lost my temper at the office—I would never want my colleagues to think I couldn't control myself. But rarely a week goes by in which the sparks of family life don't provide good tinder for a roaring fire of anger.

We put on a good show at the office and our social gatherings, but *how you are behind the closed doors of your own private castle is how you really are.* At the end of a long, hard day at the office, when you pull up the drawbridge to your castle, your family gets to live with the *real you.*

Take a look at 1 Corinthians 13—"the love chapter" of the Bible. What does it say in verse 5 about the relationship between love and anger?

_____

_____

How are you reflecting that atmosphere of love as you relate with your wife and children?

_____

Or is anger destroying the quality of your personal life? Your marriage? Your health? Do you want a remedy?

Angry words aimed at our wives and children are like arrows released from an archer's bow. Once released, traveling through the air toward their target, they cannot be withdrawn, their damage cannot be undone. Like the arrows of the archer, our angry words pierce like a jagged blade, ripping at the heart of their target. When anger pierces the soul of the home, the lifeblood of the family starts to drain away.

You may notice that your secretary seems to find you attractive. You reflect on how your wife no longer appreciates you. It never occurs to you that the problem may be you, that if the secretary knew the *real you*—the angry you that lives secretly behind the closed doors of your home—she would find you about as desirable as a flat tire.

Who has been the primary target of your anger?

___

What has usually been the result?

___

Three Angry Men

Check how you would describe your anger:

_____ *I have a low flash point. I get angry quickly and often.*
_____ *I have a long fuse, but when it finally burns down, watch out for an explosion.*
_____ *I never have angry outbursts, but rather plot revenge as I seethe with anger.*

Now let's look at some specific types.

Number One

"Freddie Flash" has a short fuse. He is an angry man looking for a place to be angry, exploding at the slightest provocation, though his anger subsides just as quickly. He thinks the harm he does is inconsequential. His anger problem is a "frequency" problem, but it hasn't dawned on him that it's not the single occurrence but the frequency that has branded him as someone to avoid.

If you are "Freddie Flash," which of your relationships are in trouble because of your anger?

___

Number Two

"Cary Control" doesn't become angry every day. But, boy-oh-boy, when Cary's long fuse finally burns down, the dynamite explodes! He loses control and strikes out with a verbal tirade that makes his wife's knees wobble and his children flinch in terror. His anger problem is an "intensity" problem.

Cary's bitterness about his station in life consumes every waking moment, and sometimes the pressures of life just overwhelm him. The intensity of his anger frightens him, but he just can't seem to keep the lid on it all the time. Sometimes he has to let off steam.

If you are "Cary Control," which of your relationships have been damaged by the explosions?

Number Three

"Gary Grudge" never has an outburst. Instead, he seethes with anger and plots revenge. His counterattacks are designed to discredit the man he hates. Gary often wakes in the middle of the night, a cold sweat reminding him of the one who has done him wrong. His anger problem is a problem of "duration."

The toxic juices of anger burn on the lining of his stomach like rust remover on an old, corroded hinge. He feeds his ulcer the right foods, but his high blood pressure and colitis require a doctor's prescription.

If you are "Gary Grudge," what has this done to your body?

"Freddie Flash," "Cary Control," and "Gary Grudge"—they show us the three main symptoms of our anger: a *low flash point* (a frequency problem), *losing control* (an intensity problem), and *holding a grudge* (a duration problem).

Now we need to look at *why* we become angry.

What Makes Us Angry That Shouldn't?

Seven reasons for anger stir up our sinful nature and hamper our efforts to live by the Spirit. In a life fully surrendered to the Lordship of Jesus Christ, these seven reasons for anger are opportunities either to become angry or to trust God with yet another area of our lives.

1. Violations of Rights

Everyone believes he has certain rights. On a physical level, we each feel we have "space" rights. Psychologists tell us we consider an eighteen-inch zone in front of our faces as private. One reaction to the invasion of this is to fester in anger.

We feel we have many other rights (for example, common courtesies). *Name some of these other rights we may feel are violated.*

(1) _____

(2) _____

(3) _____

Write Proverbs 19:11 and memorize it (this is one of my favorite verses):

_____

_____

How should we respond to such violations of our rights, according to the Bible?

_____

2. Disappointment with Station in Life

Many men become bitter when they suspect that their "oyster" doesn't have the pearl they wanted. Some of us need to accept our lot in life as from the Lord, provided we have been faithful with our abilities. For others, the answer is different. *Write Proverbs 19:3:*

_____

_____

Remember, fewer slots exist at the top than men trying to fill them. *The issue is not getting more, but learning to be content with what we have.*

3. Blocked Goals

Setting and achieving realistic goals can be a source of personal satisfaction. Everyone sets goals, though some are not consciously aware of the process. When we are blocked from achieving our goals, for good cause or not, we frequently respond with anger.

Look up Psalm 37:5–8. How should we conduct ourselves when setting goals and responding to the outcome?

_____

_____

4. Irritations

Life's little irritations often weigh more heavily on us than our true dilemmas. Think of these quotations: "She squeezes the toothpaste from the top, but I squeeze it from the bottom!" or "Billy! How many times do I have to tell you: Don't bounce that ball in the house!"

Recall two "little irritations" in the last month that have raised anger within you.

(1) _____

(2) _____

Now write Ecclesiastes 7:9 and read it twice:

_____

According to that verse, what type of person gets angry over little irritations?

_____

5. Feeling Misunderstood

Many years ago, I heard Dr. Henry Brandt say something that made an indelible impression on me: "Other people don't create your spirit; they only reveal it." *With that in mind, when your feelings get hurt, and anger begins its predictable rise within, you have to confess that the other person (complete the sentence)*

_____

_____

6. Unrealistic Expectations

I expect strangers to let me down, but when *Christian friends* do so, I can become very upset. The problem is that I often set unrealistically high expectations for my friends and family. They would have to be perfect to live up to some of my expectations.

The apostle Paul had a word for people like me. *Read Ephesians 4:31– 32, then write verse 32 here:*

_____

_____

Now ask God to enable you to do it.

7. Pathological/Psychological

Occasionally a man will have a problem with anger because of an illness or emotional disorder. A man abused as a child has a higher statistical probability of having the same anger problem as his own father.

A man whose frequent and intense eruptions of anger permanently alienate family members, or worse, cause him to strike family members during his angry outbursts, should seek professional counseling.

Now, let's review. What two characteristics (named earlier) do all seven of these reasons for anger have in common?

(1) _____

(2) _____

We are happy as clams when people agree with us, let us have our own way, and give us what we want. But they don't always see it our way, and our *selfishness* and *impatience* often lead to angry outbursts.

Is Anger Ever Justified?

What usually makes us angry but shouldn't includes such things as our mother-in-law calling as the family is sitting down to dinner, an associate who is habitually late, or the subcompact that dives into the space in front of us as we slow down for a red light.

The things that usually don't make us angry, but should, are racial prejudice, abortion, declining moral values, and similar injustices.

When was the last time you became angry enough about such injustice to try to do something about it? Yesterday? Last month? Last year? Ever? _____

When we observe a miscarriage of justice, a controlled, focused anger —*righteous indignation*—can work for a positive result. Anger over injustice, when the stench of prejudice and bigotry rises to the nostrils, consumes righteous men with a passion to correct the evil. The greatness of our country rests on the bedrock of our hatred of injustice.

Betrayal by a friend when done with malice is fair cause for anger. A secret told in confidence and then betrayed also seems cause enough for anger. Or an untrue rumor that threatens our reputations seems just cause to make our anger burn.

Yet what should our response be, even then, according to the Bible? Transcribe Proverbs 29:11:

_____

_____

The Promise for the Undeserved Curse

I would like to share a wonderful secret with you. Actually it's no secret—it's in the Bible. But few men know about this "promise for the undeserved curse."

The first time I started to spread my wings in business to fly higher, the pellets started to whistle by my ears! "He will never be able to get the financing for that office building." "He doesn't have the expertise to make it fly."

When was the last time something like that happened to you?

I learned a quick lesson: The visible target is the one that gets shot at. You can disappear in the middle of the flock, or you can set yourself apart for excellence and become a target.

As the undeserved rumors and snide remarks made their way back to me, I was devastated. I was trying to rise above the quagmire of mediocrity, and the shotguns were all aimed at me!

One morning, as I lamented to the Lord over this unfair criticism, He kindly guided me to a proverb that has changed my life. No longer do I concern myself with what others might say about me. Instead, I simply recall His promise to each of us who is wrongly maligned. *You'll find that promise in Proverbs 26:2. Write it here:*

How have you seen this proverb work in everyday life?

In some mysterious way, by the power of the Holy Spirit, an undeserved curse goes in one ear of the hearer and out the other. God miraculously helps the hearer discern what is true.

The Most Vicious of All

What's the most vicious rumor mill of all?

If you said, "The Christian grapevine," or some close variation, you are correct. Worst of all, this grapevine sometimes has the dual function of a "prayer chain."

Here's how it works: I hear that Tom has been seen at lunch with another woman. I am much too respectable to pass on such unverified gossip. However, at lunch with Ed the next day I discreetly inquire if he knows anything about Tom for which we should be in prayer. Ed looks surprised, and then he becomes suspicious. Exactly what I was hoping.

He asks if there is something going on with which he might help. I say, "Well, I probably shouldn't say anything, but I heard Tom is *having an affair* [note the change from "seen at lunch" to "having an affair"]. We'd better pray for him."

That evening Ed and his wife have dinner with the Thompsons. Ed mentions during dessert that Tom is in need of prayer.

"Oh, why is that, Ed?"

"Well, I heard that Tom is thinking about leaving Jane. He has been keeping a girlfriend in an apartment downtown. Let's ask the Lord to intervene."

Is it any wonder Tom is seething with the anger of betrayal? But Tom doesn't need to worry. The promise for the undeserved curse will soon straighten everything out.

Do men in your environment gossip? *Name two rumors of this nature in which you have been a subject:*

(1) _____

(2) _____

Now name two rumors that you helped to pass on:

(1) _____

(2) _____

What was the result in each of those instances?

_____

_____

> **Remember, fewer slots exist at the top than men trying to fill them. The issue is not getting more, but learning to be content with what we have.**

What Happens When We Become Angry?

When my son was eight years old, he began to spill his chocolate milk with a bit of regularity. One night at dinner he knocked over a full sixteen-ounce glass, which splattered everywhere. In a huff, I stormed into the bedroom like a pouty little child and refused to return to the dinner table.

In one word, what had my anger made me? _____

If you said "foolish" you agreed with Proverbs 14:17: "A quick-tempered man does foolish things."

Here is an illustration of a more complex result: Our company once had an executive who became angry at the slightest provocation. He had terrorized the secretarial staff, and the other executives hated him.

I continued to forgive and forget, until finally word came back to me about the impact of his anger. It seems he had alienated most of the leasing brokers in town, upon whom we rely heavily to help lease our buildings. The straw that broke the camel's back was when I learned he was chewing out tenants who were calling in routine maintenance requests.

One morning I asked this executive into my office and said, "Fred, I love you—I really do. But the business portion of our relationship has come to its natural conclusion. You're fired."

Anger has its own consequences, just as promised in Scripture. *Write Proverbs 19:19:*

_____

_____

Recall the last time you saw this in your own life.

_____

_____

Another result of our anger affects our health. Doctors estimate that 60 percent of all disease is caused by emotional stress. The secretions of anger from the adrenal, thyroid, and pituitary glands release their toxins into our bloodstream. *Name four or more diseases possibly caused by anger:*

(1) _____

(2) _____

(3) _____

(4) _____

When Is Anger a Sin?

The answer is that anger is *usually* a sin; or at least, it usually works its way into sin. When we're angry, we spark the anger of others. Before we know what's happened, our remark about the other fellow's ugly tie has escalated to questions about our mother's heritage! But if—as urged in James 1:19–20 quoted at the beginning of this chapter—we are patient and slow to speak, there is peace.

The very best guideline for anger is found in Ephesians 4:26–27. *Look it up and write those verses here:*

_____

_____

The implication of that passage is that it is possible to be angry without sinning. How?

_____

_____

What do you believe Paul meant with his reference to the sun's going down?

_____

_____

Clearly, this was an important point to Paul. He actually offered three bits of wisdom in the passage. First, control yourself and don't sin in your anger. Second, never go to bed angry. Get down on your knees, forgive, and ask forgiveness. Third, when you are angry, your self-control is at risk. You can explode into sin. The devil may see a crack in the door and seize a foothold.

The practical center to the admonition, then, is to never let the sun go down while you remain angry. That's when anger will become sin.

*L*ooking Closer in the Mirror:

Scripture makes it clear that as Christians, we are to imitate God's character. Is God an angry God? Read Psalm 103:8; 30:5; 78:38–39; Jonah 4:2; 2 Peter 3:9. Based on what these verses tell us about God, what should our attitude be?

_____

_____

_____

Following are four guidelines for responding to the temptation to sin in your anger. After each write a two- or three-word command to yourself that captures the essence of the verse. For example, the first one might be: "Keep Control."

• "A fool gives full vent to his anger, but a wise man keeps himself under control" (Proverbs 29:11).

_____

• "A man's wisdom gives him patience; it is to his glory to overlook an offense" (Proverbs 19:11).

_____

- *"Do not make friends with a hot-tempered man, do not associate with one easily angered, or you may learn his ways and get yourself ensnared"* (Proverbs 22:24–25).

- *"A gentle answer turns away wrath, but a harsh word stirs up anger"* (Proverbs 15:1).

According to Galatians 5:16–17, how would you describe the two forces at work within you? How can a man live by the Spirit?

_____

_____

_____

Now, if necessary, look at yourself in the mirror as you tackle the next three parts:

(1) Are you an angry man? If so, and you want to overcome your anger, isolate the reasons for your anger:

_____

_____

_____

(2) Ask God to reveal the depth of your sin in the area of anger and write it down:

_____

_____

_____

(3) Ask God to show you the people you have hurt through your anger, and to show you how and when you need to seek forgiveness. Write down what He brings to your mind.

_____

_____

_____

This is an important step in overcoming the temptation to anger and its sins. Go to those you have hurt with your anger and ask for their forgiveness. If you have wounded them deeply, they may not respond right away. That's all right. As you change, they will respond to the new you. What could be more exciting than the prospect of restoring your home from a torture chamber to a castle?

MIRROR WORK

*I*t's important that you ask God to forgive you for your sins of anger and to change you into an unselfish, patient man. Write out your prayer:

_____

_____

_____

_____

In the next chapter . . .

"I am the master of my fate; I am the captain of my soul." Most of us are familiar with the quote. But is it true? No. We're about to embark on a journey to discover the difference between taking responsibility for our lives and trying to live independently of God.

19 The Desire to Be Independent

I am the master of my fate; I am the captain of my soul.

WILLIAM ERNEST HENLEY

I know, O Lord, that a man's life is not his own; it is not for man to direct his steps.

JEREMIAH 10:23

> **"The turning point of our lives is when we stop seeking the God we want and start seeking the God who is."**

As our children grow to their teens, they make their "Declaration of Independence" as an act of rebellion against our authority as parents. These can be long days. I wonder if that's why Jesus emphasized, "Let the *little* children come to me," because He knew their desire to be independent came with an innocent trust rather than rebellion.

As adults we spread our wings and make our own sort of "Declaration of Independence." But in a real sense, we are still children of our Father in heaven, and we, like our own children, can choose to trust Him or live in rebellion against Him.

The Problem

We are raised to be independent. From their earliest homilies, Mom and Dad taught us to be independent and to make our own place.

How early do our children make the first moves in their "Declaration of Independence" from us, their parents?

_____

_____

What was your first such move that you recall?

_____

Most men are taught to pull themselves up by their bootstraps. "Life is what you make of it!" we're told. We learn early the thoughts expressed by William Henley at the beginning of this chapter—that we can author our own destinies.

Men want to control their own lives. Even if we were not taught to seek independence, our own human nature would pull us in that direction. We want freedom. We want the power to shape the events of our lives. And in following our desire, we often break ranks with God and go our own independent ways.

There is a difference between taking "responsibility" for our lives and trying to live "independently" from God. Describe that difference:

_____

_____

Yes, we are to take responsibility for our lives—no one will go to work in our place, and no one will pay our bills. The key, then, is this: Responsibility recognizes *our part* and *God's part*. Our part is to trust God and faithfully fulfill our duties. God's part is to provide for our well-being.

Independence rebels against God's influence. The independent man thinks, "*I* will do *what* I want to do, *when* I want to do it, *wherever* I want to do it, with *whomever* I want to do it. *I* will be in control. *I* want to satisfy my ambitions. *I* won't depend on anyone. *People let me down. God will let me down. I can make it on my own.*

"If I can be independent then I will not need to rely upon anyone else. I will not have to trust anyone else, and I will be able to avoid the pain of being disappointed and disillusioned.

"If I can be independent then I can be in control of my own life. I will have the power, whether through money or influence, to get my own way; I will have the freedom to come and go as I please."

Describe the similarity between this attitude and the one that drew Adam and Eve to yield to temptation in the Garden of Eden.

_____

_____

> *Men want to control their own lives. . . . And in following our desire, we often break ranks with God and go our own independent ways.*

Our desire to be independent, of course, usually disguises itself. It's subtle, not open rebellion. Nonetheless, we really don't seek God's counsel, and we often shun His advice. We simply do our own thing.

Name the last two times you did your own thing, knowing deep inside you were acting independently:

(1) _____

(2) _____

Remember, the opposite of desiring independence from God is to trust Him. The man who does not trust God trusts in himself and the philosophies of this world. This is the epitome of independence.

The Human Potential Movement

I was very active in the human potential movement in the early 1970s, both before and after I became a Christian. Every book expounding the merits of willing-your-way-to-success was in my library. "What the mind can conceive and believe it can achieve," went the reasoning.

I believe in many ways my life is a product of the human potential movement. It would have been difficult, indeed, to be in the marketplace during the self-centered seventies and the alienated eighties and not have been at least partly influenced to believe "you can have it all." We Christians, although we have the Holy Spirit residing within us, don't have any special inoculation against the desire to be independent.

After all, it's true. By the strength of our hands, we *can* achieve many worldly successes. The opposite of desiring to be independent from God is to trust Him. The man who does not trust God trusts in himself and the philosophies of this world, which is the epitome of independence. The missing word is *trust. God doesn't want us to trust in man. He wants us to trust Him.*

Can you recall any Madison Avenue slogan or exhortation that promoted the human potential movement?

Describe any evidence you've seen that the human potential movement infiltrated the Christian church.

Trust in Man and Trust in God Contrasted

Jeremiah, the weeping prophet, records a vivid contrast between the fate of the one who trusts in man (the independent man) and the man who trusts in the Lord (the dependent man).

First, write Jeremiah 17:5–6 and reread it carefully:

The man God speaks of in this passage is not necessarily some wicked sort of fellow. He might even be a valiant man—a winner by all external appearances. But inside he has turned away from the Lord.

What is the fate of the self-reliant man?

> We all know men who live in opulence, yet the creases in their faces betray that they live in a parched land.

Like a bush bearing no seed, he tumbles along producing no fruit, headed nowhere. The independent man can never satisfy his thirst for significance and purpose.

Could his "wasteland" be a state of mind just as easily as a place? Tell how:

_____

_____

Have you experienced something like that? Explain and give specific examples.

_____

_____

We all know men who live in opulence, yet the creases in their faces betray that they live in a parched land.

President Lincoln once turned down a job applicant, citing as his reason, "I don't like his face." One of his Cabinet members expressed surprise and let the president know he didn't think that was a sound reason. But Lincoln wouldn't bend, saying, "Every man over forty is responsible for his face."

A man's face betrays whether he has lived a life of independence or dependence. What does the face you see in the mirror tell you?

_____

Now let's look at the man who stands on the other side of this ledger. Write Jeremiah 17:7–8 and reread it carefully:

_____

_____

_____

If the independent man will be miserable, we are pleased to learn that the dependent man will be blessed. But look closely at the last two sentences. He is promised no cakewalk. The Christian is not exempt from hard times. He is, however, promised freedom from two things. *Write them down:*

(1) _____

(2) _____

God causes rain to fall on the wicked and the good. So hard times come to all men—it's just part of life. Everyone suffers.

The difference between the man who trusts in God and the man who trusts in himself is not in the *circumstances* but in his *response*. The man who trusts God has a positive attitude. He knows hard times will come, but he doesn't fear them; he doesn't worry when life's inevitable trials strike. He believes God will take care of him, and it shows on his face.

Again, how do you measure up when hard times strike? How does it show on your face?

Getting to the "Root" of the Matter

The wind howled, and the rain blew sideways. New Orleans had not seen such a storm in fifty years. Mike huddled his family under the staircase, and they listened intently to a portable radio, waiting for some word that the storm was letting up.

Mike had planted two trees in his yard many years ago. One was an oak, and the other was what they call a "hackberry" tree. The two grew tall, and their branches spread shade over half the backyard.

The next morning, when the storm had passed, Mike surveyed the damage. To his surprise, the giant hackberry tree had been torn up and lay horizontally across his neighbor's fence.

"There are no roots!" he exclaimed. His hackberry tree didn't have any deep roots to provide support. The oak stood alone, a solemn reminder that when the storms of life sweep over us, we need deep roots.

The independent man has the shallow roots of the hackberry tree—a "bush in the wastelands." The dependent man has deep roots like the oak.

Why does the dependent man have deep roots that are so well nourished? If you need help answering that question, look back at Jeremiah 17:7–8.

The Illusion of Power

If we were going to be independent we would need power. *Name three kinds of power to which most men gravitate:*

(1) _____

(2) _____

(3) _____

There is no doubt that such power, or the position that such power gives, can cause a man to *think* he's qualified to be independent from others.

But what is *genuine* power? The kind of power we usually think of is ultimately impotent. Genuine power is the exclusive province of God and those to whom He imparts it. *Without the power of Christ no world would exist. Why? The answer is found in Colossians 1:16–17; write those verses and read them carefully:*

_____

_____

_____

That passage says a lot, of course, but *write the one truth from it, aside from creation, that proves my statement above that "without the power of Christ no world would exist":*

_____

In comparison, the Bible is explicit in telling the things men do not have the power to do. *Write those things as found in the following verses:*

Matthew 5:36 _____

_____

Matthew 6:27 _____

_____

James 4:14 _____

_____

Acts 27:20 _____

_____

So where is our power? We have no genuine power except as Christ grants it to us. The games we play to become independent produce dwarf-scale power. The power we use on each other makes us like a bunch of little blind ants.

Christ alone can heal the sick. He alone can satisfy our need to be significant, and grant an eternal extension to our eighty-year-long "inch" of life on earth.

The Turning Point

Now we come to one of the most important statements I've ever written. *I want you to memorize it and then write it from memory: There is a God we want and there is a God who is. Many times they are not the same God. The turning point of our lives is when we stop seeking the God we want and start seeking the God who is.*

_____

_____

_____

Before we take this turning step, we seek our independent way and try to remake God the way we want Him. In history that's called idol worship.

We Americans, and indeed all Westerners, may think we are more immune to the sin of idolatry than are our counterparts in other parts of the world. After all, we live in nations built on Christian principles. But the bottom line is that we tend to individualize God for ourselves by devising our own compact, concise definition of who God is.

John White spoke of it this way:

> During the past half century He has in fact been *trivialized,* packaged for entertainment, presented as a sort of psychological panacea, a heavenly glue to keep happy families together, a celestial slot machine to respond to our whim, a formula for success, a fund raiser for pseudoreligious enterprises, a slick phrase for bumper stickers, and a sort of holy pie and ice cream.[1]

In some ways, God is like the President of the United States. *How well do you know our current president?*

_____

We hear information about our president; we listen to his news conferences and read about his ideas. Some have toured the White House, and a few of us have even shaken his hand. But how well do we really know him? Most of us don't know him at all.

It's the same with God. We have only a small glimpse of Him so far. But we could know more about Him if we made the commitment. We don't know Him as He is because we have never really gotten to know Him as He is.

The ultimate escape from the treachery of trying to lead an independent life is to start seeking the God who is.

⌐ *Looking Closer in the Mirror:*

Look up Proverbs 3:5–6 and write it here:

_____

_____

_____

The key, of course, is that you must trust in the right God. Read Deuteronomy 5:7. Now consider that today we have many substitute gods (or idols). Name five:

(1) _____

(2) _____

(3) _____

(4) _____

(5) _____

Have any of these been your substitute gods? Give specific examples.

_____

_____

Such pursuits, even when they're important, have a dreadful danger: They reduce our time with the one true God.

Unfortunately, instead of changing their focus, many men choose to remake God the way they want Him to be. According to this chapter, what can be the turning point of a man's life?

_____

_____

List three steps you can take to start seeking the God who is:

(1) _____

(2) _____

(3) _____

When we know the God who is, He will help us decipher His mysteries and show us how to attain the pinnacle of trusting completely in Him.

■ *THE PRIMARY STEP*

Are you ready to take the primary step to stop seeking the God you want and start seeking the God who is?

You know He requires us to forsake our desire to be independent. Earlier in this workbook you had an opportunity to receive Christ into your life. Perhaps you weren't quite ready, but you have been thinking things over. Or perhaps you *are* a Christian, but you realize you've been playing games with God. You don't know Him as He really is. You're a cultural Christian.

Maybe you've reached a turning point in your life. If you are ready to make the commitment to follow Christ and seek the God who is, whether for the first time or as a deeper commitment, then the following prayer is one way you can express your desire to Him. We receive Christ by faith as an act of the will, through a decision, not by a prayer. Yet prayer is an excellent way to express the desire and attitude of your heart and mind.

Here is a suggested prayer. Read it aloud, prayerfully. If it expresses the desire of your heart and mind, I suggest you then kneel and perhaps say it silently, between you and Christ, phrase by phrase:

> Lord Jesus, I confess that I have sinned against You by seeking my own independent way, rebelling against You and trusting in myself. I have not known You as You really are but, instead, have sought the God I wanted. I am now beginning to realize the difference. Forgive me, Lord. I open the door to my life and receive You as my Savior and Lord. Thank You for dying on the cross for my sins. Take control of my life and make me into the man You want me to be. Amen.

If you sincerely prayed, welcome to the family!

Now, review the three steps you wrote earlier as you noted what you needed to do to seek the God who is. And share what you have done with someone close to you. Go to a church on Sunday where Christ is honored and the Bible is held in high regard.

Genuine power is the exclusive province of God and those to whom He imparts it.

MIRROR WORK

Lord Jesus, teach me what I need to do to discover the freedom of dependence on You. Give me the courage to rest in Your care—to quit striving to make my own way and be my own man. Help me to be Your man. Amen.

In the next chapter . . .

No one wants to suffer, but the simple fact is that all of us eventually will suffer in some way. Some of you are saying, "Eventually! Man, I'm already there!" Certainly, God wants to bless us. But sometimes suffering is part of His plan. Keep reading to discover why that is true, and how we should deal with the circumstances that cause us pain.

20 Avoiding Suffering

God prepares great men for great tasks by great trials.

J. K. GRESSETT

We sent Timothy . . . to strengthen and encourage you in your faith, so that no one would be unsettled by these trials. You know quite well that we were destined for them.

1 THESSALONIANS 3:2–3

"When we suffer we can be confident Jesus knows exactly what we are going through."

John fought off the wolves for months and months, but every day was just another day in the jaws of financial turmoil. The pressure turned his love for God and family into a stale loaf of bread. He would have done anything to avoid more suffering.

Weary, John went home early one afternoon, as he was doing more often lately. Driving down the highway, his heart quickened when a gigantic bolt of lightning flashed on the horizon. If the road had continued straight, the scorching lightning rod would have burned a hole right through the asphalt pavement.

John couldn't help wishing, if only for a moment, that he was under that lightning bolt. How wonderful to go out in a literal blaze of glory! That would solve all of his problems. He would be with the Lord.

He would never seriously consider suicide, but, if natural causes could take him away—well, John would be grateful to escape his suffering.

What kind of suffering has caused you to question God's purposes for you?

_____

_____

With those thoughts, what is your opinion of the quotation by J. K. Gressett that opens this chapter?

_____

_____

The Problem

We have to face it—life is a struggle. Most men want to be happy, to avoid pain and suffering, and to escape from the bleak life of woe that so many men seem to lead. We want to live the good life, and why not? What fool would seek out a life of suffering?

Certainly it's true that God *does* want to bless our lives with abundance. Yet the Bible also teaches that suffering is part of God's order. We shouldn't go looking for it, but neither should we be surprised when it finds us. *Everyone will suffer. The only decision is whether you are going to suffer with Christ or without Him.*

You see, a unique fellowship with Christ comes into our lives when we suffer, as shown in 1 Peter 4:12–13, "Dear friends, do not be surprised at the painful trial you are suffering, as though something strange were happening to you. But rejoice that you participate in the sufferings of Christ, so that you may be overjoyed when his glory is revealed."

What do you believe it means to "participate in the sufferings of Christ"?

_____

_____

Has your suffering been a participation in the sufferings of Christ, or simply suffering? Explain.

_____

_____

> **Sometimes we are just minding our own business, and then all of the sudden, life happens.**

Martin Luther endorsed Peter's point this way: "No man ought to lay a cross upon himself, or to adopt tribulation . . . but if a cross or tribulation come upon him, then let him suffer it patiently, and know that it is good and profitable for him."

Despite these assurances, how have you answered these questions when suffering has come to you:

Does God care about me? _____

Does He really know my agony? _____

Does He want to help me? _____

Is He able to help me? _____

What is His will for me? Is it to help me or let me fall? _____

The plain truth is that when life goes our way we don't carefully examine our ways. God can't receive the glory for blessing us, because we often take the credit. If nothing else, suffering *does* get our attention. *But why, truly, do men suffer? Check the answer you think best answers that question.*

_____ *God causes it.*
_____ *God allows it to happen.*
_____ *It happens independently of God.*
_____ *Other (Please explain).* _____

Seven Reasons Why Men Suffer

Picture a loving father comforting his teary-eyed son. We don't know why the boy is crying, but we notice how concerned the father is. The son tells his dad exactly how he feels, though we can't make out the words. Finally, the father embraces his son, and the comfort and consolation of the father's love begins to flow into his boy.

In the same way, we come into the presence of our heavenly Father when we suffer, and He dries our tears. *To find out what I mean, look up 1 Peter 5:6–7 and record it in the space provided:*

_____

_____

Have you ever humbled yourself before God? Explain.

_____

_____

Explain this verse's promise regarding that kind of humbling. What will be the result? Then think: Have you seen that promise work in your own life? Describe it.

_____

_____

_____

Now let's go back to the father-son scene, and look at seven reasons that might explain not only this situation, but our own as well. *Check those you know have caused you suffering:*

_____ *An innocent mistake.*
_____ *An error in judgment.*
_____ *An integrity problem.*
_____ *The environment changes.*
_____ *Evil happens.*

_____ *God disciplines.*
_____ *God tests.*

Now let's explore those reasons. Assume our little boy—let's call him Billy—has been playing baseball in the street with his friends.

First Reason: An Innocent Mistake

Perhaps through carelessness, the baseball rolled down the storm sewer —gone forever. It wasn't anyone's fault—but he still suffered; and he ran home, crying over his disappointment.

Similarly, a man named Jack invested in a speculative oil venture that checked out great, but he lost all his money and had to pay taxes on phantom income. Like Billy, he had made an innocent mistake.

Why is it so difficult to handle innocent mistakes?

Athough we all make innocent mistakes, we still have to suffer the consequences, and they can be drastic.

Second Reason: An Error in Judgment

Another possibility: Suppose young Billy hit the baseball through the neighbor's window! That's a different mistake.

Billy knew he shouldn't play so close to Mrs. Winters's window. But still, he's done nothing dishonest. He simply made an error in judgment. Not knowing what punishment might result, he fearfully told his father. Dad decided Billy would have to tell Mrs. Winters what happened and then pay for the window from his allowance. Intentional or not, the error carried consequences.

Similarly, Ned cosigned his brother-in-law's bank note for a car loan. Six months later the bank was leaning on Ned for the payments. Cosigning a loan in this type of situation is an error in judgment, according to the Bible. That doesn't mean Ned violated a law, but rather a principle, supported by a Federal Trade Commission study that found 50 percent of people who cosigned bank loans ended up repaying the debt themselves.[1]

An error in judgment differs from an innocent mistake in this: Some guideline exists to prevent an error in judgment, while no guideline exists to prevent an innocent mistake.

Innocent or not, you still suffer. And we all use poor judgment from time to time. *How have you personally experienced this? Explain.*

If you are getting the idea that suffering is not easily avoided, you have the right idea.

Third Reason: An Integrity Problem

Little Billy may be crying because he stole the baseball bat the kids played with from the boy down the street and was caught. He is crying because he received a sound spanking.

At the adult level, suppose a salesman lied about the features of his product. His prospect bought on that basis, and when he realized the salesman had lied, he phoned the man's boss, and the deceptive salesman was fired.

Sometimes men do wrong with malice—they sin—and they must bear the moral and other consequences of their decisions. In addition to principles to live by, the Bible also contains the parameters of sin, which are commands to be obeyed. And, further, we must submit to civil laws.

Can you recall suffering yourself because of an integrity problem? Explain.

Fourth Reason: The Environment Changes

Maybe Billy was enjoying a great game of baseball in the street, only to have a policeman run him and his friends off. He told them about a recently passed municipal ordinance that prohibits playing in the street. Billy is upset over the change.

Sometimes we are just minding our own business, and then all of the sudden, *life happens.* Congress passes a tax reform package that threatens to put us out of business, or the stock market crashes and we face a margin we can't pay. Or maybe a disabling traffic accident strikes our daughter or son. When the environment changes beyond our control, we may suffer dire consequences, though we may have done nothing wrong.

Does this sound familiar? Give a specific situation where you have seen this happen.

Fifth Reason: Evil Happens

Billy may have been having a perfectly enjoyable game of baseball when, out of nowhere, the bully from down the street sneaked up and punched him.

Similarly, Ron worked for months on the sale of an insurance policy to an executive who had purchased several other policies from him over the years. The day before he was to close the sale, an unscrupulous agent convinced the executive to cancel all his old policies and replace them with far inferior ones.

Did Ron or Billy do wrong? No. Regardless of how much we wish it weren't so, evil exists in this world. Unfair things happen. And we can suffer.

Tell the most recent case of your suffering from evil in the world.

_____

_____

_____

Sixth Reason: God Disciplines

Billy's father may have sent Billy to his room as punishment for knocking the ball through the neighbor's window. Billy suffered because his father disciplined him.

Similarly, Ted, after serving as an elder for eight years, became proud. If he said it, that settled it! Eventually God led the other elders to quietly ask Ted to step down.

Those in authority may not catch a man doing wrong. But even though no one else is aware of a man's sin, God knows. And when God knows, He may discipline. Regardless of the reason for our suffering, God uses such situations to mold our character. *Look up Hebrews 12:7–8 and write it here:*

_____

_____

Recall the last time you knew you were being disciplined by God for your own good.

_____

_____

Seventh Reason: God Tests

Billy's father may have told him he couldn't play baseball until he helped his mother wash the dishes. Interested in his character and conduct, he wanted to know how much Billy was willing to contribute to the family.

You will recall that God tested Abraham to raise his blade and slay his son Isaac. As he prepared to drive the knife through the boy's heart, God called out to him, "'Abraham! Abraham!'

" 'Here I am,' he replied.

" 'Do not lay a hand on the boy,' he said. 'Do not do anything to him. Now I know that you fear God, because you have not withheld from me your son, your only son' " (Genesis 22:11–12).

God tests us to see if our character is pure. *Write Proverbs 17:3:*

_____

_____

Are you ready for God to test and strengthen your heart and character, bearing in mind that He loves you enough to do that?

_____

If you are getting the idea that suffering is not easily avoided, you have the right idea.

- We can suffer because it's our own fault or because it's someone else's.
- We can suffer by innocent mistake or as a consequence of sin.
- God may test us or discipline us.
- Sometimes the environment changes, and sometimes evil overtakes us.

Whatever the reason for our suffering, what must our response be? (See 1 Peter 5:6–7, which you recorded earlier.)

_____

What will the outcome be?

_____

Resisting Suffering

Before we humble ourselves, we often go through stages of resistance or rebellion. If we resist suffering, we also block our ability to learn from the pain.

There are five ways we try to avoid suffering:

1. We plead. When we suffer, one of our first reactions is to plead with God's sense of fairness. Is God treating us fairly compared with what we deserve?

Describe the last time you did this and why.

_____

_____

Now look up Psalm 34:19. In light of that verse, explain God's absolute fairness.

_____

_____

2. We compare. We compare ourselves with others, pointing out that we are better men and, therefore, deserving of mercy. Or we compare ourselves to other men and wish we were them instead of ourselves.

To whom did you compare yourself when you were suffering, and how do you feel about it now?

_____

_____

Now look up Psalm 49:16–17. What does it say regarding the situation you just described?

_____

_____

3. We pout. We become discouraged over our circumstances and have a pity party. We pout about our suffering and feel sorry for ourselves. We lament as the psalmist, "This is what the wicked are like—always carefree, they increase in wealth./Surely in vain have I kept my heart pure; in vain have I washed my hands in innocence./All day long I have been plagued; I have been punished every morning" (Psalm 73:12–14).

Name the things you have pouted about recently.

_____

_____

4. We shout. We become angry and shake our fists and raise our voices at God because of the pain of our suffering. Will He give us no relief? But this is futile, as explained in James 1:20. *Write that verse here. How is your anger doing lately?*

5. We doubt. After our suffering settles in on us and we realize how devastating our anguish can be, we doubt that God is real and become afraid. But as we read the Scriptures, we find so much of His faithful mercy and compassion for us that we cannot help being encouraged. *Write Isaiah 41:10 here, memorize it, and speak it aloud when doubt and discouragement hit you:*

List the ways you have doubted, and then release them aloud to the Lord:

After the Pleading, Comparing, Pouting, Shouting, and Doubting

The true solution to our suffering is not in getting it over with, but in learning to enjoy the fellowship of sharing Christ's suffering, to be anxious for nothing, to endure patiently, and to walk in the power of the Holy Spirit. *Recall the times you have experienced this victory:*

Sometimes God will deliver us according to our desires, but more often He has bigger plans for us, and He doesn't deliver us quickly. Our part in His plan is to cast all our anxiety on Him. *Write Psalm 40:11–13 here to understand how David did this so gracefully:*

Sympathy for Our Suffering

When we suffer we can be confident Jesus knows exactly what we are going through. *On the basis of Hebrew 4:15–16, write in your words why this is true:*

_____

_____

_____

Because Christ suffered as we do, we can look to Him as our model for our own attitude. The apostle Paul did. *With that in mind, write in today's terms what Paul meant when he said in Philippians 3:10, "I want to know Christ and the power of His resurrection and the fellowship of sharing in His sufferings":*

_____

_____

The Privilege of Suffering

We find a very powerful dialogue between God and the apostle Paul in 2 Corinthians 12:9–10. Paul was discussing his own "thorn in the flesh," perhaps an affliction of the eyes. Three times he "pleaded" that it be taken away, but God finally spoke a terribly significant refusal and explanation. *Memorize this first sentence of 2 Corinthians 12:9–10: "My grace is sufficient for you, for my power is made perfect in weakness."*

Now write the remainder of the passage to see Paul's response:

_____

_____

_____

Remarkably, Paul delighted in suffering. Remember, though, it was not suffering just for the sake of suffering; it was suffering for the joy of sharing fellowship with Christ.

Suffering for doing good is part of the Christian experience. That is why Paul exhorts us, "For it has been granted to you on behalf of Christ not only to believe on him, but also to suffer for him" (Philippians 1:29).

Frankly, until we have suffered, not in some superficial way, such as not getting a new car we wanted, but as a Christian, filled with anguish over whether God cares or not, we will not fully understand the personal ministry of the Holy Spirit. You may know in part, but until you come to the point where you feel you will die unless Jesus shows you some compassion, only then will you trust Him completely.

Once you pass through this threshold of His grace, you will have incredible power to overcome anxiety. The tempter cannot terrorize you with any uncertainty that you have not already known; you will have seen the hands of God reach down, responding to your faith.

If we resist suffering, we also block our ability to learn from the pain.

▱ *L*ooking Closer in the Mirror:

■ *THE RESTORATION OF GOD'S PEOPLE*

Have you made it a life goal to avoid suffering? Explain your answer.

_____

_____

Avoiding suffering is impossible. Even the man who is so security-conscious that he never sticks his neck out will sooner or later find the sorrow of suffering. Our posture is to look favorably on our suffering.
Write James 1:2–4 and read it a couple of times:

_____

_____

Do you believe James exaggerated when he said to "consider it pure joy"? How does one do this?

_____

_____

No matter how rough life gets, remember, it isn't over till it's over. Never quit. God will *always* restore His children. That's why Job was able to maintain his integrity before God when he suffered, because he trusted God completely; he knew God was in control.
Write 1 Peter 5:10. Why not memorize it so you will be prepared to console yourself or a Christian friend when suffering comes, for it is the finest of promises?

_____

_____

Based on that verse, what is our promise as Christians when we suffer?

_____

_____

Do you truly believe God will always restore the suffering Christian? How does He do it?

_____

_____

■ READY TO DIE

At the beginning of this chapter, John thought about dying as the ultimate escape from his suffering. Sometimes we ache so much that dying sounds good. But death is no answer.

Paul lived and suffered for Christ as perhaps no other man ever has. He didn't seek death as an escape, yet he knew death would be sweet for him. He would be united with Jesus. *Look up his own statement regarding this in Acts 21:13, and record it:*

_____

_____

Death will be sweet for us too. The Christian is ready to die for Christ. But, that being said, it is more important that we enter the pain of our suffering and learn to live for Him.

MIRROR WORK

*L*ord Jesus, help me learn to live for You, regardless of my circumstances. Help me to live in such a way that I won't require Your discipline, but outside of that, please enable me to accept suffering and join You in the fellowship that it brings. Amen.

In the next chapter . . .

Dishonesty is so prevalent in our culture that many of us have accepted it as the norm. So many people lie and cheat, that even some Christians have shrugged and said, "If you can't beat them, join them." We've succumbed to worldly standards of integrity. But God calls us to a higher standard. Our next section will help us solve our integrity problems.

PART SIX

Solving

Our

Integrity

Problems

Integrity: What's the Price?

21

If you tell the truth, you don't have to remember anything.

MARK TWAIN

A malicious man disguises himself with his lips, but in
his heart he harbors deceit.

PROVERBS 26:24

Hal was a small building contractor known for the quality of his work. A sizable company awarded him a job larger than any he had built before.

Thousands of minute details required exacting coordination. As the deadline for the grand opening neared, he drove his men to the brink of mutiny. He swore he would be done on time, and he was.

But the top man at the company—the man who hired him—realized that Hal didn't have the clout of a large outfit. So, he withheld payment. He said the quality of Hal's work wasn't right, so he deserved a discount. He refused to pay.

Hal desperately needed the final payment to meet his payroll. He finally gave in and lowered his bill, and in the process, he gave up his profit on the job.

How would you react if you were in Hal's place?

❝Unless we hold on to absolute integrity . . . we grieve God and cut ourselves off from the blessing we want, and the blessing God wants to give us.❞

Now, suppose Hal knows that the head of the company that "did him in" is a Christian. What recourse does He have?

The Problem

Integrity is hard to come by these days. Perhaps that is partly because it is so hard to recognize the lack of integrity in our own lives.

Have you ever gone to the refrigerator looking for a particular thing, say peanut butter, only to be frustrated that it was nowhere to be found? You yell to your wife, "Where's the peanut butter?" She walks into the kitchen, reaches onto the second shelf, and hands you the jar with a "you lose" grin on her face.

Sometimes things are so obvious that we miss them. Dishonesty is like that. It's so obvious that we often don't notice how completely it tints every aspect of life. If we take off our rose-colored glasses, however, we see a world painted in a whole different hue—the washed-out shades of dishonesty.

Frankly, dishonesty is so prevalent that we have accepted it as the norm. Just consider the regularity with which dishonesty is featured in the news. *List several examples of dishonesty that have hit the headlines in recent months.*

_____

_____

Stories that make the news usually feature gross dishonesty. In the big picture, though, true integrity is often a question of honesty in the little things.

A man sitting next to me on a plane ordered a drink—a bourbon and Coke. The busy flight attendant said she would come back for the money, which he left lying on his tray. Eventually it became obvious that the flight attendant had forgotten. After she had made a half-dozen trips past us, my aisle-mate reached over, picked up his money, and slipped it back into his coat pocket.

Integrity. What's the price? He sold his for a two dollar drink.

The simple fact is that integrity isn't valued very highly these days. Most men "cut corners" on little things. They run yellow lights, speed, promise four weeks delivery when they know it will take six. *Do you agree or disagree with that statement? Explain your answer and give examples, both personal and observed.*

_____

_____

_____

Is absolute integrity a reasonable goal in today's society? Why or why not?

_____

_____

What about Christian men? As heinous as are the crimes of the headlines, the dishonesty that tints the daily life of a Christian man grieves God just as much, perhaps more.

Most men are trapped in the lie of maintaining a "Christian image" for honesty, when in reality they wink at integrity every day. How have you found yourself caught in that trap?

_____

_____

What is the result?

_____

_____

Unless we hold on to absolute integrity in every situation, no matter how big or small, we grieve God and cut ourselves off from the blessing we want, and the blessing God wants to give us.

The Common Thread

We see the value of integrity in the great heroes of the Bible. Certainly, they came from diverse backgrounds. Some were kings. Others, like Gideon, came from the worst families. Samson was a powerful figure, while timid Moses nearly feared his own shadow. Jonah doubted, yet David had unswerving faith.

What, then, was the common characteristic that these men possessed besides their faith in God? What attracted God to these men of such diversity?

The answer will be painful to some of our ears, because the bottom line is that *God knew He could trust these men when they were all alone.*

God is looking for a few good men. He always has been. You don't have to be the smartest, best-looking, most articulate man to get the job on God's team—you just have to be faithful.

If we take off our rose-colored glasses, however, we see a world painted in a whole different hue—the washed-out shades of dishonesty.

The Lower End of the Scale

If we limit our faithfulness to major matters, we miss the point that to be trusted with much, we must first prove trustworthy with little. In God's eyes, we are just as guilty when we stuff our suitcases with motel towels as we would be if we robbed a bank. The consequences may be different, but the verdict is still "guilty as charged."

Let me illustrate. One evening I stopped by the home of a business colleague to drop off some papers. Next to his phone was a note pad with the company logo. The company manual stated that no office supplies were to be consumed for personal use.

From that day forward, my confidence in him was never quite the same. That was an expensive pad of paper—it cost him my opinion of his integrity.

In many ways, this same scenario plays out in our spiritual lives as well. Look up Luke 16:10 and write it here.

_____

_____

The principle of that verse is, "As it goes with the little things, so it will go with the big things." Do you agree with this principle? Or do you think it's possible to maintain two sets of standards—one for the "little" and one for the "much"? Why do you believe that?

_____

_____

Now continue reading in that passage, looking at Luke 16:11–12. Jesus asks two rhetorical questions in these verses. How would you answer them? Why?

_____

_____

_____

In light of this passage, what kind of witness have you been giving in respect to your honesty and integrity?

(1) At home _____

_____

(2) Where you shop _____

_____

(3) Where you work _____

_____

Most men are so mired in the quicksand of dishonesty that an average, hard-working, honest man looks very good to God. God will use you if He knows He can trust you. Can He? Explain your answer.

_____

_____

A Matter of Disobedience

All of the Ten Commandments require obedience. At its very essence, disobedience is dishonesty. For those dedicated to Christ, we take a pledge to be like Him. So anytime we break one Commandment, it is an act of dishonesty.

Among those ten rules, three apply to the issue of integrity: lying, cheating, and stealing. *What are some contemporary ways in which men break these commandments? List some ways we gloss over our sins of lying, cheating, and stealing in "the little things."*

_____

_____

_____

The Little White Lie

Integrity generates trust. When we don't keep our commitments, trust is broken, and our integrity falls into question.

John told Bill he would be at the open house for Bill's new offices. But John didn't show up. Later Bill learned that, before saying yes to the open house invitation, John had scheduled an appointment at the same time, an appointment he kept.

"Why didn't he just tell me he had already scheduled something else?" Bill asked when he found out.

What do you think happened to their relationship?

Relationships are built on trust. That fragile thread is easily broken. The white lie fractures many relationships.

"I'm glad you called. I was just getting ready to call you."

"Let's have lunch sometime."

"I'll be praying for you."

Have you been hurt by a white lie similar to these? Describe how it affected you.

Have you been guilty of white lies such as these? Describe how they affected your relationships.

John Ruskin reminds us that we lie in so many ways. "The essence of lying," he says, *"is in deception, not in words." How do people lie without saying anything?*

Ruskin added:

A lie may be told by silence, by equivocation, by the accent on a syllable, by a glance of the eye attaching a peculiar significance to a sentence. All these kinds of lies are worse and baser by many degrees than a lie plainly worded. No form of blinded conscience is so far sunk as that which comforts itself for having deceived because the deception was by gesture or silence instead of utterance.[1]

In light of that, are we any less guilty for having lied silently? Explain your answer.

The Narrow Road

As in so many aspects of the spiritual pilgrimage, the right way is often the path least traveled. The street named "Honest" is not particularly crowded. It's a little like the way that leads to eternal life. *Look up Jesus' words regarding that particular road. You'll find them in Matthew 7:13–14. Write those verses here.*

What makes it so difficult to travel that road with your wife or children?

What makes it so difficult to travel the narrow road of honesty when you are in business or at work?

Three Reasons a Deal Goes Bad

As I see it, business deals rest on integrity. But they rest on other things as well. Business deals can go sour for one or more of three reasons: judgment, environment, and integrity.

Error in Judgment

The western extension of a major boulevard was to be completed in 1975. The road didn't actually open until September 1987. The investors counted on being in and out of the land deal in two or three years. When the road plans were delayed, everyone threw in the towel.

Everyone makes mistakes. Unfortunately, sometimes in business the mistakes involve a lot of money. And sometimes it's other people's money. It has been my experience, though, that people are pretty tolerant of busi-

In God's eyes, we are just as guilty when we stuff our suitcases with motel towels as we would be if we robbed a bank.

ness deals that don't work out because of an error in judgment, provided that good communication takes place.

How has an error in judgment affected a business deal you or your employer was involved in?

_____

_____

How did that affect you personally?

_____

_____

Change in the Environment

At the end of World War II, three brothers started a flying school for veterans under the G.I. Bill. They taught thousands of returning soldiers how to fly. Without warning, four years after the end of the war, Congress amended the G.I. Bill so flying lessons no longer qualified for tuition assistance. Their business immediately went under, and they had to liquidate in pieces, one propeller at a time.

Regardless of how good you are, the vagaries of the business environment—competitive or regulatory—can sneak up on you more quietly than a lion stalking its prey. Before you know it, you are face-to-face with calamity, and there is nothing to do but make the best of a bad situation.

Describe an environmental change that affected your business or your job security.

_____

_____

How have you handled it?

_____

_____

Integrity

The third reason business deals go sour is the problem of integrity. Men who cut corners to put transactions together are like the first of the three little pigs. The house built from straw collapses at the first high wind that blows.

Lying to prospects, concealing information that would probably kill the sale, squeezing for a better price by using a competitor as a stalking horse (when you know you really won't buy from the competitor), withholding pay increases from those who are deserving, not paying your bills as agreed when you are able—these are of chief importance to God, for as I noted previously, He is looking for a few good men.

⫽▱ ooking Closer in the Mirror:

How important is personal integrity, even in the "little" things? How important is it to God, as He searches people's hearts looking for faithful followers? You'll find the answer in Leviticus 6:1–5.

_____

_____

Does this passage apply to us today? If so, what are the implications?

_____

_____

Specifically, do you believe restitution is a valid scriptural principle for modern times? How would it impact our contemporary view of integrity? Explain your answer.

_____

_____

_____

Do you need to make restitution to anyone? If so, whom? And what type of restitution is necessary?

_____

_____

_____

■ A CASE-BY-CASE APPROACH

Look up Deuteronomy 5:32–33. What does it say about the importance of our obedience to the Ten Commandments?

_____

_____

Our prosperity has everything to do with our obedience, for honesty permeates God's commandments.

During the course of a day, we all have scores of opportunities to be dishonest. If we must decide each time we make a decision whether or not we will be honest, we consume a lot of energy and run the risk of making a sloppy decision and compromising our integrity.

By settling the issue once and for all, and deciding to always choose the narrow road—to always have integrity—we can liberate ourselves from the bondage of making hundreds of daily decisions. We won't have to worry about those tiny decisions which, like water tapping on a rock, can wear down our character. We can remove the taint of dishonesty that colors the lives of so many men.

Are you willing to make a once-and-for-all commitment to integrity? If so, write out your commitment here, sign it, and date it. Photocopy this page and put your copy in a place where you will see it regularly—perhaps your Bible—so it will serve as a daily reminder of your pledge.

Commitment: _____

_____

_____

_____

_____

Signed: _____   **Date**: _____

MIRROR **WORK**

*L*ord Jesus, I want to be pure. But I understand that sometimes integrity issues are hard to pin-point. Please search me. Find any lack of integrity in my life, and bring it to my attention. Then show me how to correct it. Amen.

In the next chapter . . .

Integrity isn't just what we do—it's also what we think. Would you be embarrassed if your friends knew what goes on in your mind? You're certainly not alone. Keep reading to discover how to handle your secret thought life.

Leading a Secret Thought Life

22

The secret thoughts of a man run over all things, holy, profane, clean, obscene, grave and light, without shame or blame.

THOMAS HOBBES

We take captive every thought to make it obedient to Christ.

2 CORINTHIANS 10:5

Three of us were eating deli sandwiches at a streetside table on the picturesque main street of town. Paper-thin translucent leaves glistened as the sun diffused through the new growth of early spring.

As we were about to leave, a very lovely woman passed by on the sidewalk. She was beautiful, fresh, and sophisticated. She seemed a perfect match for the day. Many heads turned as she walked by, including those of the men with whom I was sitting.

I watched their eyes follow her, and I could tell they undressed her in the secrecy of their private worlds. Because Christians are expected not to lust over women, I carefully concealed my thoughts, for I was aware that the only difference between us was that I had more carefully controlled my eyes.

I knew that pretending not to notice was counterfeit. I knew I was leading a secret thought life different from the image I projected. I was embarrassed by it. I thought it was exclusively my problem. *Maybe my sins are not forgiven after all, or maybe I'm not even a Christian,* I thought.

It never occurred to me that other Christian men might struggle with the same problem. After all, no one really talks about it. *Why do Christian men not talk about their secret thought lives?*

> ❝ 'Take captive every thought to make it obedient to Christ.' *That's the essence of living our thought lives by the power of the Holy Spirit.* ❞

List some results of our refusal to talk to one another about this area of our lives.

The Problem

I'd be willing to bet my car that you could relate to the story I just shared. That indicates that all of us, regardless of the length of our experience in the Christian life, probably need to face some tough questions.

- Am I leading a secret thought life significantly different from the "me" that I show to other people?
- Would I be embarrassed if my friends and associates knew what goes on inside my mind?
- If my thoughts were audible, would my wife want a divorce?

How is your secret thought life most different from the life you present visibly to other people?

_____

_____

_____

The Battle for the Mind

Am I leading a secret thought life significantly different from the "me" that I show to other people?

It would be easy to reduce this chapter to a discussion regarding the problem of lust. The simple fact, though, is that the battle for the mind involves a lot of areas.

For example, one morning I was driving to speak at a men's Bible study. I slowed for a traffic light, relieved to see I would make it through the intersection on the next green light.

As I braked, the driver next to me saw a "hairline crack" and, without warning, swerved in front of me. I slammed on the brakes and checked the rearview mirror. Anger grabbed me, but since I was on my way to speak at Bible study, I recovered and kept my spiritual glow.

Then the light turned green and the long line of cars inched toward the intersection. The car ahead of me made it, but I was stuck first in line at the red light. That did it, Bible study or not. I let out an audible expletive that came from a part of me not fully surrendered to God.

How would you react in this same situation?

_____

_____

Each day we battle to "take our thoughts captive"—to control our minds. What are the areas in which you do battle?

Describe the apostle Paul's battle, as he presents it in Romans 7:15–24.

When we begin to grasp the simplicity of this battle, we can equip ourselves with some firepower to take control of our secret thought lives. Paul, by the way, answered his own question later. "Who will rescue me from this body of death?" he asked. "Thanks be to God—through Jesus Christ our Lord!" was his reply (Romans 7:25).

Does his approach seem too simplistic for such a deep problem? Explain your answer.

Mind X and Mind Y

Perhaps it will help if we agree on a basic principle which I have labeled *"Mind X and Mind Y."* It's based on an interesting business management theory developed by Douglas McGregor, a professor at M.I.T., which goes by the name *"Theory X/Theory Y."*

The *Theory X* manager believes people are basically lazy and irresponsible and will do a poor job unless constantly supervised. *Theory Y* managers, on the other hand, believe people generally want to do a good job and will respond to clearly defined objectives. If only supported and encouraged, people will get the job done.

There may be some biblical basis to applying this theory to the human mind. The Bible depicts two parts to the mind: one controlled by the sinful nature, which we might call *Mind X*, and a second controlled by the Spirit, which we might call *Mind Y*.

As followers of Christ, we are not left on our own to squirm with the sinful nature of our *Mind X*, but we have been given the Holy Spirit to teach and guide our *Mind Y*.

If we understand the workings of our two minds, we can conquer our secret thought lives. The decoder for all of this is in Romans 8:5–6. Look it up and write it here.

Where is the fuzzy line that separates temptation from sin?

_____

_____

_____

Now, in every place where that passage refers to the sinful or carnal mind, cross it out and replace it with "Mind X," and in every place where you referred to the mind controlled by the Holy Spirit, cross it out and replace it with "Mind Y."

What happens when we do what our "Mind X" suggests? Provide a specific example.

_____

_____

What happens when we let "Mind Y" exercise control? Provide a specific example.

_____

_____

The Fuzzy Line

The problem, of course, even for those of us who are trying to let our *Mind Y* exercise control in our lives, is that not all situations are clearly black-and-white. Sometimes the line between temptation and sin gets fuzzy.

It's somewhat like little Johnny, who drew a line in the sand and said to his brother, "You'd better not cross that line or I'll beat you up!" Little Jimmy defiantly stepped across the line and folded his arms across his chest in triumph. His brother Johnny paused, then drew another line in the sand and repeated, "You'd better not cross that line or I'll beat you up!"

Where is the fuzzy line that separates temptation from sin? Is it etched in stone, or in shifting sand? Can we redraw it when we don't like the immediate results? What is the difference between temptation and actual sin in our thought lives?

Temptation Is Not Sin

The thoughts that enter our lives are not sin. In fact, a Christian may very well be tempted with more negative thoughts than he was before his conversion. Why is that?

The tempter would like nothing better than to discourage us about our faith. Perhaps you remember that, in the story I shared at the beginning of this chapter, I began to wonder if my sins really were forgiven, and if I truly was a Christian.

Many men suffer this same discouragement. We find ourselves thinking, "How could I be a true Christian and still have these thoughts? I must not have a genuine faith." When we think like that, who wins, and why?

We really have no more control over our thoughts than over the vulgar language of a man sitting next to us at a restaurant. We hear them both—we can't "turn them off" like a radio.

True, we can put so much junk into our minds that they are predisposed to tempting thoughts. Even so, thoughts are merely thoughts. Tempting thoughts can become sinful thoughts—but only if we let *Mind X* have its own way and cross the fuzzy line.

Why is it so difficult to accept tempting thoughts for what they are, and to refuse to feel guilty as if we have sinned?

When Temptation Crosses the Line

The best illustration for the difference between temptation and actual sin in our thought lives falls in the area of sexual attraction. Since men are physically attracted to women, when does mental attraction become sin? *Is there some definable threshold over which we cross from mere temptation to actual sin?*

When our normal observations become abnormal preoccupations, then we have crossed the fuzzy line. Dr. R. C. Sproul, in his book *Pleasing God,* noted these thoughts:

> Lust is not noticing that a woman is sexually attractive. Lust is born when we turn a simple awareness into a preoccupied fantasy. When we invite sexual thoughts into our minds and nurture them, we have passed

from simple awareness into lust. Luther put it this way: "We cannot help it if birds fly over our heads. It is another thing if we invite them to build nests in our hair."[1]

Concealing Sin

Unfortunately, one major problem blocks our dealing with sin in our thought lives—the bottom line is, it's so easy to hide. Sometimes we can fool even ourselves.

Tom, for instance, enjoyed girl-watching. Whenever he traveled, he liked to sit in the airport terminal, checking out the women who came and went. After he became a Christian, Tom sensed his obsession displeased God. But it was his one private secret. "Besides," he reasoned, "everyone's entitled to a minor vice, aren't they? Nobody gets hurt. It's a victimless crime."

Can you relate to his attempt to explain away his sin? Look up Proverbs 28:13. What evidence do you see in your own life or in the lives of others to demonstrate the accuracy of this verse?

_____

_____

How does Tom's excuse match up to this scriptural warning?

_____

_____

We can't hide anything from God. He knows every word we will speak, even before it is on our lips. Our goal for our secret thought lives, then, since they are no secret to God, should be to think in a way that demonstrates personal holiness.

Visibility to Others

I would rather go to jail than be seen in a bar. Frankly, the reasons are not spiritual, but selfish. I don't want my reputation to be tarnished. This has less to do with what Jesus might think than with what my friends might think.

From this simple example you can see that the *visibility* of our speech and actions helps us keep them in line. *How does visibility bring some discipline to your life?*

_____

_____

_____

What, then, is the result of the low visibility of your thought life?

_____

_____

High visibility is not all bad. It helps us exercise self-discipline—and it can actually cause us to seek God's righteousness in our lives.

Awareness by Me

While others may take note of our sins because of their visibility, we may be aware or unaware of our own sins.

As new Christians, we brought all of our excess baggage with us to our newfound faith.

Even before becoming Christians we disguised much of our secret thought life, but once we became Christians, we became skilled concealers of these secret thoughts. We carefully controlled our speech and actions to keep in step with our perception of the new job description, mostly because it served our purposes.

Low awareness sins are blind spots. These areas provide the battleground for some of the fiercest fights for our minds.

The psalmist referred to this in Psalm 19:12–13. Look up that passage and write it here.

_____

_____

How does the Christian share the concern which the psalmist described in those verses?

_____

_____

> *Our goal for our secret thought lives, then, since they are no secret to God, should be to think in a way that demonstrates personal holiness.*

The Visibility/Awareness Connection

Figure 22.1 provides a clear picture of the visibility/awareness relationship.

VISIBILITY

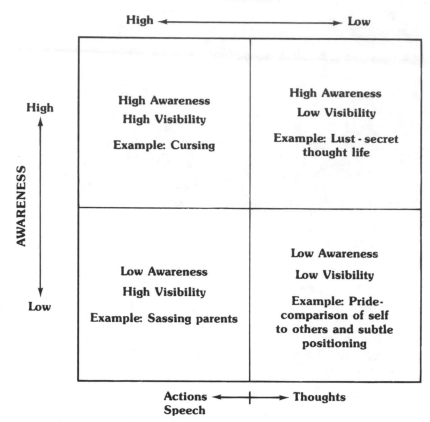

High Visibility/High Awareness

As you can see, high visibility/high awareness sins are the most blatant ones—sins that anyone (even the nonbeliever) would recognize as wrong. For me, before I received the Lord, every other word had four letters imaginatively arranged. That was a high visibility/high awareness sin.

High Visibility/Low Awareness

These sins are often the sins of nonbelievers, but not always. One man I know became a Christian, but after several years he still was known for his temper. When approached about it, he said he thought it was perfectly normal to let off steam. No one had ever made him aware that anger can be sin. He has made substantial progress since then.

Low Visibility/High Awareness

Low visibility/high awareness sins are the nemesis of the Christian man. "I know this kind of thinking is wrong, but I'm just not willing to give it up."

Once a friend offered to help me obtain a business loan through one of his contacts. But when I went for his help, I couldn't get him to follow up on it. My feelings were wounded. I was angry beyond forgiveness, and soon I became bitter.

I was highly aware of the sin in my secret thoughts, but the low visibility didn't require me to become accountable to anyone. Finally, the Holy Spirit's conviction became so strong that I reconciled with the man.

Low Visibility/Low Awareness

The most sly sins of all are the low visibility/low awareness ones. Not only does no one else see it, but we don't either. And since we rarely give our lives introspective self-examination, we can be oblivious to the wrongness of our wrong thinking.

A few years ago, I realized that I am a "critiquer." I critique everything. That alone would be no problem, but I also realized that I add to my critique a comparison of myself. Very subtly, I was putting others down to make myself feel better. This is the essence of pride, which we have discussed in a previous chapter.

Which of those four categories best characterizes the sin you find you must battle most regularly? Specifically explain your answer.

_____

_____

_____

> **Unless we develop a solid understanding of how our thoughts, motives, and ambitions are shaped, we will have impure secret thoughts, wrong motives, and selfish ambitions.**

The Mind That Plays Tricks on Itself

A brewery that made regular and light beer surveyed people who drank their product. "Do you prefer regular or light beer?" they asked. Amazingly, people reported they preferred light beer three to one.

For years this brewery had produced nine times as much regular beer as light. *If you were in this situation, would you change your production?* _____ *Yes* _____ *No* _____ *Don't know.*

This brewery didn't. Rather, they assumed that, in essence, people had interpreted the question to mean, "Do you prefer the beer of refined discriminating people, or do you only drink regular beer?"[2]

We have a remarkable capacity to kid, trick, and fool ourselves. Our self-image is so important to us that we will believe almost any reasonable explanation for our failures, as long as we end up as the hero. The prophet

Jeremiah noted this when he said, "The heart is deceitful above *all* things and beyond cure. Who can understand it?" (Jeremiah 17:9, italics added). *According to the words of Jeremiah 17:9, why do we skew things to make ourselves look good or feel smart?*

_____

_____

Unless we develop a solid understanding of how our thoughts, motives, and ambitions are shaped, we will have impure secret thoughts, wrong motives, and selfish ambitions. If we don't leave a sentinel posted in the watchtower, then the enemy can slip into our thoughts under the cover of low awareness.

Self-deceit is subtle. John decided to buy a new car because the gas mileage on the old one wasn't very good. The new car John bought depreciated $3,000 the first year, but he saved $200 in gas. *What did John really want?*

_____

_____

Look up Proverbs 16:1–2. How does John's action reflect the principle outlined in that passage?

_____

_____

ooking Closer in the Mirror:

Look up Jeremiah 23:24. Based on that verse, do you believe God knows your thoughts? Why do so many men emphasize living right before their peers, but they don't make a priority of living right in their thoughts, which are lived out before God?

_____

_____

Describe a situation which, at the time seemed harmless, but now you realize you crossed the line between temptation and sin.

_____

_____

Now make a clear line for yourself, so you won't continue to repeat that mistake. Mark a line that you will not cross. Explain how you chose the place to put your line, and describe how it will affect your lifestyle from now on.

_____

_____

_____

■ CONQUERING THE SECRET THOUGHT LIFE

To paraphrase an old cliché, you can fool some of the people all the time and all the people some of the time. You can even fool yourself. But you can't fool God.

Look up Proverbs 20:27. What does this verse mean for you?

_____

_____

Write that in a prayer, asking God to accomplish it in your life.

_____

_____

Compare your prayer to the one recorded in Psalm 139:23–24. What similarities or differences do you find?

_____

_____

What kind of thoughts is the psalmist particularly concerned about in that passage?

_____

_____

■ TAKE CAPTIVE EVERY THOUGHT

Learning to control our thoughts can be like raising children. Some friends of mine decided their daughter could not go to PG-13 movies until she was thirteen. All of her friends could go when they were ten and eleven. Every weekend she would ask to go to this or that movie, always rated PG-13. She always tested the limits.

Our thoughts are like that. Every week they seek permission to cross the line we've drawn. It takes discipline and effort to keep our *Mind Y* in gear and our *Mind X* disengaged.

According to Ecclesiastes 12:14, what are the consequences if we refuse to do that?

_____

_____

_____

That's a scary thought. But we can avoid harsh judgment. Remember we quoted 2 Corinthians 10:5 at the beginning of this chapter? *"Take captive every thought to make it obedient to Christ."* That's the essence of living our thought lives by the power of the Holy Spirit.

MIRROR WORK

Lord Jesus, I believe You never ask me to do anything without providing the power to accomplish it. You've asked me to take every thought captive. Now, help me to draw a line that I will not cross. Amen.

In the next chapter . . .

Howard Ball has said that "living the Christian life isn't difficult, it's impossible." Perhaps after reading this chapter, you really believe that's true. No man has the strength to always make the right decisions. But by building a structure of accountability, we can order our lives in a way that gives us the best chance for success.

Accountability: The Missing Link

23

Our society displays far too little correlation between its purported beliefs and its behavior.

ANONYMOUS

The kisses of an enemy may be profuse, but faithful are the wounds of a friend.

PROVERBS 27:6

I played men's doubles tennis with a partner who always became angry when I netted the ball. Finally I told him, "Give me a break. I would never intentionally hit the ball into the net!"

In the same way, nobody who trusts Christ disobeys Scripture *intentionally*. Men don't fail on purpose. Yet, we see men falling short of their potential every day.

Why is that? Christians don't fail because they want to. The simple truth is that all genuine Christians want to live obedient lives through faith in Jesus Christ. But alas, "the spirit is willing, but the flesh is weak," and in this life, temptations wait around every corner.

What evidence do you see that while we do not intentionally disobey, the flesh is weak when it comes to standing against temptation?

> **"One of the greatest reasons men get into trouble is that they don't answer to anyone for their lifestyles."**

No man has the strength of purpose to always make the right choices. Just when we think we are getting ourselves under control—zap! As the apostle Paul reminds us, "So, if you think you are standing firm, be careful that you don't fall!" (1 Corinthians 10:12).

The Problem

One of the greatest reasons why men get into trouble is that they don't answer to anyone for their lifestyles. If you were to ask around, you'd find very few men who have built significant accountability into their Christian lives.

I call accountability the *missing link* of Christianity.

What about you? Are you falling victim to the missing link? Beyond God Himself, to whom do you feel most accountable for what is going on in your spiritual life?

_____ *Your wife*

_____ *Your pastor*

_____ *Your small group leader*

_____ *A close friend*

_____ *Your father*

_____ *Other (Please specify)* _____

At what level are you sharing your life with that person to whom you feel most accountable?

_____

_____

We get caught in a web of cutting corners and compromise, self-deceit and wrong thinking, which goes unchallenged by anyone in our lives.

Every day men fail morally, spiritually, relationally, and financially, not because they don't want to succeed, but because they have *blind spots* and *weak spots* which they imagine they can handle on their own. They can't. And they lose their families, their businesses, their jobs, their savings, and damage their relationship with God.

Some men have spectacular failures where in a moment of passion they abruptly burst into flames, crash, and burn. But the more common way men get into trouble evolves from hundreds of tiny decisions—decisions which go undetected—that slowly, like water tapping on a rock, wear down a man's character. Not blatantly or precipitously, but subtly, over time, we get caught in a web of cutting corners and compromise, self-deceit and wrong thinking, which goes unchallenged by anyone in our lives.

List some recent examples that have made the news—situations where politicians, businessmen, and even clergy were finally exposed for a series of small actions that became a headline-making pattern.

_____

_____

What was the missing link in their lives that allowed that kind of behavior to persist?

_____

What does that imply for you?

_____

_____

God's Word teaches us how to guard against falling away. "Solid food [God's Word] is for the mature, who by constant use have trained themselves to distinguish good from evil" (Hebrews 5:14). Yet, men *do* fall away because they don't have to answer to anyone for their behavior and beliefs.

In a world where evil often triumphs, how can a man order his life to have the greatest likelihood of succeeding? The answer—the missing link—is accountability.

The Purpose and Definition of Accountability

The purpose of accountability is nothing less than to each day become more Christ-like in all our ways and ever more intimate with Him. What is accountability anyway? Accountability is like nuclear fusion. Everyone has heard of it, everyone knows it's important, but few people can actually explain it.

Here is a working definition for Christian accountability: *To be regularly answerable for each of the key areas of our lives to qualified people.*

Now that I have defined it, would you say you are part of an accountability structure? ____ *Yes* ____ *No* ____ *Don't know*

If you are, what have you gained from that relationship? If you are not, what could you gain from an accountable relationship?

Now, let's explore that definition by breaking it down into four parts: *answerable, key areas, regularly,* and *qualified people.*

Answerable

In commerce, every man is accountable to someone. Even the self-employed owner is accountable to his customers and clients. I own my own business, but I still must give financial and management accountings to limited partners and lenders.

You are probably part of a business structure. List some ways you and others in your organization are held accountable.

Unless we are *answerable* on a regular basis for key areas of our personal lives, just as we are for our professional lives, we will stray. Submission to someone else's inspection grates on the desire to be independent. But let me assure you, Scripture establishes a pattern of accountability.

Describe the kinds of accountability in the following passages, and note the value of that accountability.

Galatians 6:1–2 _____

_____

_____

Philippians 2:4 _____

_____

Ecclesiastes 4:9–10 _____

_____

_____

Proverbs 27:6 _____

_____

Proverbs 27:17 _____

_____

We must find someone to whom we can *answer* for the *goals* we set and the *standards* by which we live. We should each set goals to help us accomplish God's purposes and priorities for our lives. Then we need someone to whom we can be answerable—to give an accurate report—about how we are progressing toward those goals.

The Bible delineates general guidelines for our character and conduct which apply to all Christians. We also need people in our lives to challenge and encourage us to live up to those standards.

List some spiritual goals and priorities you have established for which you could make yourself accountable to another person.

_____

_____

Key Areas for Accountability

An iceberg is one of nature's most spectacular and dangerous phenomena. The visible portion is beautiful—like the "best foot" we each put forward with our friends. But only one-eighth to one-tenth of an iceberg can be seen. The rest is hidden below the surface of the water. *That's* where the danger lurks.

Perhaps you remember the Titanic, considered by experts to be un-sinkable. But on the night of April 14, 1912, it defied those experts, sinking in one of history's largest sea disasters. Fifteen hundred people perished as the submerged part of a mountain of ice ripped a three-hundred-foot gash in the hull of what was considered the greatest ocean liner in the world.

Figure 23.1

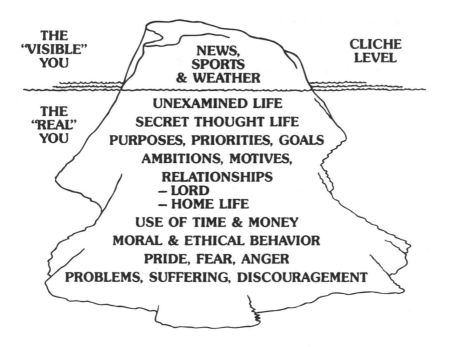

THE ACCOUNTABILITY ICEBERG

Figure 23.1 shows our accountability iceberg. It illustrates how most of our conversation revolves around the cliché level of life—news, sports, and weather. *How does this illustration mirror your experience?*

The areas of our lives that need accountability lie beneath the surface of our own personal icebergs. They go beyond the "visible" you and touch the heart of the "real" you.

Those areas can be examined from different angles. One distinction, which we have already touched briefly, is *personal* versus *professional* accountability. The men who hold us accountable with our careers and ethics may not be the same men we ask to help us maximize our relationships with our wives and kids.

Another distinction zeros in on areas *all men* need to address versus *personal high risk* areas—those with which we have special struggles. A man who is a credit card "junkie," for instance, may need to answer weekly to someone in that area alone.

But perhaps the most useful distinction is *categorical*. The key areas in which we all need accountability are:

- Relationship with God
- Relationship with wife
- Relationship with kids
- Use of money and time
- Moral and ethical behavior
- Areas of personal struggle

Regularly

For sixteen years I have met weekly with a friend who serves as my accountability partner. We hold each other responsible for our relationships with the Lord and, to a lesser degree, our families. We also have great fellowship and times of prayer.

Is this regularity important? In my experience, the answer is yes. One on one accountability is a major emphasis of the men's Bible study I have taught in Orlando for eight years. I have found that men who don't meet weekly eventually stop meeting altogether.

What would you have to do to set up a weekly meeting with an accountability partner?

Picking Accountability Partners

All of this probably has made sense to you so far. But let's face it—no one really wants to bare his soul to just anybody. So, how do you choose a good accountability partner?

The overarching qualification for partners is that they love Christ, they want to see you succeed, and they also sense a need for accountability.

Beyond that, based on Proverbs 13:20, what qualification would you want to see in your partner?

Chances are that an existing friend is a good candidate. To work through the process of choosing a friend for that special relationship, perhaps you will want to re-read the chapter titled "Friends: Risks and Rewards" in the context of accountability.

You may want to ask different men to hold you accountable in different areas: moral, spiritual, financial, and relational. How tragic to achieve a high degree of success in your relationships with your family and with the Lord, only to go bankrupt because of a foolish financial decision that could have been averted through accountability.

And let me note a word of caution. Men should not have accountable relationships with women other than their wives. That is an invitation for disaster. In my opinion, however, wives are particularly helpful in areas of personal weakness, where vulnerability is a sensitive issue.

Do you agree or disagree, and why?

> *The peace and joy of our daily lives springs from the integrity and balance we maintain in key areas of life.*

Sadly, we all have been stung by leaks of confidential information. The fear of betrayal by a friend keeps many of us from taking the risk of opening our lives up to someone. *How can we avoid leaks of confidential information shared in this type of relationship?*

To wrap up this section, I suggest that as you seek someone to hold you accountable, you should look for someone with whom you can enter a true partnership. Instead of looking for a "boss," find a fellow struggler so you can help each other.

Avoid asking men who may have hidden agendas. If you owe someone money, for instance, you probably shouldn't ask that person to hold you accountable in the area of your finances.

Finally, don't go overboard. Time is limited. Since you will probably meet regularly, you don't want to have so many accountable relationships that you feel bogged down. One or two men should be all you need— maybe three in some circumstances. If you form a group, the different skills of the other men will probably help cover all the key areas.

Here and There

If accountability can become so sticky, then why should we consider it important? The ultimate reason we should be interested in our accountability *here* in this life is our accountability *there* in eternity.

List some ways we are accountable to God, according to the following Scriptures.

Matthew 12:36 _____

_____

Romans 14:12 _____

_____

Romans 2:6, 16 _____

_____

The tighter we hold the reins here, the more God will be pleased when we stand before Christ's judgment seat. And on a practical level, the peace and joy of our daily lives spring from the integrity and balance we maintain in key areas of life. Whether moral, spiritual, relational, or financial—the "big four" areas—when we handle our lives with skill and wisdom, we experience a sense of personal satisfaction. Without the help of others in accountable relationships, none of us really can attain our potential.

Counsel Versus Accountability

Given what you have read so far in this chapter, describe the difference between seeking counsel and seeking accountability.

_____

_____

Many men seek Christian counsel and think they have fulfilled their duty. Plainly, seeking counsel adds value to our decisions, and frankly, most of us should seek more of it. *But seeking counsel alone does not go far enough.*

Seeking counsel is based on our initiative. Being held accountable gives another person the right and responsibility to take initiative. To seek counsel is to look for answers to our questions. To be accountable is to give answers to the questions we are asked.

Would you say you have sought counsel or accountability?

_____

Now that you recognize the difference, to whom would you go for:

Counsel _____

Accountability _____

Fellowship Versus Accountability

Based on what you have read so far in this chapter, describe the difference between fellowship and accountability.

Early in my spiritual pilgrimage, I was among six men who committed to meet weekly. We discussed a wide range of subjects, but we mostly met for fellowship. One member of our group was writing a Christian book on how to handle money and possessions, so we spent part of our time looking over his ideas.

Suddenly, another member of our group quit his job, divorced his wife, abandoned three infant children, and married his secretary—all of which came as a total surprise to the rest of us. How could we possibly not know, you ask? We simply did not ask each other the hard questions.

This experience taught me that fellowship without accountability has a very good, limited value, if any at all. Fellowship is good, but it is no substitute for accountability. Accountability doesn't evolve naturally. It results from a purposed decision to live in a "fish bowl" before someone we trust.

Unfortunately, despite all of the benefits of accountability, *most of us would prefer to stick to the level of fellowship. Why is that?*

> *Unless we face our propensities for sin and self-deceit, and acknowledge that we need help, we will never stick with a program of accountability.*

Why Men Are Not Accountable

Even after we are captured by Christ, we continue in a lifelong power struggle between the old man of the flesh (*the Mind X*) and the new man (*the Mind Y*). Our old man really doesn't want to be held accountable and resists that notion with all of his resources.

Let me share with you the most common reasons why we don't submit ourselves to accountability.

The Problem of Willingness

The National Football League suspended Lawrence Taylor, the New York Giants' perennial All-Pro linebacker, for violating its substance-abuse policy. He was quoted in the September 1, 1988, edition of *The New York Times* as explaining, "God, I didn't mean for it to happen. I wish it hadn't, but I made a bad decision and I'll have to pay the price for it . . . I really wasn't allowing the Giants to help me. I wasn't allowing my wife to help me. I was doing it by myself because I wanted to say I could do it on my own. It doesn't work like that. Boy, I found that out."

What are some reasons why Lawrence Taylor was not willing to be held accountable?

_____

_____

Unless we face our propensities for sin and self-deceit, and acknowledge that we need help, we will never stick with a program of accountability. We may start one, but after a few testy moments, we will abandon those nosy, uncomfortable questions.

The Problem of Strong Personality

Once I tried to develop an accountable relationship with another man. After a short time, I sensed he wasn't really interested. He was willing to meet, but he failed to submit his ego to the pruning character of the hard questions on how he was doing with the Lord, his wife, and his kids.

If you have a strong ego, how have you reacted to this chapter?

_____

_____

What possible conflict could you anticipate if you get involved in an accountability relationship?

_____

_____

The Problem of Success

Recently I asked a successful businessman if anyone held him accountable for his decisions.

"Over several years," he said, "I have become aware that I have no one to whom I must answer. As I have become more successful, everyone assumes I have my act together. The worldly prestige that comes from success intimidates most people from asking how I am doing. *There appears to be a presumption that since I am successful in business, then every other area of my life is in order.* Frankly, I operate without answering to anyone."

Why do successful men also need accountability relationships?

_____

_____

The Problem of Vulnerability

The price of friendship is personal vulnerability. The price of an effective, accountable relationship is also personal vulnerability. In friendship personal vulnerability is *voluntary,* but in an accountable relationship it must be *mandatory.* To get past news, sports, and weather, a man must be willing to reveal that part of him which is hidden below the surface.

To be vulnerable means to risk the disapproval of your accountability partner. Let's face it—none of us naturally goes looking for someone to whom he can exhibit his blemishes. Accountability is a decision of the will, because we sense we will receive a higher reward from the Lord Jesus when we pay the price of having a brother sharpen us "as iron sharpens iron."

Describe how you feel about being personally vulnerable to another person.

_____

_____

Why do we sometimes deceive our partners, even when we really want to be in an accountability relationship?

_____

_____

Why is it best to move slowly in our efforts to make ourselves personally vulnerable?

_____

_____

I have done many shameful things. We all have. Within an accountability relationship, we don't need to air all of our old dirty laundry to be personally vulnerable. If you are clear with Christ about an area, I think some things are better left alone. Yet for those areas where we *continue* to struggle, we *do* need help that can only come from making ourselves vulnerable to an accountability partner. If any guilt remains from the past, talk about it—Jesus wants us to be healed.

The Problem of Structure

Recently I asked a group of men about the frequency of their golf game. The few who said they played regularly also said they have a standing game—a structure. Among the majority who didn't play regularly, no one had a standing game.

Accountability works the same way. The only men who are consistently having accountable relationships have planned and committed them-

The only men who are consistently having accountable relationships have planned and committed themselves to a specific structure or game plan.

selves to a specific structure or game plan. *What kind of regularity and struc-ture are you prepared to commit to?*

◨ *Looking Closer in the Mirror:*

Review from within this chapter, from the section titled "Key Areas for Accountability," the six categories in which I believe we all need to be held accountable. List them here:

(1) _____

(2) _____

(3) _____

(4) _____

(5) _____

(6) _____

Now ask yourself, what are your own personal weak spots—your "personal high-risk areas"?

In what areas of your secret thought life do you struggle most?

Do you really want to know your own "blind spots"? Why or why not?

List some questions you don't really want anyone to ask you.

Whom could you trust to ask you those tough questions?

Why do you need to be accountable regarding those questions?

_____

_____

Getting Started

Within this chapter, you have already listed men you would feel comfortable inviting into an accountability relationship. Review those names. Perhaps you will want to add or subtract some friends or acquaintances.

Now, outline a strategy for asking them to read this chapter and enter into such a relationship with you.

_____

_____

At the end of this chapter, I have included *The Weekly One-Hour Accountability Check-Up*. It is designed to help you and those who are willing to enter this relationship with you.

Don't be fooled, though. All of this sounds fairly simple. Yet only about 15 percent of any group of men introduced to the idea of accountability actually develop accountability relationships. *What will keep you going if the men you have named reject your invitation?*

_____

_____

Keep in mind—accountability is worth the effort it requires. If you are part of the vast majority of men who don't have anyone asking them Who? What? Why? and How? then let me challenge you to fill in this missing link in your life. It may be the component that enables you to synchronize your behavior with your beliefs, and keeps you from spinning out of control.

MIRROR WORK

Lord Jesus, I know now that it's impossible for me to live this Christian life the way You intend all by myself. Lead me to people who will hold me accountable in the various areas of my life, and help me to fulfill that responsibility for them as well. Amen.

In the next chapter . . .

This book has contained some important information, but it can't make you change unless you want to. True change results from daily decisions. Keep reading— let's discover how to incorporate those changes into our daily lives.

The Weekly One-Hour Accountability Check-Up

To be accountable is to be regularly answerable for each key area of our lives to qualified people.

Suggested Guidelines:

(1) Try to ensure each person gets equal "air time." However, if one of you has a particularly hard struggle one week, be flexible enough to focus on that issue, even if it takes the whole hour.

(2) Let each person work through a section at a time, then let the others answer. This will keep things moving better.

(3) Don't neglect the prayer time.

(4) Try one-on-one. Small groups of three to five men work well if everyone speaks succinctly. One hour will go by very quickly.

(5) Re-read the chapter, "Accountability: The Missing Link" at least once each year and discuss the questions included in your workbook. You will be surprised how your understanding of accountability will change over the years.

(6) Stick it out. You will want to quit, perhaps often. Ask God to strengthen you when you want to give up.

(7) Hold each other accountable for the *goals* you each set and to the *standards* of God's Word.

(8) Never forget the purpose of accountability: To each day become more Christ-like in all your ways. Remember, *Jesus* is the object of our search, devotion, sacrifice, and affection. Anything less than intimacy with the living Lord will be a pallid achievement of your time together.

(9) Finally, if you are uncomfortable with the format, feel free to alter these questions and type up your own accountability checklist. The substance is more important than the form. You may want to divide the key areas among more than one accountability partner.

Questions to Start Off the Meeting:

(1) How has God blessed you this week? (What went right?)

(2) What problem has consumed your thoughts this week? (What went wrong?)

Spiritual Life:

(1) Have you read God's Word daily? (How long? Why not? Will you next week?)

(2) Describe your prayers (for yourself, others, praise, confession, gratitude).

(3) How is your relationship with Christ changing?

(4) How have you been tempted this week? How did you respond?

(5) Do you have any unconfessed sin in your life?

(6) Are you walking in the Spirit?

(7) Did you worship in church this week? (Was your faith in Jesus strengthened? Was He honored?)

(8) Have you shared your faith? In what ways? How can you improve?

Home Life:

(1) How is it going with your wife? (attitudes, time, irritations, disappointments, progress, her relationship with Christ)

(2) How is it going with the kids? (quantity and quality of time, values and beliefs, education, spiritual welfare, and warfare)

(3) How are your finances going? (debts, sharing, saving, stewardship)

Work Life:

(1) How are things going on the job? (career progress, relationships, temptations, work load, stress, problems, working too much)

Critical Concerns:

(1) Do you feel you are in the center of God's will? Do you sense His peace?

(2) What are you wrestling with in your thought life?

(3) What have you done for someone else this week? (helping the poor, offering encouragement, providing service)

(4) Are your priorities in the right order?

(5) Is your moral and ethical behavior what it should be?

(6) How are you doing in your personal high-risk area?

(7) Is the "visible" you and the "real" you consistent in this relationship?

Prayer:

Close the one-hour accountability check-up with ten to fifteen minutes of prayer. Focus on concerns of the week.

PART SEVEN

Conclusion

How Can a Man Change?

24

Few people think more than two or three times a year. I have made an international reputation by thinking once or twice a week.

GEORGE BERNARD SHAW

The knowledge of the secrets of the kingdom of heaven has been given to you, but not to them. Whoever has will be given more, and he will have an abundance.

JESUS, MATTHEW 13:11–12

T he turnpike from Miami to Orlando stretches endlessly, monotonously for over two hundred miles—the world's most tiring highway. We had just finished a wonderful but compact two-day visit with Patsy's parents.

But on the drive back to Orlando a frustration with life swept over me. I began to ask questions. Nonstop, for an hour and a half, plaintive questions poured out, one right after the other. I had no idea where they were coming from.

God let me vent. Frankly, I couldn't tell you today what any three of those questions were. Patsy saw the full spectrum of emotions—from top to bottom. We had been married for only a few months, and I feared she would think I had flipped. I was a brand-new Christian, and my head reeled with questions for God. Then, as quickly as it had begun, the gusher stopped.

Have you ever bombarded God with questions? Explain.

> **We didn't become the men we are overnight, and neither do we change overnight.**

When I finished, my impression was that God said, "Look, I appreciate your concerns, but you just don't need to know all that right now. Don't worry about it. Just trust Me. I'm all you need. You can't solve all those problems. That's what I'm here for."

A peace swept over me, though I still didn't have any answers. I sensed God loved me—that's all that mattered. *Would you be satisfied with that outcome, even without answers? Explain.*

I'd like to report that this was all I needed and that I've never questioned God since, but you know that's not true. Still, it *was* enough for the moment.

Life is a big question mark. God is a big answer. No matter how down or up, tired or strong, befriended or betrayed, upright or dishonest, hurt or happy, rich or broke, successful or failed, famous or unknown: God is the answer. He is all we need.

That's what I discovered on the turnpike. I felt my resistance melt. I lost that sense of wanting to be in control, and I surrendered anew to Him. As I've done many times since, I found a deeper level of pilgrimage—a deeper sense of relationship. And my life began to change.

> **The Kingdom of God starts here— in this, God's world, where good and evil live side by side as enemies.**

The Problem

As we began this book, I posed the question, *"Why do men think the things they think, say the things they say, and do the things they do?"* By now we both have a much better understanding of the answer to this important question.

But in a few minutes you will set aside this workbook and move on to the next chapter of your life—a life lived in the crucible of this world. Tomorrow morning, when the phones start ringing and customers start complaining, life gets real.

List some demands and tests you expect tomorrow to bring.

Americans have come to expect simple, streamlined solutions to perfectly packaged problems: "The three easy steps to a happy this . . . " or "The four foolproof ways to be a successful that . . ." But life is more complex than "this and that." We didn't become the men we are overnight, and neither do we change overnight. Patient, trial-and-error effort, diligently grinding it out on a day-to-day basis—that's the pathway to change.

In this final chapter, let's lay out some practical, daily steps we can take to change and move our lives to the next level. Let's really answer the question, "How can a man change?"

The Case for Daily Effort

You can save a fortune by using rechargeable batteries. But if you don't recharge them on schedule, they won't do the job. In the same way, the Christian must recharge his spiritual batteries every day. *If you fail to do so, what happens?*

_____

_____

The Christian pilgrimage is a moment-by-moment, daily journey. It requires daily effort. *Proverbs 19:27 tells us about that effort. Record that verse in the space provided.*

_____

_____

The Kingdom of God starts here—in this, God's world, where good and evil live side by side as enemies. Their struggle dominates all of our literature, news, movies, television shows, and so on. It dominates because it's one of life's most real characteristics. And to the extent that we don't stand guard *daily,* the other side successfully plots to break down our resistance.

Practical Steps to Daily Change

Each year the Houston Astros come to central Florida for spring training. Do these million-dollar athletes come to Florida to learn about obscure but rarely used baseball strategies? No. They practice fielding, running, batting, and conditioning—the basics. Every day they hit, run, and field.
How does the Christian journey compare to spring training?

_____

_____

Now that we've established that Christians must "return to the basics," let's take a look at how we can accomplish that.

(1) Daily Preparation

A man's first spiritual discipline is to prepare daily for life in a world in which good and evil live side by side. *List the daily spiritual disciplines that prepare us for that life.*

_____

_____

> **A man's first spiritual discipline is to prepare daily for life in a world in which good and evil live side by side.**

Whether done in early morning or in the evening, daily *Bible reading and study* coupled with *prayer* make up the first essential building block for real change. Underline Bible passages that capture your interest. Memorize passages for strength, courage, and faith. Write down impressions, ideas, and prayers. You may want to keep a journal of what you pray about and record the answers in it.

I use the acronym ACTS to help me pray. "A" is for adoration—praising God for His attributes. "C" is for confession—asking forgiveness for the sins I have committed. (Learn to keep "short accounts" with God.) "T" is for thanksgiving—expressing gratitude for His blessings and answers to my prayers. "S" is for supplication—asking for anything and everything that comes to mind for myself and for others.

Beyond all that, Scripture tells us one more thing about prayer. What can we learn from Luke 11:5–13?

_____

(2) Daily Temptation

Everyone is tempted to sin every day. God promises He will provide an escape—a safety valve—if we will choose it. *You'll find that safety valve explained in 1 Corinthians 10:13. Write that passage in the space provided.*

_____

_____

Based on that verse, when you are tempted, I encourage you to reject the thought and thank the Lord for giving you power for victory. Whatever thought pops into your mind, take it captive. Make it obedient to Christ.

(3) Daily Sin

Everyone sins. Inevitably, we sometimes are overcome and give way to temptation. *When you become aware of sin, what should you do?*

_____

Yes, confess it to the Lord and thank Him for forgiving your sins—past, present, and future—according to His promise in 1 John 1:9. *If you can, write that verse from memory. If not, look it up and record it in the space provided. Then memorize it, for it will provide a tremendous reminder of how to be cleansed from your sins.*

_____

_____

Then, invite Christ again to take control of your life, and get on with the next part of that life. This is the essence of living in the power of the Holy Spirit.

(4) Daily Power

When Jesus controls our lives, the Holy Spirit's power works in us.
Write John 14:26:

_____

_____

Write John 16:13:

_____

_____

Write Romans 8:9:

_____

_____

The Holy Spirit is given to all believers *(read 1 Corinthians 3:16)*. But not all believers enjoy this power because they resist Him and choose to sin. Even more, most Christians do not understand how to live in a moment-by-moment, daily fellowship with God.

The fruit of God's Spirit—love, joy, peace, patience, kindness, goodness, faithfulness, gentleness, and self-control—belongs to the surrendered man who yields control of his life to the mind of Christ every moment.

If we crucify our own ambition, confess our sins, and give Jesus Christ first place in our lives, then the Holy Spirit's power is available to meet every need. *Based on previous chapters (see Chapters 21–23), how do you crucify your own ambition?*

_____

_____

Living by the Holy Spirit's power requires an intense, moment-by-moment love relationship with the living Christ in which we soar on wings like eagles, or, having sinned, we tearfully confess and are restored.

(5) Daily Witnessing

If Christ is truly preeminent in our lives, then we will want to tell others about Him. Every Christian has the *command* and the *power* to witness. *Write Acts 1:8 and memorize it:*

_____

_____

Furthermore, the Great Commission does not say, "Therefore, *37 percent* of you go and make disciples of all nations." *According to the verse you just recorded, who is responsible to go and make disciples?*

_____

Do you have the desire to see others come to faith in Christ? Why or why not?

_____

_____

Do you have the ability to show someone how to trust Christ for the first time?

_____

If not, obtain training (read 1 Timothy 2:3–4 and 1 Peter 3:15). Can anything else really matter if we don't address the need of the human soul?

(6) Daily Pilgrimage

Life is a struggle. Each day is part of a pilgrimage that prepares us for our eternal destiny.

Each day we should set apart Christ in our hearts as the Lord. *Can you do that?* Focus on the good you see and hear. Testify, simply as a witness to the jury, about the changes occurring in your own life. Encourage those around you, and meet together regularly for friendship, accountability, Bible study, and prayer.

List some practical things you can do to be involved in those types of activities.

_____

_____

_____

To *encourage* someone is to *inspire* them to have *courage*. I believe we need to inspire others to have courage. We need to attend church where the Bible is believed and Christ is honored. Join a weekly Bible study group. Form an accountable relationship. Pursue your job as a holy vocation. Remember the poor when you give your resources. Be a faithful steward. Stand against bigotry and racial prejudice. Increase your love for God and for people. Remember, no amount of success at the office can compensate for failure at home.

> *Each day we should set apart Christ in our hearts as the Lord.*

The Sin of Partial Surrender

Some of us will try to go just halfway with that commitment. We will be like a congressman who was once asked about his attitude toward whiskey. He replied, "If you mean that demon drink that poisons the mind, pollutes the body, desecrates family life, and inflames sinners, then I'm against it. But if you mean the elixir of Christmas cheer, the shield against a cold winter chill, the taxable potion that puts needed funds into public coffers to comfort little crippled children, then I'm for it. This is my position, and I will not compromise."[1]

Many of us go back and forth like this between the life with Christ and the life in the world—we compromise; we have only partly surrendered to the Lord Jesus Christ. The challenge is to be a certain kind of man—the kind we have described in these pages, a man committed to the Christian life view, a biblical Christian.

Looking Closer in the Mirror:

What makes people resist change?

More specifically, what makes you resist change?

Do you have complaints against God? Do you have questions you would like Him to answer? The bottom line is that He is the answer. Do you really need to know all the answers, or is it enough to know God? Explain.

■ FINAL WORDS

No amount of success at the office can compensate for failure at home.

Men's last words betray them. They often reveal that the priorities by which these men lived didn't really satisfy their longing for meaning and purpose. Some men attain great esteem, but at the end of their lives, how many really find peace? You may be surprised to learn the final or near-final comments of some great men who have gone to their graves.

Tolstoy, for instance, remarked, "Even in the valley of the shadow of death, two and two do not make six."

Seneca noted, "All my life I have been seeking to climb out of the pit of my besetting sins and I cannot do it and I never will unless a hand is let down to draw me up."

A lifelong agnostic, W. C. Fields was discovered reading a Bible on his deathbed. "I'm looking for a loophole," he explained.

And Socrates, revered through the ages for his wisdom, said, "All of the wisdom of this world is but a tiny raft upon which we must set sail when we leave the earth. If only there was a firmer foundation upon which to sail, perhaps some divine word."

We have the Divine Word he longed for—but what are we doing with it? We should be living by it.

Record what you want to be remembered as your last words:

Are you prepared to make the daily effort to make that goal a reality in your life? _____ Yes _____ No.

■ *THE NEED FOR DAILY EFFORT*

In what ways can you personally identify with this statement? "Americans have come to expect simple, streamlined solutions to perfectly packaged problems."

_____

_____

What specifically are you prepared to commit to do in daily preparation, such as Bible study and prayer?

_____

_____

Specifically, how do you plan to prepare to deal with daily temptation?

_____

_____

Specifically, how will you prepare to handle daily sin?

_____

_____

Do you understand how to walk in the power of the Holy Spirit? Explain.

_____

_____

Do you have the desire and training to see others come to a saving faith in Jesus Christ? _____ Yes _____ No

If not, what are you prepared to do to correct that situation?

_____

_____

■ *PARTIAL SURRENDER*

Have you been guilty of the sin of partial surrender? Are you trying to have your cake and eat it too? Are you willing to make a "clean break" with the old man? Explain your answer.

_____

_____

_____

Is it time for you to stop going through the motions and get serious about your eternal destiny and earthly purpose?

My father once had an employee who said, "Mr. Morley, I need to make more money. If you will just pay me more money, I promise I'll work harder."

With a twinkle in his eye, my dad responded, "I can see you have a need. I'll tell you what; I'd like to help. Why don't you go ahead and work harder, and then I'll pay you more money."

We often want God to increase our "pay" without putting forth any effort. To receive the higher wage, though, we need to take some daily steps to know Him as He is.

Is it time for you to stop going through the motions and get serious about your eternal destiny and earthly purpose? Take a moment and direct your answer to God, not to me. Tell Him anything else you feel you should. The pen is in your hands now, so go ahead—write the next chapter!

_____

_____

_____

_____

_____

MIRROR WORK

Lord Jesus, I want to be the man You intended for me to be—I want to change. I know now that I need to seek You daily. I need to be involved in the daily disciplines that will lead me into closer and closer relationship with You. I commit myself to a life of devotion and study of God. Then I will go into the world as a changed man— called to walk with You and to work for You. Amen.

Congratulations! You have successfully completed what I hope has been a life changing experience.

As you continue to look in the mirror each day, remember to view yourself through the loving eyes of Jesus and to strive for an even deeper relationship with him.

Pat Morley

Notes

Chapter 2

1. Francis A. Schaeffer, *A Christian Manifesto* (Westchester: Crossway Books, 1981), 17–18.
2. Reprinted from Lane Cooper, *Louis Agassiz as a Teacher*. Copyright 1945 by Cornell University. Used by permission of the publisher.

Chapter 3

1. Schaeffer, *How Should We Then Live?* (Westchester: Crossway Books, 1976), 205.
2. Ibid.

Chapter 6

1. Emily Morrison Beck, ed., *Familiar Quotations* (Boston: Little, Brown and Co., 1980), 818.
2. Ralph Matteson and Arthur Miller, *Finding a Job You Can Love* (Nashville: Thomas Nelson, 1982), 123.

Chapter 8

1. Sandy and Harry Chapin, "Cat's in the Cradle," Copyright 1974, Story Songs, Ltd.
2. James C. Dobson, *Straight Talk to Men and Their Wives* (Waco: Word Books, 1984), 35–36.
3. Myron Magnet, "The Money Society," *Fortune* 6 July 1987, 30–31. Reprinted by permission.
4. "Teen Life Puts Strain on Health," *The Orlando Sentinel,* 10 August 1988, 1.
5. Gordon McDonald, *The Effective Father* (Wheaton: Tyndale House, 1977), 79.

Chapter 10

1. Albert M. Wells, Sr., compiler, *Inspiring Quotations, Contemporary and Classical* (Nashville: Thomas Nelson, 1988), 76.

Chapter 11

1. Magnet, 30.

Chapter 13

1. Louis B. Barnes and Mark P. Kriger, "The Many Sides of Leadership" (a draft, April, 1985), 1.
2. Ibid.
3. Peter F. Drucker, "Getting Things Done—How to Make People Decisions," *Harvard Business Review,* July-August 1985, 1.

Chapter 19
1. John White, *Putting the Soul Back in Psychology* (Downers Grove: InterVarsity Press, 1987), 79.

Chapter 20
1. Howard Dayton, Crown Ministries.

Chapter 21
1. Wells, *Inspiring Quotations*, 90.

Chapter 22
1. R. C. Sproul, *Pleasing God* (Wheaton, IL: Tyndale House, 1988), 79.
2. Vance Packard, *Hidden Persuaders* (New York: Pocket Books, 1981), 12–13.

Chapter 24
1. *The Little, Brown Book of Anecdotes* (Boston: Little, Brown Company, 1985), 586.

About the Author

Patrick Morley, best known as an author and speaker, began his career as a businessman. He founded Morley Properties which, during the 1980s, was one of Florida's 100 largest privately held companies. He has been the President or Managing Partner of 59 companies and partnerships.

Morley's vision is to help bring about a spiritual awakening in America. Through his ministry Morley speaks at outreach events and city-wide evangelistic missions throughout the U.S. and abroad.

He graduated with honors from the University of Central Florida, which selected him as its Outstanding Alumnus in 1984. Morley is a graduate of the Harvard Business School Owner/President Management Program and holds a One Year Certificate in Theology from Reformed Theological Seminary. He also serves on the Board of Directors of Campus Crusade for Christ and teaches a weekly Bible study to 125 businessmen.

Morley's previous books include *The Man in the Mirror, Walking with Christ in the Details of Life,* and *The Rest of Your Life.* He resides with his family in Orlando, Florida.

PATRICK MORLEY *Ministries*

Would you like to learn more about the ministry of Patrick Morley?

The vision of Patrick Morley Ministries is to help bring about a spiritual awakening in America in this generation. Ministries include:
- city-wide missions
- evangelistic speaking
- publishing
- teaching
- men's ministry

If you would like to receive information and be placed on our mailing list, please cut this from the book, complete and mail.

Name _____

Street _____

City_____ State _____ ZIP _____

Tel (_____) _____ Fax (_____) _____

Patrick Morley Ministries
P.O. Box 574222, Orlando, FL 32857-9936   (407) 331-0095